THE EDGE OF THE FOREST

Land, Childhood and Change in a New Guinea

Protoagricultural Society   E. Richard Sorenson

Smithsonian Institution Press, Washington, D.C.

Copyright © 1976 Smithsonian Institution   All rights reserved
First edition
Smithsonian Institution Press, Washington, D.C. 20560
Designed by Elizabeth A. Sur
Edited by Jeannette R. Mueller
Printed in the United States of America by Meriden Gravure
Company

Library of Congress Cataloging in Publication Data
Sorenson, E. Richard.
The edge of the forest.
"Abstracts of the initial body of research
films": p.
Includes index.
1. Fore (New Guinea people)   2. Social change—
Case studies.   3. Socialization—Case studies.
4. Moving-pictures in ethnology.   I. Title.
DU740.42.S67   301.29'95   76-608117
ISBN 0-87474-875-5

All illustrations by E. Richard Sorenson except for following
figures by: **U.S. Army Airforce** (courtesy U.S. Army
Topographic Command) 1, 2, 47, 49a, 57, 58, 59, 60, 61, 63,
64, 65; **Dr. D. C. Gajdusek** (courtesy National Institutes of
Health), 10, 11, 12e, 15a, 21d, 25d, 29a, 33a, 33d, 34a-f,
36a-b, 41a, 41c-d, 55, 136, 137; **Edward Gollub** (courtesy
Dr. Sylvan Tomkins), 69.

Contents

Figures

Maps

Tables

Foreword

This is a unique book in many ways. The seven-year period over which the fieldwork was carried out included five separate trips to the Fore of Papua New Guinea and was unusually long. Extraordinary circumstances were provided by the incidence of kuru, "the laughing death." During the period covered by Dr. Sorenson's expedition, the South Fore were transformed from a slash-and-burn, stone-tool-using culture to a modern coffee-raising culture with an annual income of $250,000 (Australian). Emerging from his work was a theory and method of the use of film for scientific inquiry.

First taking what pictures he could on Carleton Gadjusek's expeditions to study kuru, Dr. Sorenson began delineating his ideas on research film, defining it as total field footage in sequence, annotated by place, time and situation and appended by a special commentary by the fieldworker. He was able to design a method of work that extended over three phases: initial exploratory, undirected and opportunistic filmmaking; hypothesis construction based on laboratory analysis of the films; and hypothesis testing through a return visit.

The range of his fieldwork, over a large section of the Eastern Highlands, provided a macroscopic view of the economic development of the area. Combining the techniques of aerial photography, blood typing and historical reconstruction in adjacent areas, the author has provided a basis for his identification and description of a protoagricultural society, an evolutionary phase he has placed between hunting and gathering and the settlement patterns that develop after land has become limited. When he first encountered the South Fore, they were still pushing out into virgin forest; their loose, polylocal and easily segmented society was well adapted to the existence of an open frontier. In the North and progressively in the South, as population increased, this expansion option was cut off, and by the end of the period of observation, the South Fore were beginning to return to previously abandoned cultivated lands. The description of these open frontier conditions is a welcome addition to the study of ecological evolutionary conditions and may, at a more abstract level, have implications for the settlement in the future of such open continental areas as North America, Australia and Siberia.

With impressive care, Dr. Sorenson has examined the methods of child care and their relationship to the development of a personality open to the opportunistic and enthusiastic pursuit of new situations. Exploration and independence develop in the security of early Fore childhood, bulwarked by both adult and sibling affection and tolerance of haphazard aggression. There is an extraordinary absence of sibling rivalry among Fore children; indeed, women are able to breast feed the knee baby as well as the new infant without inciting jealousies. Film analysis and later corroborative observation document the extensive nonverbal communication used in the formation and maintenance of elective friendships among young children and congenial adults. The observance of such congenial groupings, lightly related to kinship ties, is a valuable addition to existing ethnographical accounts, in most of which the binding demands of kinship create an atmosphere involving at least some rejection, rebellion and aggression.

Felicitously, Dr. Sorenson has demonstrated that, as the flexible, open-minded Fore adapted to the demands of commercial coffee cropping, a settled way of life in larger villages and a competitive economy, the tolerance of childhood impulses decreased and the incidence of aggression among children increased. This kind of aggression had not been observed when the Fore had lived in dispersed hamlets where difficulties could always be solved by moving away into new lands easily available for cultivation. These results are congruent with the findings of other ethnographers among the Kung Bushmen and among African nomads who have become sedentary. They confirm the growing emphasis on the speed of change among primitive peoples under contact conditions, an alteration often obscured by the amnesia informants display in describing immediately preceding conditions.

A careful technical monograph, the book is divided into chapters, each of which is capable of standing on its own, with its own illustrative materials—photographs, stills from film, aerial maps and details from surveys. The reader, whether he is interested in the disproportionate death of females from kuru, the way blood typing or aerial mapping can reveal earlier migration and contacts, or child behavior data, can, because of the extensive subheading, illustration and indexing, use each chapter separately.

The Edge of the Forest validates the methods of film use, preservation and research that Dr. Sorenson has systematically advocated and is now employing as director of the National Anthropological Film Center at the Smithsonian Institution in Washington, D.C. Through the Film Center, other anthropological filmmakers are able to assemble, preserve and analyze comparable materials.

Margaret Mead
The American Museum of Natural History
New York, January 3, 1976

Acknowledgments

I am indebted to Peter and Toshi Seeger for the inspiration provided by their humanity and clear-sighted grasp of the human condition and for that basic understanding of motion-picture filming that led me to take my cameras into the world to learn. I have also been profoundly influenced by Dr. Margaret Mead, whose sustained encouragement and example has made it easier for me to bring these somewhat suspect filming contraptions into the field of anthropology as tools of scholarly inquiry. I also thank Dr. Carleton Gajdusek for supporting and participating in some of the early phases of this effort and for making the initial field trip to New Guinea possible.

Dr. Frank D. Schofield paved the way for my initial work among the Fore, and Dr. Jonathan Hancock and District Officer Mert Brightwell gave me considerable support. However, without the sustained assistance, advice and friendship of that group of Fore individuals who stuck with me over the years, this study would not have been possible. I give special thanks, therefore, to Anuma, Karako, Malagei, Agaso, Anua, Usumu, Koniye, Igiwaki and Koiye.

I am very grateful to Dr. Bernard J. Siegel for his encouragement and his very careful and helpful readings of my work and for his advice on how to proceed with this manuscript. I also thank Dr. Margaret Mead, Dr. J. Peter White, Dr. George Spindler, Dr. A. Richard Diebold, Dr. Charles O. Frake, Dr. George Collier and Shirley Lindenbaum for reviewing and commenting on parts of the early draft.

I give special mention to Mathias Maradol for the keen Micronesian insight he applied in helping me select and assemble many of the photographic displays. Sensitive in his appreciation of word meanings in relation to human affairs, he supplied comments and criticisms of the written manuscript that were also of particular value. I thank Dr. Steven Weisenfeld and Peter E. Kenmore for their invaluable assistance in working out the blood-genetic differences in regional populations across the Eastern Highlands and within the Fore region. I also thank Dr. Lim Su Chong for his careful reading of the initial draft and George Kim for assistance in assembling the final manuscript.

Initial fieldwork was supported by the Study of Child Growth and Development and Disease Patterns in Primitive Cultures of the National Institutes of Health. Additional fieldwork and analysis were supported by the University of California Medical School San Francisco, The National Geographic Society, Stanford University, and privately. This book is an extension of my Ph.D. dissertation written for Stanford University (1971).

A number of previous publications have touched on aspects of this work. Some of these have been rewritten for inclusion here, others simply deal with aspects of the same subject (Sorenson 1967ab, 1968ab, 1971ab, 1972, 1973abcd, 1974a, 1975; Sorenson and Jablonko 1973; Sorenson and Kenmore 1974; Sorenson and Gajdusek 1963, 1966, 1969).

Notes for all text references begin on page 243.

Chapter 1 **The Situation**

In the 1960s, an ecological and demographic situation that once may have been widely distributed throughout the world, still supported a way of life different from that of either hunting-gathering or settled agriculture. In the Highlands of Papua New Guinea, vast regions of unexploited virgin land, a low population density and a staple food plant that could be progressively introduced into the adjacent ecology to human benefit, supported this way of life.

Because it was molded by ecological and demographic conditions that preceded the filling of the land with agricultural settlement, I have called this way of life *protoagricultural*. In the larger perspective, it supersedes hunting-gathering and precedes settled agriculture, although there is evidence that at least semisettled agriculturalists may sometimes revert to a protoagricultural existence when a new crop opens new lands to exploitation.

Protoagricultural society may be a major kind of human organization. Not just an unstable transition state between two more permanent kinds of society, it should persist as long as its ecological and demographic prerequisites persist. As an important and possibly long-lasting evolutionary connection between hunting-gathering and settled agriculture, it may have played a significant role in the cultural and behavioral development of humankind and in the associated ecological evolution of the world.

Before humankind turned to cultivation for subsistence, populations were, for the most part, sparsely distributed as small bands of hunter-gatherers. As hunter-gatherers would have been the first to introduce a staple, cultivable food plant, this introduction had to be in accord with their established hunting-gathering patterns of behavior and culture.

It is well understood now that a crucial development in human history was the invention of horticulture. Although its significance was probably not so clear to those hunters and gatherers who were responsible for the initial horticultural innovations, it moved humankind into a new realm of power—the purposeful manipulation of ecology to apparent human benefit. Horticulture freed humanity from dependence on the providential production of wild foodstuffs. It provided an ability to produce to meet required consumption.

Horticultural needs focus human interest and daily life in one way, hunting-gathering in another. Relying on horticulture necessitates a new pattern of human organization. A gardener does not search for his food across an extended range; he concentrates effort and attention on manipulating small, selected sites of food production. Territorial focus becomes narrower, and economic behavior is territorially altered. Social behavior is exercised in a daily arena requiring qualitatively different behavioral practices. This territorial and economic refocusing sets the stage for the emergence of protoagricultural social organization.

Ultimately the horticultural innovation spawns population growth and often leaves in its wake progressive ecological disturbance of major proportions. The seemingly limitless virgin land opportunities of the first horticulturalists eventually prove to be finite as the lands begin to fill up and the original ecology is transformed. Eventually the conditions once permitting protoagricultural development disappear, and a new stage is set leading to another major kind of human organization, which we may call settled agriculture.

The South Fore, the subjects of this study, were still protoagricultural at the time of Western contact. Because these horticulturalists were still able to expand into extensive surrounding unoccupied virgin rainforest, their way of life could be termed protoagricultural. But their neighbors to the north, including the North Fore, were reaching the end of this development and were becoming ecologically and territorially circumscribed. They seemed to be in transition toward a more restricted kind of agricultural existence.

The South Fore populated a fringe pioneer region extending southward from the central divide of New Guinea into vast regions of unexploited rainforest. They maintained an informal social structure, which facilitated group segmentation and resettlement. The North Fore occupied the edges of a large deforested core region where dispersive segmentation had become less practicable. They were afflicted by a time of troubles marked by intervillage raiding and warfare.

Because of these differences, the Fore provide information not only about New Guinea Highland protoagricultural life, but also on how protoagriculturalists may abandon their gardens of opportunity to cope with emerging and more limited territorial conditions.

It is important to recognize that analysis of a single New Guinea group is not sufficient to outline the full range of protoagricultural social and cultural possibilities; nor is it sufficient to formulate a final definition of the protoagricultural way of life. However by examining the protoagriculture-related aspects of Fore territorial, economic, social and behavioral organization, we gain new insight into an important kind of existence that may have been common in the past. Such data, even from a single society, can inform us about the general condition, allowing us to formulate a framework in which to place other evidence on human cultural and economic evolution.

Until the mid-1950s, the Fore were remotely situated in the mountains of central New Guinea. Isolated from outside commercial and technological cultures, they were without metal or cloth. They did not know of salt water, nor of the sea surrounding New Guinea. Neither missionary nor government influence had yet penetrated their mountainous homeland.

The first serious contact was in the early 1950s, when a pioneering anthropological study of Eastern Highlands people by Ronald and Catherine Berndt included some northern hamlets of the North Fore. But not until 1957 was the first government patrol post established in the region. It was also in 1957 that a series of medical scientists began epidemiological and clinical studies of kuru, an infectious neurological disease unique to the Fore and their immediate neighbors. In 1961 and 1962, Robert and Shirley Glasse conducted an intensive study of anthropological factors associated with kuru from a base in the South Fore.

I arrived among the South Fore in September 1963 to participate in the study of kuru and to initiate a study of child behavior and development. My fascination with the unexpected situation I encountered led me beyond these initial objectives to a total of five field trips between 1963 and 1970, spending approximately a year and a half in residence among the South Fore.

During the 1960s, changes in the Fore lifestyle began to occur rather quickly. Unusually adaptive, the Fore were quick to shed indigenous practices in favor of the Western example. Even when I began my fieldwork, there were some Fore in daily contact with Western government officers, missionaries and scientists. Some worked as servants or day-laborers in and around Western households and stations; others had lived as workers on Western-administered plantations outside the Fore. Recently esablished were four resident missionaries and a government patrol post at Okapa.

The seven years embracing my field trips to the Fore comprised a period of remarkable cultural and material change. This isolated, primitive people proved to be startlingly receptive to new ideas and practices; they were rapidly altering their neolithic culture to adapt to Western law, government, religion, materials and trade. During the first years, I encountered "cargo-cult" beliefs and a disorganized abandoning of earlier practices and beliefs. During the later years, there was rapid, almost breathtaking economic development.

During the entire period, the pattern of change was spotty—as if the cultural change were an epidemic disease, irregularly striking hamlets in a somewhat haphazard order, outward from site of infection. Hamlets nearest the patrol post, the missions or the new jeep track were afflicted first; those more remotely situated tended to be struck later. But rapid change could also affect a remote site while intervening hamlets remained less affected. During all of my field trips, there were some hamlets where a more traditional style of life continued and others where life had been drastically altered.

Sometimes, change was so rapid that many people seemed to be afflicted by a kind of cultural shock. An anomie, even cultural amnesia, seemed to pervade some hamlets for a time. Some individuals appeared temporarily to have lost memory of even recently past events of their own lives and made factual errors in reporting them—a situation vaguely reminiscent of the kind of identity crisis children seem to pass through when they learn to talk and again as they enter adolescence. Some Fore even forgot what type and style of traditional garments they had worn only a few years earlier, or that they had used stone axes and had eaten their dead close relatives. Others were confused about the taboos they had only recently abandoned. Such difficulties in recounting the past were temporary and disappeared when they became accustomed to the new way of life. However, because of this cognitive disorder, I approached oral information cautiously.

It has been suggested that the forgetful individuals might have been dissimulating in an effort to appear more modern. Yet, the Fore were so unassuming and so open in all other respects that I dismissed this theory. Furthermore, I noted that the apparently amnesic Fore would excitedly recall what they had forgotten when presented with clear reminders, as by photographs or the comments of associates. Under these conditions, they would brighten up, laugh and even excitedly call attention of others to the interesting evidence, as they somewhat proudly exhibited their own revived recollections.

Underlying this cultural and cognitive confusion seemed to be a remarkable receptivity to change. There seemed to be little emotional commitment to traditional views. Ideas and practices, in themselves, did not seem to have much of a hold on the Fore. This markedly open-minded people so readily accepted reformulations of identity and practice that even the slightest suggestion or example by the new government officers, missionaries and scientists was a sufficient basis for spontaneous alteration of tribal affiliations, identities, personal names and rules governing conduct. For example, when the first Australian patrol officer began to map the region, a problem in communication led him to refer to the people who lived in this region as the Fore. Actually, this was their own name for a culturally and linguistically different people (now called the Awa) across the Lamari River. They did not correct the Australian patrol officer but adopted his usage and now universally refer to themselves as the Fore. They were also quite willing to be affiliated with formal regional groupings arbitrarily established by the early govern-

ment officers and to identify themselves by the names given to these groups.

During the early period, government officials and missionaries sometimes characterized the Fore as friendly, compliant and among the easiest people to work with in New Guinea. "But," they sometimes added, "wasn't it too bad they were so dumb?"—apparently because of the seemingly uncritical willingness of the Fore to do whatever they suggested. I did not hear this comment after 1967 when they were making a quarter of a million dollars per annum from cash cropping.

The extraordinary readiness of the Fore to abandon traditional identities and practices was worrisome to me. I had not heard of anything quite like what I was encountering. However, the nature of this problem did not begin to become fully clear until fairly late in my fieldwork. Initially, I saw it only as a hinderance to data collection, not as an unusual culturally generated human trait worthy of study itself.

This difficulty also made reliable information from informants hard to get—a problem compounded by the unfamiliarity of the traditional Fore to question-and-answer discourse. In the small peer groups comprising their communities, there was little indigenous need for an interrogative approach to communication. Precontact Fore social horizons did not extend much beyond one's small community, where daily familiarization with everyone, since childhood, led to an understanding and intimacy that made the question-and-answer style of discourse unnecessary. Instead, human interaction was based largely on common feeling, personal rapport and familiarity. Subtle interactive behavior, not questions or instructions, communicated needs, desires and interests. Questions, like demands, were an indication of alienation and were often treated as threats or insults.

Because the interrogative style had not evolved as a significant part of the Fore communicative repertoire, many individuals displayed uncertainty, hesitation and confusion in the face of questions. Some were completely tongue-tied; others trembled and perspired profusely or looked wildly about. The least acculturated were most afflicted; they often seemed bewildered, even fearful in the face of the kind of communication that Westerners take so much for granted.

The subtle, informal and personal style of communication characteristic of Fore comments was quite consistent with the sociopolitical organization. Economically opportunistic and socially egalitarian, the small, continually dispersing bands of Fore protoagriculturalists had no chiefs, patriarchs, medicine men, priests or the like, to whom anyone was accountable. Solidarity and allegiance stemmed from personal familiarity and regard. Bad feeling led to segmentation and divergent settlement.

In this situation, a cultural barrier, more fundamental than difference in language alone, stood in the way of any widespread effort to obtain information by interview. Questions were an open recognition of alienation. To interview was to be threatening or insulting. It was an arrogant extension of a communicative technique specific to our own culture; and among the Fore, it caused emotional and communicative dissonances unknown in the Western world, where the interrogative style of discourse has firmly settled in with the help of a system of institutionalized education.

This problem in communication was partially circumvented by the eagerness of the economically opportunistic Fore people to adopt Western practices. This, they thought, was the key to obtaining lavish shipments of extraordinary goods and materials of the sort that so dramatically blessed us, alien newcomers to their lands.

Because of such "cargo-cult" beliefs, it was easy to obtain native assistants and associates eager to do things in our way. This greatly enhanced the possibility of working among the Fore, in spite of a basic difference in approach to social interaction and information exchange. But even this receptiveness to things Western did not fully solve the communication problem. It was also necessary to develop some degree of personal familiarity to avoid the emotional and communicative dissonance triggered by direct questions or instructions.

Because such problems made it hard to interview any but my closest associates, I turned my efforts primarily to phenomenological documentation and analysis. I relied primarily on my motion picture and still cameras, and I began a systematic sampling of visual data from the behavioral and environmental situations I encountered. Fortunately I had already formulated procedures governing the investigation of nonrecurring phenomena; and I had come with two motion picture cameras, two still cameras and an amount of film that was unusual in those days.

I began to film immediately; I did not wait to understand what I was filming first. Moving into one, and then another South Fore village and roaming the rest of the Fore lands, I relied primarily on my cameras to gather information on the socioenvironmental situation in regards to childhood. Still photographs were used to document the setting. With cinema, I recorded naturally occurring Fore social interaction and behavior. From this work, the theory and method of the research film emerged. *(See Appendix 1)*

The cognitive and communicative confusion, which had so obstructed data gathering by interview in 1963–64, had diminished considerably by 1968. People who had trouble recalling the past in 1963 had little difficulty five years later. Nearly everyone was able to discuss intelligently and agree on past events and practices, including those that had occurred before contact. The Fore were generally more confident and much less disconcerted by our style of communication. They had become more secure in a new way of life. Their new crop of coffee was delivering a handsome profit.

But the general situation had also changed. Fundamental changes in residential organization had swept all hamlets. There were no more segregated collective men's and women's houses. Family houses had been generally adopted by married couples, changing the social and territorial arena for the young children who had been accustomed to treating all the members of their hamlet as close kin. It also territorialized hamlets in a way previously unknown. Not having a men's house to live in and being uncomfortable in the family houses, boys between nine and 16 began to gather in "boy's houses," away from the adult men with whom they had previously lived. Mothers began to wear blouses, altering the freer pattern of unrestricted infant access to the breast, which had prevailed earlier. Episodes of infant and child frustration, not seen in traditional Fore hamlets, began to take place. In the larger, consolidated modernized hamlets, anger, withdrawal, aggressiveness, stinginess and increased interest in controlling the behavior of others began to appear.

These newer patterns of activity seemed to affect children more than adults; emerging from the play of the modernizing children were occasional angry yells, impetuous pushings and a decreased tolerance of younger children.

Chapter 2   **Conditions of Existence**

Along the valleys and ridges of the rugged mountain backbone dividing the north of the island of New Guinea from the south, many small, neolithic cultural enclaves remained isolated from the attractions of the outside commercial world until the middle of the 20th century. Although the origin of these peoples is still unknown, archaeological evidence indicates that the present inhabitants are at least materially the cultural heirs of the earliest inhabitants.[1]

A dissected topography, densely covered with rainforest and tropical grasses, presented severe physical barriers to travel. Off-trail movement was very difficult. What trails there were had to be cut and kept open with stone implements. These conditions tended to isolate areas of habitation; and, as communities were virtually self-sufficient, there seemed to be little interest under normal circumstances in traveling very far beyond one's home region. Introduction of horticulture seems to have been fairly recent, although it is still impossible to date.[2]

The physical isolation of these highland communities was sufficient to permit divergent adaptation. This, in turn, imposed additional linguistic and cultural barriers to interregional movement. Only in regions where the need for land began to be a problem was community isolation significantly breached by incipient congestion and dispersive migration.

The Fore can be seen as pioneer peoples on the edge of the major Highlands populations. Remotely situated in the southern fringes of the high Central Range until the 1950s, they carried on an isolated protoagricultural way of life, beyond the reach of modern commerce and government and uninfluenced by any of the world's major ideologies or religions. In this rugged land of steep valleys and high ridges, thick tropical rainforest alternates with tracts of dense grassland.

Flat areas are rare. Peaks rise over 9,000 feet; valleys descend to 1,000 feet above sea level.

Situated on an irregular mountainous wedge of about 400 square miles, the Fore homeland extended southward into uninhabited lands from the Kratke range. On the southeast these lands were sharply bounded by the spectacular Lamari gorge, which descends more than 5,000 feet below some populated regions. On the northeast, they terminated somewhat irregularly on the ridges above the Puburamba River, a tributary to the Lamari. The Fore lands extended westward, across the Lamari-Yani divide, and in some places up to the edges of the Yani River. The Fore wedge was bounded roughly by the Lamari and Yani Rivers. Its point penetrated a vast, uninhabited region of virgin rainforest *(maps 1 and 2).* Populated regions were characterized by clusters of hamlets and gardens situated on the dividing line between two ecologies: between the retreating edge of the forest and the advancing edge of abandoned grassland.

Linguistic Setting

This part of the Eastern Highlands was a region of considerable linguistic diversity, and the Fore were surrounded by peoples speaking seven mutually unintelligible languages—languages that have been formally divided into four linguistic families, three stocks and at least two phyla *(map 3).*[3] The Fore language itself can be formally divided into three dialects.[4] However, many Fore thought of themselves as having four distinctive ways of speaking *(map 4).*

At the time of contact, the Fore did not have a name for the language they spoke, nor did they have a name for themselves as an identifiable dis-

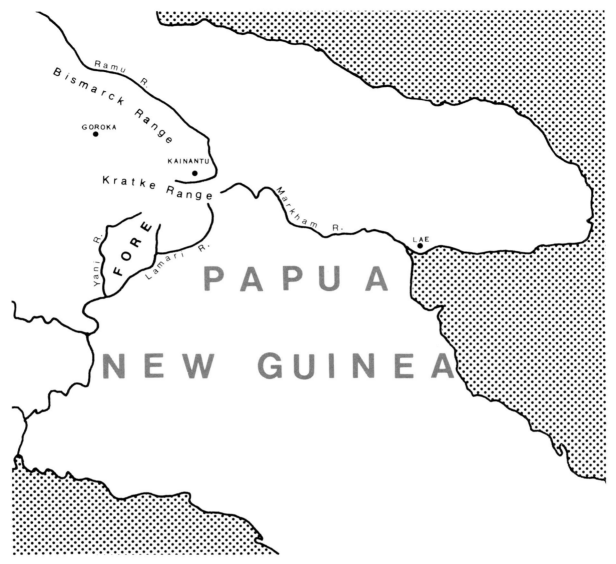

MAP 1. THE FORE REGION IN THE EASTERN HIGHLANDS OF PAPUA NEW GUINEA

tinct group of people. They were aware that some neighbors spoke similarly enough to be understood. Yet, this mutual intelligibility was not grasped as a basis for a common name. In part, this may have been a consequence of lack of agreement from region to region on the limits of the intelligibility. But more likely it is a result of isolation of the various regions from each other.

Boundaries between dialects and between adjacent languages were never very clear. People in border regions could usually communicate with the inhabitants of the neighboring villages without thinking they were speaking more than one language—their own. To them their full communicational repertoire was their language. It didn't matter that elements may have been acquired from different sources. Rather than thinking of themselves as bilingual, they simply understood which other villages they could manage in, and the degree to which this was usually possible.

Instead of being separated by distinct language frontiers, languages tended to fade into one another. Shared vocabularies and shared styles of speaking united most adjacent villages through a kind of dialect chain. Even into regions of rather marked linguistic difference, communication was almost always possible between individuals in neighboring villages. For example, my Fore friends from the Atigina region *(map 5)*, were able to understand at least some of what the residents of the Awa village of Yakia were saying, in spite of the fact that linguists would formally place the Awa language in an entirely different language family. But these same Fore were unable to understand much in the village of Amoraba situated more deeply in Awa territory. Individuals from the Fore village of Abomatasa, immediately adjacent to the Awa region, could manage communication with both Yakia and Amoraba residents. Similarly, Fore from Okasa village had no difficulty understanding the Auyana spoken in Indona but had a harder time in Kawaina.

Habitation Patterns

Centrifugally dispersing outward from common sites of origin, the segmenting Fore groups slowly moved their hamlets and gardens into the retreating forest around them and left uninhabited grasslands in their wake *(fig. 1)*. In the south, uninhabited forest surrounded most communities, but in the north, there were also large zones of grassland, particularly in the river valleys *(fig. 2)*. In both north and south, hamlets and gardens tended to be irregularly situated adjacent to the forest *(fig. 3)*.

Around all inhabited areas were pseudopodlike projections of garden and grassland, where the Fore had extended gardens and hamlets into the forest. Intruding somewhat further into the forest were small satellitelike clearings, marking sites where more deeply penetrating segmenting groups had chosen to settle or make their gardens *(fig. 4)*.

Precontact hamlets were small, varying in size from two or three small dwellings to a cluster

MAP 2. SKETCH OF THE FORE TERRITORY

containing up to a half dozen separate men's and women's houses *(fig. 5)*. The one or two large men's houses in a hamlet provided shelter for all the men and older boys, typically between 10 and 20 residents and their visiting friends. The larger number of smaller women's houses nearby were usually occupied by two married women who had been childhood friends in the village from which they had been purchased through traditional bride exchange agreements. With them lived their unmarried daughters and young sons under six or seven years of age.

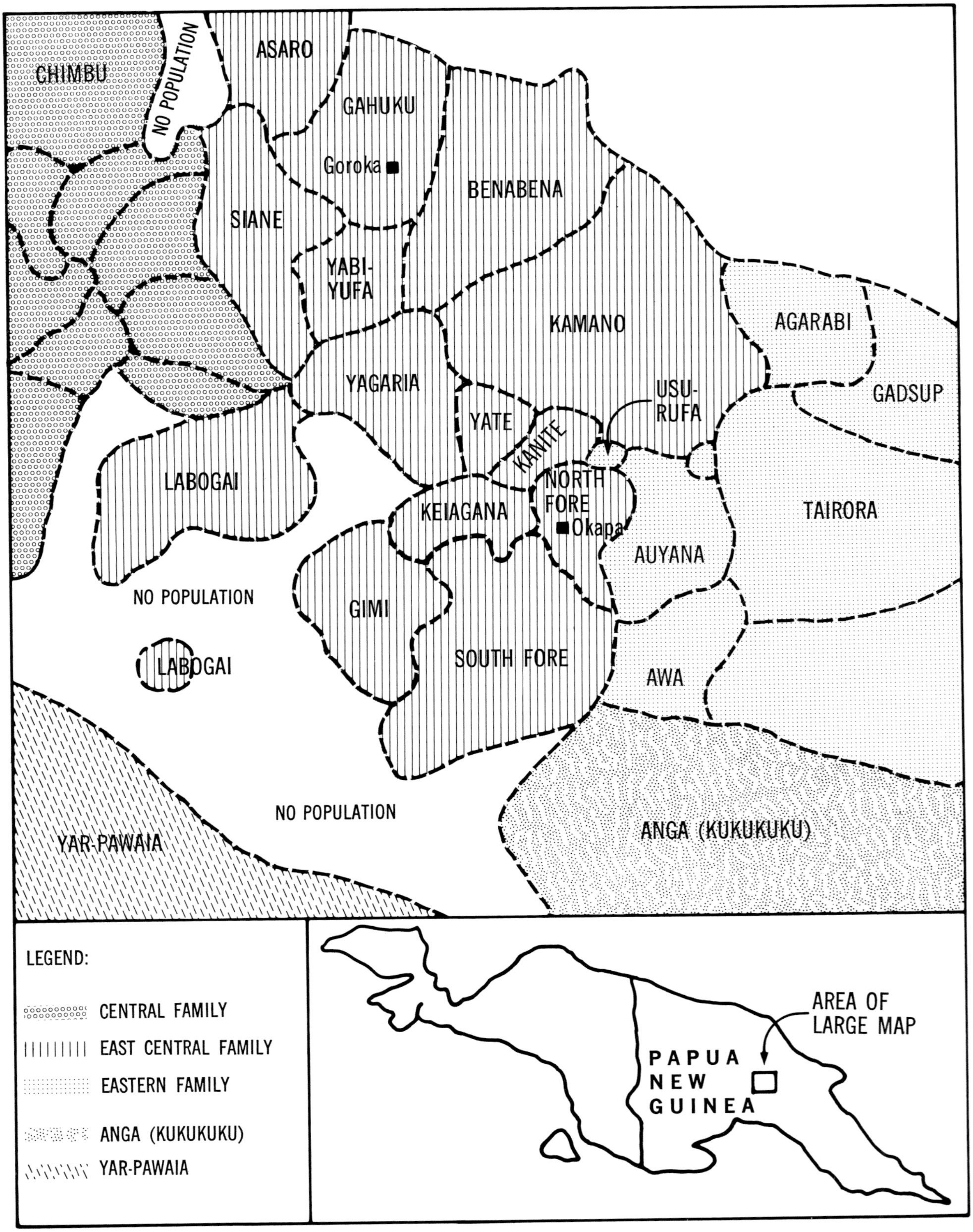
CHIMBU
NO POPULATION
ASARO
GAHUKU
Goroka
BENABENA
SIANE
YABI-
YUFA
KAMANO
AGARABI
GADSUP
YAGARIA
USU-
RUFA
YATE
KANITE
LABOGAI
NORTH
FORE
Okapa
KEIAGANA
TAIRORA
AUYANA
NO POPULATION
GIMI
LABOGAI
SOUTH FORE
AWA
NO POPULATION
YAR-PAWAIA
ANGA (KUKUKUKU)
LEGEND:
CENTRAL FAMILY
EAST CENTRAL FAMILY
EASTERN FAMILY
ANGA (KUKUKUKU)
YAR-PAWAIA
AREA OF
LARGE MAP
PAPUA
NEW
GUINEA

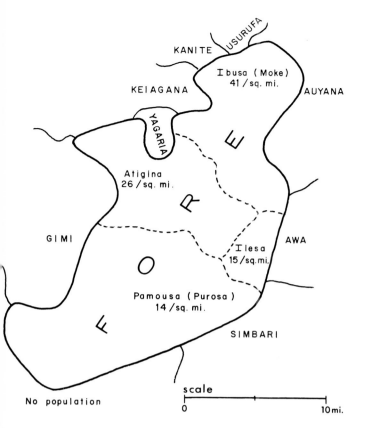

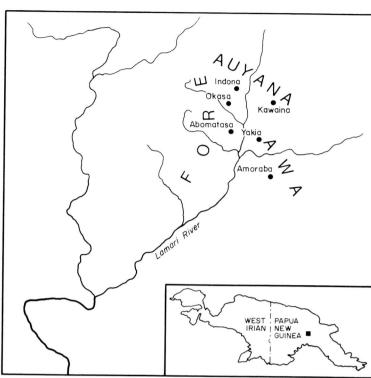

MAP 4. FORE DIALECTS AND THEIR POPULATION DENSI-TIES. Although Scott (1963) showed three dialects of Fore, many Fore refer to the Ilesa speech as distinctive as well. Scott spoke of the northern (Ibusa), central (Atigina and Ilesa), and southern (Pamousa) dialects. Here I have also indicated the territory of the Ilesa. Surrounding languages are shown in upper case. The Yagaria-speaking people of 1958, shown on this map, had adopted the Keiagana language and culture by 1963 and thus do not show on later maps.

MAP 5. THE DIALECT CHAIN PHENOMENON. Atigina Fore can communicate with Yakia Awa but not Amoraba Awa. Abomatasa Fore can communicate with both Yakia and Amoraba Awa. Okasa Fore can communicate with Indona Auyana but not with Kawaina Auyana. Indona and Kawaina Auyana communicate easily, as do Yakia and Amoraba Awa.

MAP 3. LINGUISTIC DIVERSITY. The Fore make up part of one of the southward projections of the East New Guinea Highlands linguistic stock (Wurm 1962, 1964), represented here by the Central, East Central and Eastern linguistic families. Two of their neighbors, the Anga (Kukukuku) and Yar-Pawaia, belong to two other, quite dissimilar linguistic stocks, neither of which is even included in the language phylum containing the East New Guinea Highlands stock. In the south, the Fore lands merge into a vast uninhabited region. North Fore and South Fore are shown separately because of the earlier belief that they were differentiable linguistically.

FIGURE 1. PATTERNS OF SETTLEMENT. The fringes of deforested lands were the sites of habitation and gardening. In this 1949 aerial photograph of the North Fore region, looking westward from the Lamari valley, contiguous zones of grassland mark origin sites of several expanding population groups. In many places these groups have begun to move into the same remaining stands of forest. In other places forest lands previously separating elements of the expanding population disappeared, leaving broad tracts of undivided grassland. The path of the upper Puburamba River valley appears to the lower left, clearly demarked by the grassland. The Moke site on which Okapa was later built is under the cloud marked by an asterisk. Population clusters extending to the right from Moke include Anumpa, Kasoru, Emesa, Ibusa-Moke, Keyanosa, Etesena, Ibusa, Mage, Kagu, Opoiyanti and Kalu.

FIGURE 2. THE FORE LANDS FROM NORTH TO SOUTH. These two aerial photographs view the Fore region westward from above the Lamari valley up the three eastern river valleys: Puburamba and Waisarampa (a), and Kaza (b) (see map 2). The Purosa valley, the large clearing at the head of the Kaza River, is the site of the population clusters of Mugaiamuti, Ketabi, Ai, Purosa-Takai, Takai and Ivaki. Extensive uninhabited virgin rainforest surrounds this southern region of protoagricultural penetration. The Waisarampa River valley, to the north, also contains extensive virgin lands, particularly downriver from its source. Two somewhat different populations inhabit the Waisarampa valley: 1) the hamlet clusters in the Ilesa region; and 2) the Atigina region around its source. Further to the north the extensive deforestation of the Puburamba valley indicates that it supported protoagricultural habitation for some time. The adjacent, uninhabited great grasslands of the Lamari valley are a likely source from which the early protoagriculturalists entered the Puburamba valley.

FIGURE 3. THE EDGE OF THE FOREST. The classic location of traditional Fore hamlets was on the edge of the forest adjacent to gardens cut out of the forest by hamlet members. Typically, the gardens abutted the forest on one side and were flanked by abandoned grassland on another, where previous gardens had been deserted. Frequently on the crest of a ridge, the hamlet would be built in one of the abandoned plots.

FIGURE 4. SEGMENTATION AND RESETTLEMENT. Leaving behind the deforested Purosa valley (top), segmenting people of Takai develop new hamlets and gardens in the adjacent rainforest. Fresh clearings surround a new hamlet and its ancillary two-house, partially segmented appendage (lower left center). Gardens cover an opposing slope (lower right). Another hamlet has been established in a portion of the forest closer to the central deforested core of the Purosa valley (upper right). A third hamlet occupies a cleared pseudopod extending into yet another part of the forest (upper left). A previously gardened clearing, now abandoned to *kunai* grass reveals the earlier sites of habitation and gardening. [Purosa-Takai, 1967]

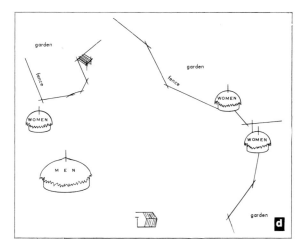

FIGURE 5. TRADITIONAL HAMLET. The Fore practiced segregated male/female residence. Before Western contact the typical hamlet would have been made up of a large men's residential-clubhouse (left house, **a**), and two to four women's houses, each housing two married women and their daughters and sons under about six to seven years of age (right house, **a**; both houses, **b**). Women's houses were sometimes astride a garden and the hamlet yard (**b**). Men's houses provided warmth and shelter for both married men and unmarried youths (**c**). The schematic drawing shows the arrangement of these houses of Akilankamuti hamlet of Waisa, 1963 (**d**).

Population Distribution

At the time of Western contact there were about 12,000 Fore people *(table 1)*.[5] Overall population density was approximately 30 per square mile, but the density was highest in the north and decreased as one proceeded toward the uninhabited lands to the south. Regional averages for the north, central and southern regions were: North Fore (Ibusa dialect), 41/sq. mi.; central Fore (Atigina and Ilesa dialects), 23/sq. mi.; southern Fore (Pamousa or Purosa dialect), 14/sq. mi. *(see map 4)*.[6]

TABLE 1: FORE POPULATION BY REGIONAL GROUPINGS—1958

Division	Dialect	Native region	Population cluster	
NORTH FORE	Ibusa (Moke)	Ibusa	Ibusa	336
			Emesa	204
5,029	5,029	1,508	Etesesa	130
			Ibusa-Moke	190
			Kagu	175
			Keianosa	109
			Opoiyanti	87
			Pusarasa	277
		Aga	Aga	147
			Aga-Yagusa	178
		442	Keiakasa	117
		Awande	Awande	264
		264		
		Okasa	Okasa	242
			Ilafo	99
		549	Kasokana	208
		Ofafina	Famia	271
			Kalu	309
		889	Tiarana	309
		Wantokabarasa	Anumpa	436
			Kasogu	169
		1,377	Kasoru	408
			Moke	241
			Mage	123
SOUTH FORE	Atigina	Atigina	Amora	160
			Higitaru	139
6,962	4,267	1,957	Kalu	110
			Kamata	116
			Kamira	288
			Kanigitasa	143
			Kume	148
			Mentilesa	147
			Waisa	170
			Wanikanto	156
			Wanitabe	153
			Wanta	52
			Yagareba	175

Division	Dialect	Native region	Population cluster	
		Kamikina	Amusi	242
			Kabuye	109
		2,301	Kaga	137
			Keiakasa	234
			Miarasa	237
			Oma-Kasoru	197
			Paigatasa	170
			Tamogavisa	172
			Tunuku	144
			Yasubi	488
			Yasu-Tunuku	180
	Pamousa (Purosa)	Purosa	Agakamatasa	102
			Ai	148
	2,327	738	Ketabi	143
			Mugaiamuti	270
			Purosa-Takai	75
		Ifufurapa	Intamatasa	156
			Ivaki	327
		1,589	Kasarai	.03
			Orie	102
			Paiti	177
			Takai	228
			Takari	81
			Umasa	145
			Urai	168
	Ilesa	Ilesa	Ilesa	134
			Abomotasa	98
	368	368	Awarosa	136

Within the Fore region there were originally at least 70 distinct population clusters. Sixty-five of these became the bases for the census units imposed by the early Australian patrol officers *(map 6)*. However, being part of defined formal territorial groups was quite new to the Fore. They had not traditionally organized themselves according to formally established regions or exclusive sociopolitical groups. Instead, social and political interdigitation existed between all populations within and immediately adjacent to the Fore. Groups tended to fade into one another along the edges in a rather haphazard way, much as did languages and dialects. Contributing to this condition was the protoagricultural way of life in which individuals or small groups were expected to break away from old communities while continuing to maintain association and residence privileges with their old hamlet-mates.

All population clusters (or villages, as they came to be called) comprised several small hamlets *(map 7; fig. 6)*. In pioneer areas these clusters could be identified ecologically by their small, central cores of grassland. In older regions, there were several clusters along the longer perimeters of a larger deforested core.

MAP 6. THE CENSUS UNITS, OR "VILLAGES" OF THE FORE AND THEIR NEIGHBORS. In precontact times the Fore did not think of themselves as belonging to named territories but, rather, as allied with other individuals in other hamlets through kinship and associational ties. With the advent of government administration, these fluctuating local affiliations were somewhat arbitrarily assigned to the named census units ("villages") shown

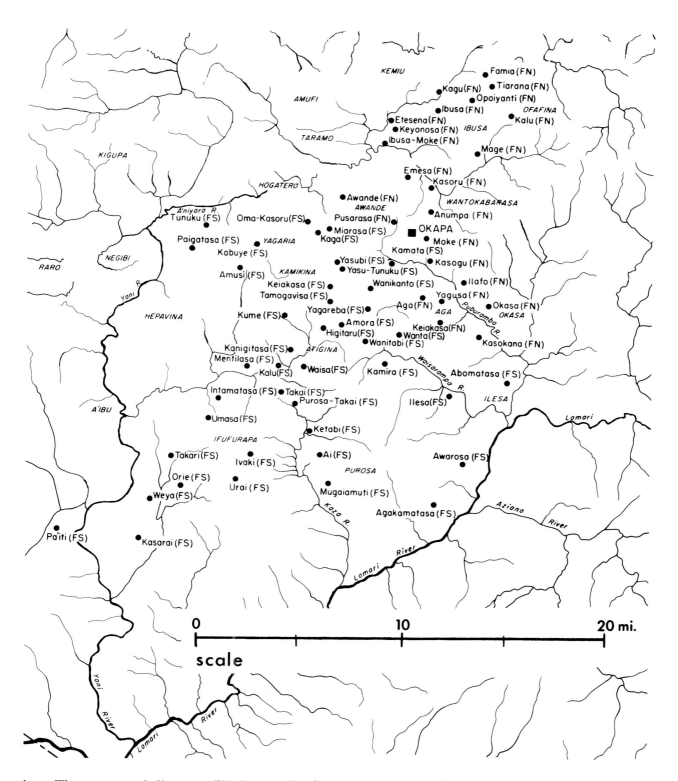

KEMIU

AMUFI

KIGUPA

TARAMO

HOGATERU

A'niyara R.

NEGIBI

RARO

Yani R.

HEPAVINA

A'IBU

Famia (FN)

Kagu(FN) Tiarana (FN)

Opoiyanti (FN)

Ibusa (FN)

Etesena(FN) Kalu (FN) OFAFINA

Keyonosa (FN) IBUSA

Ibusa-Moke (FN) Mage (FN)

Emesa (FN)

Kasoru (FN)

Awande (FN) WANTOKABARASA

AWANDE

Tunuku (FS) Oma-Kasoru(FS) Pusarasa (FN)

Anumpa (FN)

Paigatasa (FS) Miarasa (FS) ■ OKAPA

YAGARIA Kaga(FS) Moke (FN)

Kabuye (FS) Kamata (FN)

Yasubi (FS) Kasogu (FN)

Amusi (FS) KAMIKINA Yasu-Tunuku (FS)

Keiakasa (FS) Wanikanto (FS) Ilafo (FN)

Tamogavisa (FS) Yagusa (FN)

Aga(FN) Okasa (FN)

Kume (FS) Yagareba(FS) AGA OKASA

Amora (FS) Keiakasa(FN)

Higitaru(FS) Wanta (FS) Kasokana (FN)

Kanigitasa(FS) Wanitabi (FS)

ATIGINA

Mentilasa (FS) Waisa(FS) Kamira (FS) Abomatasa (FS)

Kalu(FS) Waisarampa R.

Intamatasa (FS) Takai (FS) ILESA

Purosa-Takai (FS) Ilesa(FS) Lamari

Umasa(FS)

Ketabi(FS)

IFUFURAPA

Takari(FS) Ai(FS) Awarosa (FS)

Ivaki (FS)

Orie (FS) PUROSA

Urai (FS)

Weya(FS) Mugaiamuti (FS) Aziana

Kazo R. Agakamatasa (FS) River

Pa'iti (FS)

Kasarai (FS)

Lamari River

Yani River

Lamari River

Puburampa R.

0   10   20 mi.

scale

here. They represent indigenous affiliations associated
with regions by the early patrol officers. The dialects
spoken by the residents of these census units are in
parentheses after the name: (FN)=North Fore, (FS)
= South Fore.

29

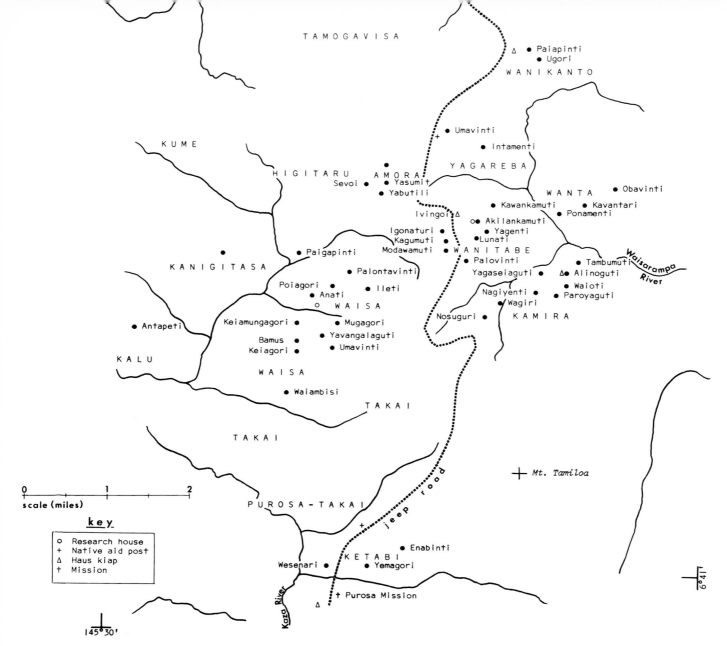

MAP 7. THE HAMLETS OF WANITABE, WAISA AND KAMIRA VILLAGES, 1963. To speak of the Fore as belonging to villages is to adopt the nonindigenous census unit organization imposed by the government for administrative purposes. The boundaries of these census units ("villages") have not yet been defined, and the territorial limits are ambiguous. They can only be given general geographic references. It is, thus, more accurate to map the Fore by their hamlet locations. This map shows the distribution of the hamlets usually attributed to Waisa, Wanitabe, Kamira and some of their neighbors. Since 1963 some of these hamlets have been abandoned and new ones have been built (cf., for Wanitabe, fig. 6). Largely due to the residential mobility of the Fore, the members of these hamlets are not all censused in the same place; they belong to different villages insofar as the government is concerned. For example, Ponamenti, the main hamlet of Wanta village, is also the residence of a number of Kamira people. Similarly, Kavantari is often thought to be a hamlet of Wanta because of its location—however, most of its residents are Kamata people, who refer to the hamlet as one of Kamata, a distant census unit off the map to the north. Kavantari is also sometimes referred to as Wanikanto or Yagareba, because it also has residents belonging to these census units. The same problem exists in some of the most modern hamlets: Akilankamuti has contingents from Yagareba, Wanitabe and Amora villages. Because of this ambiguity, even different government officials have variously referred to Akilankamuti as Wanitabe and Yagareba. The dotted line marks the route of the government jeep road.

FIGURE 6. THE HAMLETS OF WANITABE IN 1967. Clustering around one of the last stands of forest in their domain are nine inhabited sites (hamlets) of Wanitabe. Already the watercourses are becoming etched by the last remnants of the forest in this upper tip of the Waisarampa River valley. Most of the rest of the Wanitabe land is an abandoned tract of grassland continuing off the right edge of the picture. A new native-planned and native-built road (diagonally from lower left) roughly marks an informal border between Yagareba and Wanitabe villages. However, many people counted as Wanitabe in the census live in the large, modern hamlet of Akilankamuti, together with a slightly larger number of Yagareba people, making it difficult to assign this hamlet to a village. Similarly, a few Yagareba people live in the predominantly Wanitabe hamlet of Yagenti, and a few Kamira people live in Niginosi and Teteyeguti. To the left of Kagumuti, across the road, outlines of previous gardens still mark the grasslands. Residents of Akilankamuti have just begun to depart from the traditional practice of cutting small gardens out of the forest and are developing a large area of contiguous gardens adjacent to their hamlet (the large fenced area below the hamlet). Some people in the two large, new-style Wanitabe hamlets (Plovinti and Kagumuti) have also begun to experiment with grassland horticulture, but more in the traditional fashion of small plots. The most traditional people of Wanitabe still live in the small, old-style hamlets (Kalugori, Paparoti, Lunati, Teteyeguti and Niginosi) and continue to concentrate their gardening activity on forest locations.

Trails

Steep, rough, usually muddy, narrow footpaths were all that connected the hamlets with one another and their outlying gardens (fig. 7). Since the trails were primarily to connect hamlets and gardens, fences—specially strengthened at crossings—frequently intersected trails (fig. 8). Along the river edges of the Fore region, vine suspension bridges were occasionally built to provide access to new gardens and houses (fig. 9).

Following the standard practice of land rights belonging to those who were using the land or whose labor was producing something from the land, all trails were owned by the people who made and sustained them. There were no public trails or trunk trails. Instead, the trails marked corridors in the playing out of the localized Fore protoagricultural way of life. Lying at the heart of the socioeconomic system, all trails were looked on as private. Trespassing on them by outsiders or strangers was considered threatening and to be discouraged by attack or sorcery. Even personal differences between acquaintances could discourage one from using another's trail. In some cases friends would even make their way to the same destination over different trails because both were not friendly with owners of the various intervening trails.

Trails in an inhabited region formed an interlocking system with the nodes coinciding with hamlet sites; peripheral trails often touched another hamlet system. Where kinship connections made travel desirable to distant hamlets or to another region of population, a connecting trail would sometimes have been made across several hours of intervening wild land. To go further, beyond neighboring hamlets or regions, often required circuitous routing over trails owned by friends and through hamlets where one was known and accepted. Interregional travel could be quite indirect and was considered dangerous.

This phenomenon of narrow corridors of privately owned land running through otherwise unclaimed and unused land is the reverse of our own in which we have public roads passing through lands fully owned, whether used or not, by individuals or corporations. In a sense, the Fore were contained within their own lands by a usufruct concept of land ownership that included trails.

Cannibalism

Until Westernization, the Fore ate their dead kinsmen and close friends as a rite of mourning and of love and respect for the dead.[7] Close relatives and associates of both sexes took part in the death feasts, but women and children were the principal cannibal mourners. The ritual was often described as a deep desire to remain close to and preserve inside oneself the traces of dead loved ones.

Women, particularly older women, attended to the dismembering and cooking of the bodies, even to the extent of carving off the flesh, although butchery and carving of other animals was done by men. As in normal daily life, girls and young boys habitually clustered about the women, participating in their childlike ways in the carving, cooking and eating of the dead.

Men, especially older men who were closely associated with the deceased, would sometimes take part in eating the dead body as well, even though cannibalism was primarily a practice of women. Warriors usually abstained, claiming fear that cannibalism would diminish their prowess. Those men who did participate rarely ate women kinsmen, restricting their cannibalism to male relatives, on the grounds that female body essence was injurious to male strength.

All portions of the dead body were consumed. The flesh was carved from the bones with bamboo knives, and the visceral tissues carefully removed for cooking. Even the brain tissue was poured from the smashed skull into a bamboo cylinder for cooking over a low fire in the manner that the other tissues were cooked. The human flesh was usually cooked in these bamboo cylinders along with fern leaves or other greens. Occasionally, it was cooked with the vegetables in steam pits over hot stones. Human flesh was, however, a very small part of the total diet, since such cannibalism was restricted to dead close relatives.

Frequently, the body was eaten after two or three days of mourning and after decay had already set in. Cooking was rarely extensive, and partially cooked human meat was often consumed. The lower boiling temperature (less than 95° C at the elevations of many Fore hamlets) increased the possibility that microorganisms could survive the cooking.

Cannibalism seems to have had a relatively short

FIGURE 7. TRAILS. Rough footpaths are the only tradi-tional connections between hamlets and gardens or other hamlets. Frequently enclosed by high grasses or trees, trails were not dug or cleared in the usual sense. Rather, they were created through slashing and the wear of feet repeatedly going to the same place, usually a garden (a, b, c). As a result new trails were not usually well marked (d). Paths through inhabited areas often followed garden fences, reflecting their primary use to connect hamlets with gardens (e). Intervillage trails most often ascended or followed ridges, frequently through tracts of *kunai* grass kept short by repeated burning (f). Fallen logs often pro-vided bridges over the many sharply cut stream beds (b, g). Typical items transported over trails were food from gardens (g) and grass for thatching (e). Until 1957, when the new government sponsored a few public trails and a dead-end jeep track through the Fore region, all travel was via the kinds of trails pictured here. Even in 1969 most intravillage move-ment continued to be on such trails. [a, c–e, Yagareba, 1967; b, Takai, 1967; f, between Ilesa and Kamira, 1963; g, Wanitabe, 1963]

FIGURE 8. FENCES. Trails are primarily to connect hamlets and gardens. As a result, they are frequently intersected by fences, further emphasizing the private character of trails by requiring the travelers who use them to pass through clearly demarcated areas of actively owned land. In order to go through a settled region, a traveler must cross such fences frequently, passing through gardens and hamlets. A young boy with an empty produce bag perches on the edge of the fence separating a garden from an adjacent trail (**a**). Where trails cross fences, notched log ramps are frequently built to facilitate travel (**b**). In other places it is necessary to climb over a specially strengthened part of the fence (**c**). Entrance to hamlets was sometimes barricaded before Western contact, with removable upright barriers that had to be moved in order to pass (**d**).

FIGURE 9. SUSPENSION BRIDGE. In a few places where rivers pass the Fore lands, suspension bridges of vine and stick are constructed to permit travel across the river. This bridge across the Lamari River at Yamnaubinti, Agakamatasa, provides access to South Fore gardens across the river and contact with the Simbari Anga of Morandugai (Dunkwi) hamlet.

history among the Fore, probably not practiced extensively for more than 60 to 100 years before the arrival of missionaries and government officers, after which it quickly disappeared.[8] Soon after the establishment of an Australian patrol post in the Fore region, cannibalism was made a punishable offense, and participants of cannibal mortuary feasts were sometimes jailed. But also discouraging cannibalism was the quickness with which the Fore recognized the abhorrence that Westerners showed toward their method of handling the dead. Eager, in those early days, to adopt European example in the hopes of securing the kind of products, materials and wealth Europeans possessed, they soon abandoned their cannibalistic practices.

Through 1957, and on into 1958 and 1959, episodes of cannibalism were still encountered, especially in the more remote hamlets of the South Fore. But by 1960 it was all but gone, with only a suspicion that some of the older women still carried on the practice surreptitiously into 1960 and 1961.

Kuru

Kuru, an always fatal, infectious, progressively degenerative neurological disease, was occurring in near epidemic proportions among the Fore at the time of Western contact (figs. 10, 11). Related to the practice of cannibalism, it was responsible for approximately half of all deaths in some regions; people dying of it could be found in most South Fore villages. Unknown to Western mankind before 1957, it has yet to be seen elsewhere in the world. Gajdusek described it as follows:

Kuru is, primarily a disease of motor co-ordination with ataxia somewhat akin to the trunkal ataxia of midline cerebellar lesions. Its clinical course is remarkably uniform. Excitement of any sort causes exaggeration of the involuntary movements, which disappear in sleep. The onset is insidious, without antecedent febrile illness. The patient himself is aware of his clumsiness in walking before others notice it. The subsequent course of the disease can be divided into three clinical stages: in the first stage, while the patient is still ambulatory, there is fine irregular tremor akin to shivering, accompanied by a progressive locomotor ataxia, occasional myoclonic jerks, lability which is predominantly euphoric. In the second stage, the patient requires a stick for locomotion and later can walk only when supported by others. Tremors are still coarse and irregular,

and choreiform and athetoid movements and myoclonic shock-like jerks are present. Dysarthria appears and emotionalism with easily provoked inordinate laughter persists. Strabismus develops, often accompanied by nystagmoid eye jerks; tendon jerks are usually hyperactive, and there may be sustained ankle clonus. In the third stage the patient becomes sedentary, unable to walk even with support. He is dragged from the low kunai grass house to sit outdoors. Later, when he loses balance even when sitting, he is left inside, aphonic, and with dysphagia leading to starvation. Decubitus ulcers develop and terminal bronchopneumonia is frequent. The patient in this terminal stage often rolls into the house fire and is fatally burned, he may aspirate secretions or roll over and suffocate. Muscle tone may be normal or may alternate between rigidity and flaccidity. There is no sensory disturbance; muscle fibrillations appear only late in the disease.[9]

The Fore believed kuru to be caused by sorcery. Early studies by Bennett, Rhodes and Robson suggested that it was a genetic disorder determined by a single gene, dominant in females.[10] However, the recent experimental transmission of kuru to chimpanzees and spider monkeys by Gajdusek and his associates has confirmed an infectious etiology, probably a viruslike agent transmitted by cannibalism,[11] a theory first proposed by Glasse and further developed with Mathews and Lindenbaum.[12]

Since kuru was first discovered and studied by Zigas and Gajdusek,[13] it has been slowly declining in incidence,[14] probably as a result of the cessation of cannibalism.

Since the Fore often ate their dead close kinsmen, any infectious agent transmitted thereby would appear to be hereditary. Kinship, not genes, determined transmission. Genetically active DNA or RNA was obtained not from the gametes of natural parents but from classificatory relatives as a result of social customs.

Kuru affected Fore social organization, not only by intensifying suspicion and fear of sorcery, and inducing migration, but also by changing the male/female ratio of the population. In adults it was predominantly a disease of women (the primary cannibal mourners). Among Fore over the age of 20, kuru occurred nearly 20 times more frequently among females.[15] With kuru accounting for nearly one-half of all deaths in many South Fore communities, it markedly affected population structure. In 1963, for example, there were 4,521 South Fore males and only 2,748 females—a ratio of 1.64 males to females.[16] In the North Fore, where kuru did not occur as frequently, the dis-

FIGURE 10. YOUNG GIRL WITH ADVANCED KURU.

FIGURE 11. KURU VICTIMS. Six victims of kuru from one South Fore village are assembled for this photograph.

proportion was not as severe: 1,740 males to 1,291 females, a ratio of 1.36.

In the adult population of both North and South Fore, the imbalance was more severe. For example, among all South Fore over the age of 13, the male/female ratio was 1.86; over the age of 45 it reached 3.00.

In some South Fore communities where kuru was particularly rampant, the ratio of males to females, including children, was over 2.00 and among those over 13 years of age it was over 3.00!

The shortage of women for wives was the most immediate social effect of kuru, a condition that Shirley Glasse (Lindenbaum) summarized after her study of the marital history of 50 Wanitabe clansmen:[17]

During the course of their lives the men contracted a total of 76 marriages or 1.5 unions per man. Of the 76 marriages two terminated in divorce, 45 ended with the death of the wife by kuru. By comparison 52 women contracted 73 marriages, or 1.4 per women. Five marriages terminated in divorce and 15 with the death of the husband—there were no instances in the sample of the husband dying of kuru.

It is difficult to find an adult man who has not been affected by the loss of immediate kin as a result of kuru. The Luluai of Wanitabe, for instance, has lost his mother, his half sister, three wives, one son and one step-son. Pago, a Wanitabe man of about 45 years, has lost three wives and three daughters. Anagu, a Kamila man of about 46 years, has lost his mother, four wives, one sister, one daughter and one son. An extreme case, Poraka, a Kamila man of about 50 years of age has lost three wives, two sisters, two sons, one son's wife, and three daughters.

Because the ravages of kuru left the Fore without sufficient wives to enable them to adhere to the more typical New Guinea Highlands division of labor, men had to assume responsibilities that were carried out by women elsewhere in the Highlands. Particularly in the South Fore, men could be seen at work in the gardens growing their own food—sometimes with the help of their sons or other close male friends. It was harder to find this in the North Fore where kuru was less severe. Fore men also participated in the care and handling of young children—a responsibility more often left to women in other Highland cultures.

Sorcery

The Fore believed, as did most New Guinea Highlanders, that neighboring malicious sorcerers with access to one's living space, could cause sickness and death.[18] But, unlike sorcery in many other parts of the world, its practice was not restricted to professionals or to a particular class; nor did it require difficult-to-acquire technical or ideological knowledge or a long apprenticeship. Men were the principal practitioners, but anyone could be a sorcerer providing he had learned one or more of the techniques from someone who knew them.

Sorcery, as practiced by the Fore, ranged from preparation of outright poisons and the infliction of ritualized traumatic physical abuse on an enemy, to magical acts thought to induce sickness and death from a distance. Although it was customary to keep sorcery techniques secret, it was usually possible to learn some from a father or a close friend. Sometimes a sorcery secret could be purchased from a more distant associate.

Since all sorcery procedures required access to the victim or to his personal detritus (e.g.: hair, fingernail clippings, feces, semen or scraps of his food or clothing), a sorcerer had to have access to the hamlet of his victim either personally or through an accomplice. Thus, where serious disease, such as kuru, continued to occur, suspicion and discord could become acute and socially disruptive. In the face of frequent cases of kuru, segmentation accelerated and dispersal became more pronounced as individuals and small groups fled to escape what was viewed as effective hostile sorcery. South Fore who had recently settled an altogether new region usually cited fear of kuru sorcery as their reason for moving.

Thus, in the face of a severe kuru challenge, increased fear of sorcery had a dispersive effect on Fore communities, whereas under less challenging circumstances, fear of sorcery had a consolidative effect. Lindenbaum (1971a, pp. 284, 286) showed that the Fore type of social system may give rise to sorcery accusations, both as an expression of insecurity among coresidents and as a political means by which social groups express their identity:

> . . . sorcery beliefs operate as an expression of present political reality. Acts of preventive medicine, such as the refusal to eat food in another parish, or the extra care taken with food leavings in some places rather than in others, express the social distance between the men in the groups concerned, the current degree of friendship or mistrust. The location of a sorcery challenge indicates the extent of mutual loyalty felt by a group of co-residents. Sometimes the challenge is issued across parish borders, and sometimes it occurs between sections of the same parish; in either case, it signals possible political separation.
>
> Sorcery accusations are a means of easing tensions among mutually unrelated people who reside together. They also have a political role as a mechanism by which social groups define themselves.

Ronald Berndt (1962) noted that within North Fore "districts" members did not often practice sorcery against each other:

> Sorcery is brought to bear on a member of an alien group whether or not such a person is resident in one's own district, in order to avenge a perceived injury or wrong . . . Retaliatory sorcery directed against a victim resident outside the political unit can be seen as enhancing the social solidarity of that unit. The sorcerer acts with its sanction, and even if he does not have this immediately it is ordinarily not long in coming. If such sorcery is directed against a victim living in the sorcerer's own village or district, especially a woman from another district, the sorcerer must normally have majority support to insure his own protection. If he is a "strong" man he may override public criticism, if this is expressed, or he may carry out his sorcery surreptitiously. If hostile feeling is running high against a woman's lineage and village she may serve as a scapegoat or substitute; the sorcerer's action is legally valid but may serve as a focus of dissension. It embodies retaliation against the outgroup which the victim represents; but it may give rise to conflict within the district or village, depending on the relative strength of the persons concerned.

Neither Berndt nor Lindenbaum focused sufficient attention on the degree to which kuru could unbalance the consolidative function of sorcery. There was a limit to the degree of challenge that this function could survive. What made fear of sorcery change its effect from consolidative to dispersive in a Fore community was the overtaxing, by disease occurrence, of the internal trust so important to their social organization. Under normal circumstances in the New Guinea Highlands, this degree of challenge may not have occurred often. However, the near-epidemic proportions of the bizarre new disease did overtax this system. One result was acceleration of the normally slow dispersive protoagricultural movement of the Fore.

The high prevalence of kuru gained the Fore a reputation for sorcery unequaled elsewhere in the Highlands, and it critically accentuated their own concern about sorcery. Fear of sorcery was evident in all Fore villages visited and studied, but it was particularly marked in the South Fore where kuru occurred much more frequently.

Warfare

Land pressure eventually led to conflict and warfare. In the absence of customs that could govern relations adequately between increasingly closely settled alien groups, anger and fighting could easily develop in the face of conflicting land interests.

It has been possible to observe the typical pattern of exacerbation of relations that could occur between neighboring Fore: Within one's small, closely interacting group, implicit rules of give and take developed on the basis of close personal familiarity among individuals who had known each other nearly all their lives. These close associates did not fight. But this kind of rapprochement could not be extended easily, since it required the familiarity that comes with long-standing daily association. Social relations among adult strangers tended to be uncertain and awkward. It was easy to be misunderstood, to become flustered and annoyed.

Although the typical protoagricultural Fore reaction to social friction was to move elsewhere, even to altogether new lands, this became less and less practical as the lands began to fill up. Accordingly, it was in the more densely settled regions that the Fore more often stood their ground and that warfare was more common and severe.

Warfare among the Fore was usually small scale; casualties were few. Fighting alliances were temporary and informal, particularly in sparsely settled regions. Communities or peoples rarely went to war as political or geographical units. Warfare was never an affair of state. Even within the small hamlets it was unusual for all the men to participate in a raid or battle. Instead, such actions were typically conducted by a few directly aggrieved close associates who felt personally wronged. Their hostility was typically aimed against particular individuals or small groups of associates in other nearby hamlets. Any act that impaired the value of someone's personal effort or property (e.g., breaking or weakening someone's fence, damaging a garden, killing a pig, or engaging in a sexual liaison with another's wife) were typical immediate causes.

Because of the kind of informal dispersive social organization practiced by the Fore, it was not unusual for some of one's hamlet-mates to have social or kinship connections with individuals in the hamlets of the enemy. Such individuals could usually continue to make visits to their friends on the "other side" during times of fighting and were respected in many cases for their peace-making potential.

In regions where the protoagricultural era was coming to an end and land pressure was becoming troublesome, the character of warfare also began to change. More distinct sociopolitical groups were beginning to form; larger bands of combatants began to take to the field. The likelihood of direct attack on hamlets increased, requiring residents who had not yet joined the conflict to fight or flee. Hamlet populations became more united in matters of conflict and warfare. They began to have common enemies who could be identified by where they lived.

An example of this process occurred during the early 1950s in the Ivingoi region among groups from Wanitabe and others from Waisa and Kamira. As populations increased and new forest land became more scarce, the Wanitabe people began moving their gardens and hamlets into the forests to the southeast and west of their original homeland. In doing so they met groups from Waisa and Kamira, similarly expanding. Disputes developed between them and groups in Kamira and Waisa, occasionally joined by elements living in the Wanikanto, Kamata and Kanigitasa regions. Outlying Wanitabe hamlets began to be overwhelmed, sacked and burned. Wanitabes who had associations with people in other areas moved to those areas, scattering widely. Some even left the Fore region altogether to settle among the Awa, a linguistically and culturally distinct group, who welcomed them. Some Wanitabes persisted in a few heavily stockaded ridgetop hamlets, but even these finally proved untenable and were abandoned just before Australian government patrols entered the north to establish a patrol post.

Warfare was considered a curse by most Fore, and although their accounts may have elements of excitement and bravado, I have yet to hear a Fore nostalgically or enthusiastically recall it. It ceased almost spontaneously with the distant ar-rival of the first Australians. The Fore disliked warfare, and the distant presence of but a single Australian patrol officer and a handful of native police was grasped as the excuse to cease.

•   •   •

These conditions played an important role in the emergence of the Fore protoagricultural way of life. They affected not just social and political organization but patterns of human interaction and daily behavior as well. They also sustained the particular type of protoagricultural movement and migration that was so fundamental to the Fore way of life.

Chapter 3 **Subsistence Economy**

The Fore subsistence economy was based on a slow, persistent migratory slash-and-burn penetration of the surrounding virgin land. Small gardens were the center of the productive activity and, together with the hamlets, the foci of daily life (figs. 12 and 13). Supplemented by hunting and gathering, they provided the food required to sustain the Fore population and the means to raise pigs for important ceremonial events, such as marriage, initiation, funerals and intergroup political exchange. Daily life in the hamlets was patterned by the garden-based economic system (fig. 14).

Fertility of soil in gardens declined over time, bringing decreasing yields. Old gardens were abandoned after a few years, and new gardens were cut from the edge of the forest.

In places where increased population and ecological despoilage had begun to limit the availability of virgin forest land, there was some recultivation of previously gardened areas. Old gardens that had been replaced by bush rather than grassland were preferred. In these increasingly congested regions, the subsistence economy, which originally fed only the basic needs of isolated kindreds, began to support the emergence of more extended sociopolitical ties, through elaboration of intergroup pig feasts.

Gardens

Garden sites were selected by the men. Productivity of soil, ease of access, desire to avoid unfriendly people and proximity to compatible people all influenced the choice of site.

Planting could occur any time during the year. Dry periods were preferred for garden clearing, no doubt because of the greater ease of burning, but rainy periods were often preferred for actual planting. Whether the new gardens were cut from the virgin forest or reclaimed from second-growth bush or grassland, the technique of preparing the land was essentially the same: slash-and-burn (fig. 15). Branches of large trees were chopped off and their trunks girdled; small trees were felled, bushes cut away, grass and debris burned off, ditches dug for water diversion or drainage, and fences built. Men and older boys did most of this work, while women and girls cleared weeds and grass and collected the debris into small piles to burn. After the clearing was completed, the women took responsibility for preparing the soil and for transplanting the food plants from other gardens. The cultivation and tending of gardens was primarily the responsibility of the women, who planted, cultivated and harvested the major food crops. Men were responsible for constructing and maintaining the surrounding fences (fig. 16).

The gaunt, dead tree trunks and the logs, stumps and roots haphazardly situated among the crops gave the new gardens a somewhat disorderly appearance (fig. 17). Garden neatness increased with age. In many of the older-style gardens, particularly those close to hamlets, there were mixed plantings of several foods in various stages of ripening (fig. 18).

Before the 1950s, garden clearing was done with stone axes and fire-hardened digging sticks. Since then, the introduction of steel axes, machetes and spades has made this work much easier.

After sweet potato (Ipomoea batatas), the most common cultivated food plants were the several species of green-leaf vegetables collectively called kumu in Melanesian Pidgen, a dozen or so native-designated varieties of a thick-stemmed, low grass with a thick succulent heart called pitpit (Saccharum edule and Setaria palmifola), taro (Colocasia

FIGURE 12. GARDEN SITES. As the fertility of the soil is exhausted, gardens are abandoned and new sites cleared, usually from the rainforest, where the ground is believed to be more productive. As a result, new gardens are often studded with dead tree trunks and fallen logs. Such gardens are frequently found in the forest (a) or just at the edge of it (b). *Kunai* grass fields often abut gardens on one side, marking sites of earlier cultivation (c). In areas where duration of settlement or density of population has resulted in considerable loss of forest lands, gardens have moved closer to the steep banks of streams and gulleys, leaving the paths of these watercourses etched by trees. In such regions, recultivation of old garden sites is practiced, although such practice is usually confined to those sites that have grown up in secondary scrub growth instead of *kunai* grass (d). New gardens may be extended from the edges of old gardens where the land is good (e). In recent times, this has led to larger consolidated gardens, which often include a few abandoned plots (f). [a, Takai, 1968; b, Takai, 1967; c, Ilesa, 1963; d, Awarosa, 1968; e, Agakamatasa, 1961; f, Yagareba, 1968]

FIGURE 13. GARDENS IN RELATION TO A HAMLET. The protoagricultural Fore hamlets move to penetrate virgin forest lands along favorable routes of gardening. Here, the residents of Oriondamuti hamlet of the Awarosa region sustain a contiguous path of exploitation against the forested slopes of Mt. Tamiloa (1967).

FIGURE 14. THE EFFECT OF GARDENING ON HAMLET LIFE. In the early morning, smoke seeps through the thatch roofs of the houses as fires are built up to warm food before leaving for the gardens. Children go out into the hamlet yard (a). Shortly after breakfast, most hamlet residents leave for gardens. Occasionally an older woman might remain in the hamlet weaving (b). Often children pass through the hamlet, staying for a while to play as the day wears on (c, d). By mid-afternoon, groups of residents begin returning from their gardens to prepare food collectively for the late after-noon meal. Women prepare the garden produce (e), while men cut wood and prepare the cooking fire and pit (f).

FIGURE 15. GARDEN CLEARING. Land for gardens is cleared by girdling and de-branching large trees, cutting away small trees and brush, and burning. In a, clearing and burning are nearly complete and the fence already built; some of the trees, already dead from girdling, remain standing. In b, first crops grow in a recently cleared garden.

FIGURE 16. FENCE REPAIR. One of the main jobs of the men was to build and repair fences. Weak or broken fences allowed pigs to enter and devastate gardens. Vertical stakes have to be pushed back into the ground periodically and laterals firmly attached to them by short sections of vine. When these become old and weak, they must be replaced (**a**). New laterals are frequently inserted into an otherwise vulnerable fence (**b**). [Yagareba, 1967]

FIGURE 17. NEWER AND OLDER GARDENS. The newer gardens encroaching on the forest are often studded with dead tree trunks and fallen logs. Among the remains of the forest, freshly cultivated plots alternate with plantings of sweet potato, corn, banana, green leaf vegetables (*kumu*) and *pitpit* (**a**). Over time, these traces of the forest (tree trunks and fallen logs) disappear as they are taken to the hamlets for firewood, rot away or are thrown out of the garden when they become more manageable. Neatly demarcated plots of sweet potato, bean, corn, *kumu* and coffee mark the boundary between grassland and forest (**b**).

FIGURE 18. MIXED GARDENS. Older gardens, particularly those close to hamlets, often contain a variety of vegetables planted, one among the other. These four pictures show such gardens: taro, sugar cane, yam, *kumu* and sweet potato (**a**); taro, yam, tobacco, sugar cane and sweet potato (**b**); yam, corn, sweet potato and a decorative plant (**c**); young banana trees coming up among taro, beans, *kumu* and sweet potato (**d**).

esculenta and *Xanthosoma* sp.) and yam *(Diosocera spp.)*. Most hamlets also had plantings of maize *(Zea mays)*, which appears to have been introduced somewhat before Western contact, the winged bean *(Psophocarpus tetragonolobus)*, banana *(Musa sp.)*, and cucumber *(Cucumis sativus)*. In a few gardens there was also manioc *(Manihot utilisima)*, a plant introduced before contact via intervillage trade routes, and ginger *(Zingiber sp.)*. Some gardens also had bamboo clusters planted in or near them, primarily as a ready source for bamboo cooking cylinders, but also for edible bamboo shoots. There were also a few "bark" trees (probably *Gnetum gnemon*), the inner bark of which was used to make string, net bags, apparel and a crude tapa cloth.

Before Western contact, a number of European vegetables also diffused into the Fore region during the 1940s and early 1950s via intervillage trade routes: tomato, haricot bean, onion and pawpaw. Since contact, several more vegetables have been adopted: carrots, peas, lima beans, lettuce, cabbage, pineapple, pumpkin, peanut, lemon, coffee and new varieties of banana, corn and potato.

The readiness of the Fore to adopt new foods was unusual and distinguished them from many other people of the world.

Men were responsible for a few crops; but these tended to be used ceremonially rather than casually and did not contribute substantially to the overall diet. The most important of these were sugar cane *(Saccharum officinarum)*, particularly the red variety; one variety of banana; red pandanus *(Pandanus conoideus)*; nut pandanus *(Pandanus jiulianetti* or *P. brosimos)*; and at least one variety of taro. Tobacco *(Nicotiana tabacum)* was also grown and used exclusively by men. In contrast to many other parts of the Highlands, Fore men also participated, to various degrees, in the cultivation and harvesting of most of the food crops. The winged bean sometimes received more attention from the men than the other crops because its tuber was prized for intergroup feasts.

Gardens were the center of daily Fore life. During the day, hamlets were virtually deserted as friends, relatives and children went to the gardens to mingle their social, family and erotic pursuits with their garden work in a salutary and emotionally filled gestalt of garden life *(figs. 19 and 20)*.

Protohorticulture

Along the trails in higher altitude forests, nut pandanus trees were sporadically planted or cultivated, usually as individual trees *(fig. 21)*. Occasionally, in the forests of the lower valleys, the seeds of the wild *andi* (Fore) nut tree were also planted. In some regions, particularly in the western Fore, small clusters as well as individual red pandanus trees were planted on otherwise unimproved land. These isolated plantings of trees in unimproved lands represented a kind of protohorticulture carried on by the Fore men. It was only slightly removed from the exploitation of wild nut pandanus and *andi* as gathering activities.

In pioneer regions there were also unowned wild pandanus and *andi* trees, the fruit of which could be gathered by anyone. Ownership of such trees came with an investment of labor—planting a cutting or a seed or even the simple sustained clearing away of the brush around a wild tree.

Unowned wild trees were more common in the pioneer forest regions of the South Fore. In the

FIGURE 19. GARDEN LIFE. Gardens were a major focus of social life, a convivial place of social engagement, family activity and erotic pursuit. They were not just places of labor where one had to work to gain his livelihood. Work there was not thought of as onorous; it was not a task to be completed in isolation from the more pleasurable things of life and family. Love, friendship, affection, play, work and learning were mixed into an inseparable gestalt of garden life. Women and girls tended and planted at an unscheduled leisurely pace (a, b, c), while children amused themselves nearby or participated according to their pleasure in the work activities at hand (e, f, h, k). Men protectively watched over the women, took part in the relaxed social milieu, cleared the land for new gardens and built and repaired the fences (d, g, h). Behavior of girls in the gardens was expected to be seductive and coquettish, and human relations tended to be freer in the garden than in the more formally organized hamlets (i, j). Produce gathered was carried back to the hamlets, usually in mid-afternoon (m, n).

FIGURE 20. POSTCONTACT CONSOLIDATED HAMLETS AND GARDENS. Small hamlets gathered around sites of government or mission activity after Western contact, resulting in larger hamlets with extensive contiguous gardens. Earlier, small garden plots had been the rule. [Oriondamuti hamlet of Awarosa, 1967]

FIGURE 21. PANDANUS PLANTINGS. In isolated bush or forest locations, nut pandanus (a, b) and red pandanus (c, d) are planted as single trees or in small stands, sometimes as cuttings from wild trees. The pandanus bearing edible nuts is usually planted in elevations higher than the hamlets, while red pandanus thrives better at lower altitudes in damp valleys or beside streams. These semicultivated trees represent a transitional stage between gathering wild foods and gardening. Only in a few villages has the red pandanus been introduced into actual gardens. [a, Agakamatasa; b, Yagareba, 1968; c, Weya (Saburosa), 1967]

more densely settled North Fore, they were harder to find. There the nut pandanus continued to survive as an owned plant propagated in the ungardenable higher altitude forests; the *andi,* both wild and planted, had virtually disappeared.

These protohorticultural activities may represent remnants of the earliest effort by hunting-gathering forebears to increase accessibility to and yields from wild plants through direct ecological manipulation.

Sweet Potato

Sweet potato was the staple crop. It above all others supported the Fore population and made their protoagricultural way of life possible. It was the easiest to grow and the most plentiful food of the Fore; it was always available. The most garden space was devoted to it, and it was eaten at virtually all meals. It was the first solid food given to babies, and its preeminent role in diet continued to old age. Other cultivated plants played a significant part in the Fore diet, but all of these together did not equal the sweet potato.[19]

Growing rapidly and easily on the tropical mountain slopes of the Highlands, the sweet potato replaced earlier dietary staples of the New Guinea Highlanders, probably within the last 200 years in the Fore.

By the time of contact, there were abundant sweet potato gardens around all Fore settlements. Not only was much more garden land devoted to the sweet potato, but its yield per unit of land was much greater than for the other crops. I have recorded yields up to 20 tons per acre in some gardens.[20]

In spite of its crucial role in Fore diet, the sweet potato had no ceremonial significance—possibly because of its recentness as a significant food.

Pigs

At the center of the ceremonial and political life of the Fore people were the pig feasts. They provided the formal mechanism for settling disputes and debts (including bride price and death payments) and for cementing political and economic alliances. All important rites of passage, such as initiations, marriages and funerals were celebrated by pig feasts.

Though domestic pig provided most of the animal protein eaten by the Fore, it entered the diet very irregularly. When pig numbers in a village were high and requirements for ceremony and debt repayment low, pigs were butchered and cooked for informal hamlet feasts as often as once a week. However, during times of shortage, the pigs were reserved for important ceremonies and for debt payment or exchange feasts. At such times, pig meat might not be eaten for a month or more. Sometimes there were periods of several consecutive months without pork, followed by several days of glut after a ceremonial feast. On the other hand, there could also be periods of several months when pig was eaten as often as several times a week. Typically, the Fore ate pig two or three times a month.

Pig population was cyclical in the more heavily populated regions as a result of the periodic, large intervillage pig exchange feasts. More than 100 pigs might be butchered and cooked for this celebration, which occurred at five- to 15-year intervals. The number of pigs in a Fore village usually increased slowly over the course of the several years between massive exchange feasts and then dropped markedly after the slaughter.

To contribute an inferior number of pigs in such a ceremony put a group in a position of debt. Thus, as the year of a large pig exchange ceremony approached, there were efforts to increase numbers of pigs. Other important ceremonies, such as initiations, were sometimes deferred in order to conserve pigs for the coming exchange feast. Garden space was increased to meet the subsistence demands of the increased numbers of pigs. As a means to achieving parity or preeminence at an exchange feast, sometimes alliances were concluded between previously disparate groups, and their pigs pooled.

Fenced out of gardens because of the havoc they would wreak in the plantings, pigs nevertheless had free run of the hamlets, surrounding bush and trails. Women caretakers fed, lived with and cared for them from birth *(fig. 22);* in many cases the pigs were suckled at the breasts of their foster

FIGURE 22. PIG HUSBANDRY. Pigs traditionally had free run of the hamlets and quarters in the women's houses. They could usually depend on the woman who had raised them to give them a few sweet potatoes or other scraps to eat. When the individuals who cared for the pigs returned to their hamlet with food from the garden, their pigs, anticipating handouts, often followed them (a). They also tended to idle about when their caretakers remained in the hamlet (b). Young pigs were accustomed to affectionate care by those adult women responsible for them and by their daughters (c). Care of pigs extended to grooming and delousing them (d). [a, b, c, Yagareba, 1967; d, Yagareba, 1963]

FIGURE 23. SCAVENGING PIGS I. During the day, pigs often remain near the gardens being cultivated by their caretakers, where they spend their day scavenging in the nearby uncultivated lands (a) and also wait for occasional bits of garden produce to be thrown over the fence to them (b). [Yagareba, 1967]

human mothers (this practice, however, has disappeared since the late 1950s). In traditional hamlets, pigs lived in their own section of the women's houses and often had their own doors for unrestricted entrance when the human residents were away.

During the day, pigs scavenged in the nearby bush, along the trails and around the gardens of their caretakers. These women, working in the gardens, occasionally threw inferior sweet potato tubers to them (fig. 23). In the evening the pigs usually returned to the hamlets where women returning from gardens also brought food for them. When the villagers cooked, the pigs gleaned scraps, handouts and residue. During feasts, many pigs often gathered close by to consume the large quantities of waste and disposable food (fig. 24).

Since 1966, pigs have begun to be excluded from the more modernized hamlets by fences, at the suggestion of the Australian government officials. Even though a number of villagers were not in favor of this new practice, it quickly prevailed in the modernized villages where the more progressive people lived, and as the government became more insistent. The obvious disadvantages to the Fore were: 1) separating pigs from the people who liked close association with them; and 2) making the disposal of waste from meals more difficult.

As a means to mitigating these drawbacks, the Fore began to hold their feasts outside their hamlets so that pigs could be accommodated. They also built ancillary houses away from the main hamlet, where they could live with their pigs at least part of the time. However, some people simply built smaller houses, just for pigs, outside the hamlet.

As the newer pattern of pig care has developed, men began to take on more of the responsibility for looking after them. For example, men, not women, go out to live in the ancillary houses with the pigs, and men, more often, carry food to the pigs in their new pig houses.

The overall effect of the change in the manner of housing and feeding pigs is that they are slowly receiving a lessened degree of human contact, in spite of the fact that they are still generally thought to be desirable company. Youths most influenced by contact with Europeans are, however, beginning to avoid contact with pigs.

FIGURE 24. SCAVENGING PIGS II. When the villagers cook and eat, pigs glean scraps, handouts and residue. During feasts, many pigs may gather to dispose of the large quantity of waste and disposable food and make it unnecessary for the Fore to clean the area of food scraps and cooking debris after meals.

Semidomesticated Animals

Occasionally a wild young cassowary *(Casuarius bennetti)* would be tamed and raised in the hamlet, cared for and fed by women. Those captured as young chicks, especially when just hatched, would become quite tame and were allowed free run of the hamlet. They appeared to imprint on their caretakers and made no effort to escape. However, when they approached maturity, they could be dangerous and were then usually kept in pens or tethered. Eventually, like the pigs, they were cooked and eaten in a feast.

The only other wild animals occasionally kept, fed and cared for before being eaten were the many varieties of cuscus *(Phalanger* spp.*)* and, more rarely, the tree-climbing kangaroo *(Dendrolagus* sp.*)*. These were not usually kept in captivity for more than a few weeks; they could not be tamed.

Hunting and Gathering

Although gardens were the source of most of the food eaten by the Fore, a small but almost daily component of wild food entered the diet in most hamlets. Such foods, obtained by hunting and gathering, were more abundant in pioneer areas like the South Fore *(fig. 25)*. Women and girls did not participate, restricting themselves instead to gardening.

Older boys and men hunted wild pigs, cassowary, brush turkeys *(Aepypodius arfakianus)*, scrub hens *(Megapodius* sp.*)*, cuscus, tree-climbing kangaroos, wallabies *(Thylogale* sp.*)*, a number of birds of several species, eels, snakes (particularly the python), fish and occasionally wild dogs and forest rats.

Young boys, between five and eight years of age usually limited their hunting efforts to domestic

FIGURE 25. HUNTING AND GATHERING. Boys and men do the hunting. Bows and arrows (**a**) are used, and the most common quarry are birds (**b**) and cuscus (**c**). Fishing (**d**) is less common, occurring only in the few hamlets near large streams. Some beetles are considered a culinary delicacy (**e**). Wild nuts (*kurona*) are gathered (**f**), and the larva of the longicorn beetle is relished (**g**); young tree fern leaves are collected to be cooked with pig (**h**), and mushrooms, which grow abundantly in the rainforest, are frequently gathered (**i**). Women and children often gather, cook and eat insects, spiders and larvae while working in the gardens. [**a, c, g, i,** Yagareba, 1967; **b, e,** Wanitabe, 1963; **d,** Agakamatasa; **h,** Takai, 1968]

and garden rats, beetles, grasshoppers, lizards, spiders and rarely, frogs, to augment their otherwise predominantly sweet potato diet. These were often relished by the young boys and were also eaten by girls and women. Usually they were cooked on the spot by those making the catch. When women and children were in the gardens, mothers or older children would sometimes catch insects and other arthropods to cook and give to a hungry child. Women and girls also sampled this fare, but almost never did the teenage boys and men.

Small game obtained by boys was usually cooked and consumed almost immediately after return to hamlets and sometimes even at the site of the catch. The meal was usually shared within the small hunting band and with those few friends fortunate enough to be in the vicinity. Rarely was the catch large enough for a large group.

Gathering frequently went hand-in-hand with hunting. Important among the wild foods gathered were the several species of wild mushrooms growing abundantly in the rainforest. Large collections of these were frequently shared by an entire hamlet. The large *andi* nut and the wild pandanus nut were particularly prized, as were the seeds of the wild breadfruit. Honeycomb, the larvae of the longicorn beetle (*Gerambycidae* sp.) and at least one other kind of large larva were frequently collected. The large eggs of the brush turkey and scrub hen were sometimes the objectives of a particular hunt, but the smaller eggs of many other species of birds were also collected and eaten. The several wild fruits collected included the popular mango. Several species of nut were also gathered and eaten as well as some kinds of wild bamboo shoots and the heart of the wild black palm *(limbum* in Melanesian Pidgen). Wild ferns, both tree and ground, were collected and often cooked along with other foods in the earth oven. In addition there were a number of wild herbs and barks used as condiments. A number of herbs, ferns and barks were also collected for their believed medicinal properties or for use in sorcery.[21]

After a boy's initiation, food taboos prohibited his consumption of many hunted foods such as: cuscus, wallaby, kangaroo, eggs, snakes, larvae and rats. During this period, his hunting objectives tended to alter more toward the community's needs and interests. After marriage, however, many taboos were relaxed, and married men often carried their bows and arrows to their gardens, hunted and sometimes set traps in the vicinity.

The best and most influential hunters were almost always among the older men who began to spend more time hunting in the forest in their later years. Advice and participation of these older, more skilled hunters was usually sought when large hunts were organized by the village men to obtain game for special feasts.

Sometimes there were feasts featuring cuscus, kangaroo and wallaby. Such feasts were often held during rainy periods because of a belief that the killing and eating of these animals caused dry weather. Other feasts were devoted to wild pigs and cassowary.

Wild pig, cassowary, cuscus, kangaroo, wallaby, eel and rodents were trapped as well as hunted by the men. In most cases, snares were used, but there were also deadfall traps for smaller game *(fig. 26)*. Trapping, like hunting, was a skill that increased with experience and interest; some men were recognized as particularly skillful at one or more kinds of trapping.

Young boys usually restricted their trapping efforts to rodents. Not uncommonly, small snares or deadfall traps for this purpose could be found along the edge of a garden or near a house.

Eel traps were the most intricate *(fig. 26)*. They were useable even in small streams and sometimes provided large catches sufficient to feed an entire hamlet for a small feast.

Fishing was not done by all Fore, probably because of the scarcity of streams large enough to support fish. Yet those people living near large streams or rivers would fish, and a large catch sometimes made possible a fish feast that was shared with a neighboring village. Crayfish and a fresh-water shrimp were eaten occasionally in some hamlets.

Native-Made Salt

Before the introduction of commercial salt during the 1950s, the Fore in several villages laboriously made their own salt and traded it to villages that did not *(fig. 27)*. Possibly this manufacture may be

FIGURE 26. TRAPPING. Traps and snares are used to catch rodents, cuscus, cassowaries, birds and eels. Rodent snares are often set along garden fences (a, b). Cuscus are trapped in similar snares set in trees in the forest (e). Long, tubular bark eel traps, baited with witchetty grubs, are anchored in streams (c, d). Snares (a, b, e) are used more frequently than deadfall traps (f). [a, b, Takai, 1968; c–f, Yagareba, 1968]

derivative of the elaborate salt industry of the Anga salt makers of Barua, Marawaka and Amdei which it resembles; but how the trait may have spread into the Fore is unknown. It is also similar to salt-production methods in other parts of inland New Guinea.

The salt was made by burning and extracting the water-soluble salts from the ash of an indigenous tall grass *(Coix gigantea),* which was planted and cultivated on well-watered, flat ground.

Several villages specialized in salt making and were able to supply non-salt-making villages via intervillage trade routes in return for bows and arrows, stone axes and knives, bundles of orchid stem fibre, smoking pipes, cowrie shells, tobacco and bird feathers. Sometimes the salt bundles

themselves were used as a kind of rudimentary currency rather than consumed. A few villages who made particularly good salt traded it to distant villages, even across language and cultural frontiers. Different qualities of salt were recognized, and the good salts were called "sweet."

Different recipes were used by different groups of salt makers to produce distinctive salts. They could include ashes of ferns, herbs, staghorns, creepers and barks, as well as some wild grasses and even the edible garden varieties of *pitpit.*

Some salt makers claimed that certain firewoods produced better salt than others. Villages manufacturing salt required easily accessible stands of forest land in order to supply the considerable firewood required for the incineration and evapo-

FIGURE 27. SALT MAKING. Before government control of the Fore region, salt was manufactured by the natives from a locally grown salt reed. The harvested reed was incinerated on a pyre of special wood (a) and the ashes, protected from rain by a *kunai* grass shelter, were left to cool for several days (b). The ash was then placed in a leaf filter, water poured over it, and the salt solution collected below (c). The solution was then evaporated in continually refilled pandanus leaf dishes over a bed of hot coals (d). The crystallized salt was removed from the evaporating dishes and specially wrapped (e, f) for several months of curing in the smoke of house fires. [Yagareba, 1968]

ration processes.

After harvesting, the bundles of "salt reed" were piled on top of flat pyres made of logs, sometimes to a depth of a few meters. Burning usually began early in the morning before sunrise on a day when it was believed that there would be no rain. When the pyre was burned down, leaving only ash and smoldering logs, the fragments of unburned wood were removed, and a rainproof *kunai* grass hut was built over the hot ash. The ash was left to cool in the hut for two or three days. It was then removed, small amounts at a time, and placed in a large filter made of leaves

fitted into a frame made of sticks and saplings. Water was poured on the ash, and the filtrate dripping from the bottom was collected in bamboo tubes.

During the cooling of the ash and the filtering, an evaporation house was built enclosing a rectangular bed in which to hold hot coals. The filtrate was evaporated over these coals in special dishes made from pandanus leaves. As evaporation proceeded uninterrupted, these were refilled until the filtrate was completely evaporated in two days and nights. Juice from a special bark, extracted with saliva by chewing was added, and the thickening solution was allowed to crystallize, leaving a cake of salt weighing over a pound. This salt cake was wrapped and then smoke-cured over the fire in the salt maker's house for two to three months. It was then rewrapped to be used in trade. Ceremonial incantations and rituals were performed during certain times of the manufacture, and certain aspects of the production were restricted to men who knew the secrets. Women were not allowed even to look upon the site of production.

After the introduction of Western commercial salt in the 1950s, native salt went into immediate decline, and by 1959 all salt making had ceased. The North Fore, brought under administrative control earlier, received their first commercial salt in the late 1940s. The first such salt to be introduced to the South Fore was in the mid-1950s. As soon as trade salt became available, the old, carefully protected fields of cultivated salt reed were left untended, and the reed grew wild or died. Boys were no longer required to have made salt before marriage, and the secrecy, taboos and ceremonialism surrounding salt production were abandoned. The accomplished salt makers stated that as soon as they tasted the new trade salt, they lost interest in their own salt and put their energies into finding ways to get it rather than continuing to produce their own. Since the new salt was relatively cheap and frequently distributed by the early European visitors in trade for food and services, it replaced native salt quickly.

Occasionally, as late as 1963, some of the men would make small amounts for nostalgic reasons, or, as some claimed, because they thought the native salt might give some protection from kuru. In a few South Fore villages, some men believed that more people started getting kuru when the native salt was no longer being eaten, while others blamed the increase in kuru on the greater ease with which sorcerers could move about after the opening of public roads and trails and the cessation of wafare.

Casual Eating

A casualness typified the day-to-day approach to eating, and the Fore consumed much of their food as they felt the urge to eat, rather than during formal meal times. Only the occasional feasts were managed by formal planning. Cooked and uncooked food was stored in the houses for consumption as desired by both adults and children. These stocks frequently included cold cooked sweet potato, taro, yam and sometimes pork, sugar cane, raw *pitpit*, greens, pandanus nuts and peanuts. Although cooking usually occurred more or less regularly early in the morning and again in the late afternoon, it was, nonetheless, not unusual to see one or two or more individuals at any time during the day building a small fire to cook portions of food obtained from the bush or garden or to warm up snacks found in the houses.

Small children, even toddlers, took any food around whenever they desired and ate whenever they felt the urge. They were permitted to take food from the house or garden. They could also demand it from older children and adults who were cooking or eating nearby. Young children were rarely denied the food they wanted, when they wanted it, even if it was not originally intended for them. Fore young were accustomed to free access to food from their nursing days when they had unlimited access to the breasts of their mothers.

The custom of eating according to one's impulses was well established among the Fore and accepted as natural. Consequently it was not unusual at any time of the day or night to see one or two people in a group eating while others did not, or a person nibbling on raw garden products or cold food found in the house. Similarly, those who had gone to the forest or grasslands to gather wild foods frequently cooked and ate them on the spot or immediately upon returning to their hamlets.

Yet, eating was not a purely individualistic quest, solely to gratify one's private gustatory needs. Rather, underlying much of the casual irregularity were diverse social interests extending to a number of people.

Sharing food was one of the most important forms of social and political engagement among the Fore. Of considerable importance was that their casual eating practices provided a basic structural foundation for their "loose," informal sociopolitical organization. Fires and food drew friends, who came to talk, eat and (in the case of men) smoke with each other. Individual inclinations for new personal liaisons could be acted upon easily, and newcomers could be integrated into existing fraternal groups rather readily. Conversation and sharing of food were fundamental elements in the large concept of Fore kinship and friendship. This could be seen as they shared food around a fire.

Daily Meals

In addition to their casual snacks, most Fore cooked food regularly in the morning, shortly after rising and again in mid- to late afternoon. These could be considered the daily meals. They frequently consisted of *pitpit* and green-leaf vegetables cooked in bamboo cylinders, in addition to the more basic sweet potato *(figs. 28, 29, 30)*. Corn, taro or banana might also be baked in the flames or coals of a fire. And sometimes there were supplementary wild foods such as mushrooms, palm hearts, baby birds, cuscus, wild eggs, beetles, rodents or grubs *(fig. 31)*.

Attendance at meals was not necessarily expected. Daily meals were not formal affairs, and one might eat where and with whom he chose. Typically, the Fore ate in small, informal groups of associates.

Before the advent of government administration, men and women lived in separate houses and ate separately in groups of their own sex. The married women cooperated in the cooking, assisted by the unmarried older girls and, in a rather haphazard way, by the younger children. In the men's larger houses, where up to a dozen men and boys might gather, there were often three or four fireplaces allowing various small groups to cook at their own pleasure.

The rapid decline of segregated housing after 1960 led to cooking and eating together as integrated families. Boys began to establish small residences for unmarried youths where younger boys would often join them, the married men choosing to live and eat with their wives and children. However, those Fore men who still preferred to eat with their male friends could be seen cooking for themselves out-of-doors or in the houses of bachelors or widowers rather than with the women.

Feasts

Feasts were a means of collective cooking in a community cooking pit (earth oven). They united people in common effort and also provided a means to restock houses with the precooked food used for snacks and casual meals.

It is possible to speak of both formal and informal feasts, although the Fore did not categorize them in this way. Yet, they could be distinguished by the presence or absence of fraternal relationship among the participants, the size of the celebration and whether or not it required obvious negotiated planning. Since the formality of a feast depended on how closely associated the participants were, feast organization provided a key to gauging the degree of "kinship" or sense of commonality among the informally organized Fore people.

Informal feasts sustained social ties among relatively intimate peoples. They were held by voluntarily participating members of a few closely associated hamlets *(fig. 32)*. These feasts tended to be spontaneously organized among friends and daily associates. They did not require planning as much as participation. Only individuals desiring to take part did so. No one was enjoined. Such feasts were held relatively frequently (e.g., a few times a week during periods of dry weather and only somewhat less often during rainy periods.)

Formal feasts, on the other hand, reinforced political ties among nonintimate peoples. They were intervillage celebrations held among people who were not closely connected but who still had some common interest, which made liaison advantageous. Sometimes they sustained fighting alliances; more often they kept open a source of brides. They also opened routes to other regions and helped sustain trading relations. The participants could have been recent rivals or enemies and the feast, a means to rapprochement or repayment of a grievance.

Unlike the informal hamlet feasts, these formal feasts required negotiation and planning. Appro-

FIGURE 28. DAILY MEALS I. During the day, particularly in the morning and afternoon, small groups of friends and relatives built fires and cooked in bamboo cooking cylinders on the flames or coals. These meal times were usually unscheduled and depended often on the degree of hunger and conviviality of the participants. A group of women cook *kumu* just picked from a nearby garden in front of their house using bamboo cooking cylinders. A fourth woman and her daughter are outside the frame of the picture to the right (a). A group of boys have built a small fire to cook *pitpit* and *kumu* (in the bamboo tube), corn and sweet potato. This has attracted the interest of some small children who had been playing nearby (b). Banana, yam, sweet potato and possibly *kumu, pitpit* or sweet potato in bamboo cooking cylinders, cook in the flames of a fire (c). Two men who had just returned from the bush with *mareta* (red pandanus fruit) break it into small pieces for cooking (d). [a, Mugagori hamlet of Waisa, 1963; b, Ketabi, 1963; d, Yagareba, 1967]

FIGURE 29. DAILY MEALS II. As small groups of friends sat about the fires in their houses, they frequently put bits of food brought from the gardens or bush on the fire to cook and eat.

FIGURE 30. PREPARING LEAF VEGETABLES FOR COOKING. Leaf vegetables frequently augmented the sweet potato during daily meals. These were usually cooked in bamboo cylinders, often along with other foods. Water was not added, and these vegetables were left to cook in their own juices.

FIGURE 31. EATING WILD FOODS. Wild foods frequently augment the Fore diet. These are obtained by hunting, trapping or gathering and may come either from the forest or grasslands. Mice are normally eaten only by young boys, but sometimes they can be included in a feast primarily made up of catches of wild animals (a). Cuscus (*Phalanger* spp.) is considered a delicacy and is usually caught in traps set in the tops of high trees. Like the rodents, they are usually cooked whole in the fire (b). Wild mushrooms may be gathered by boys and older men to be cooked in bamboo cylinders (c) or directly on the coals of the fire (d). Wild bush fowl eggs can be found in the grasslands and are usually considered a treat. They are normally cooked in bamboo cylinders (e). The heart of the wild palm *(limbum)* may be a snack for a boy out in the forest or he may even bring a few pieces back to the hamlet to share with a few friends (f). [Yagareba, 1967]

FIGURE 32. INFORMAL FEASTS. As often as two or three times a week, a group of hamlet residents, together with some of their friends and relatives from nearby hamlets, assemble to cook assorted garden produce in a steam pit. Here, a group waits while the food, sealed in the pit with leaves and dirt, cooks. [Yagareba, 1967]

priate contributions of food, time and place had to be worked out by intervillage discussion and bargaining. Most formal feasts were held to pay bride price, death debts or damages. Initiations were always celebrated by formal feasts. But the most lavish feasts were those sustaining intercommunity alliance through the periodic dance festivals in which up to 100 pigs might be slaughtered. They were an important means of sustaining political or defense alliances.

All feasts involved gifts and exchanges of food, as well as other goods, according to a complex sense of social obligation existing among individuals.

Inception of a feast was left to the men. Some feasts were very small, involving only a few contributing participants; others brought a few hundred individuals together from several villages.

Organizing the small fraternal feasts was relatively easy, since it required little more than the spontaneous interest of several closely associated friends. Hamlets were small, and the daily familiarity of the residents allowed such feasts to materialize during the flow of daily living. Good weather or the fortuitous killing of wild game might be the spontaneous occasion for such a feast. Those interested in participating determined how to proceed. Sometimes, an hour or so was all that was necessary to get a small feast under way.

Larger feasts, which were to settle social obligations or debts with another group or village, or to consummate a marriage or an initiation, required more serious organization and were often considered delicate social or political matters. A decision to hold such a feast could require weeks, even months of discussion and negotiation. But, since recognition of outstanding debt or need for reconciliation was often a source of concern, a means of holding an appropriate feast was usually found. Too great a delay in settling intercommunity debts could cause deterioration in relations.

Since payment feasts invariably involved people from other hamlets and villages, emissaries often went back and forth to work out the details for the participation of the more distant groups. Similarly, for the wedding and initiation feasts, men having connections with the principals in the other communities worked out the details on the basis of the existing ties of friendship, kinship and obligation. Feast exchanges, which developed between communities, became easier to organize as a pattern was establshed.

On the morning of the feast, women gathered garden produce and brought net bags full of sweet potatoes, yams, taro, *pitpit* and *kumu* from their gardens. Men brought the ceremonial sugar cane, winged bean roots, pandanus fruit and wild game or domestic pig. In the case of debt payment feasts, accumulations of bark cloth and other nonedible gifts were also brought into the feast area. By mid-day, the women were seated among their friends and began to cut, peel and package the vegetables *(fig. 33)*. The men began the butchering and the laying of the fire on which to heat the stones. Boys cleaned the trash and water from the old cooking pits. Women dressed the pig intestines and other viscera.

When the fire had burned down, the men pushed the hot stones into the adjacent cooking pit with long sticks *(fig. 34)*. Leaves were brought and placed on top of the hot stones, and the bundles of vegetables *(fig. 35)* and sides of pig were placed on the leaves. When the pit was filled, the food was covered with banana leaves and dirt to retain the heat and steam. Water was poured from long bamboo containers through small openings left in the cap of the pit. Upon sealing the first cooking pit, the men would go on to fill another. If a second pit was not necessary, they sat nearby and waited. Customarily, the men sat together on one side of the feast area and the women together on another. Boys tended to gather in small groups of age-mates, sitting and walking about. Girls sat in small groups among the women. During the course of the preparation of the food, young children and toddlers roamed freely about the feast site, sampling and playing with bits of food and other objects of interest, even poking and nibbling on the raw pig as it was butchered. The young children were not discouraged from this kind of play.

An estimate of the necessary cooking time was made by the men. Sometimes estimates were such that the pit yielded semicooked pork and vegetables; other times the meat and vegetables seemed overcooked.

When the food was thought to be cooked, the men opened the pit and distributed bundles of food to the waiting guests and participants *(figs.*

FIGURE 33. PREPARING FOOD FOR A FEAST. Men carry on their tasks in separate groups from the women and children (a, b). Men do the butchering (c) and prepare certain vegetables such as grated taro (d). Children may participate in any aspect of food preparation at their pleasure and often play in the pig carcass as it is being butchered (e). Women cut, peel and bundle most of the vegetables including *pitpit, kumu* (f) and sweet potato (g), accumulating these bundles about them (h) as the men prepare the cooking pit. [a, Agakamatasa, 1962; b, Yagareba (Kinenti), 1967; c, e, Wanitabe, 1963; d, Kasokana, 1957; f, Agakamatasa, 1961; h, Waisa, 1963]

FIGURE 34. COOKING THE FEAST. Food for the feast is steam-cooked in covered pits, often called earth ovens or *mumu* (Melanesian Pidgen). Stones supply the heat for cooking, after having been heated on a special fire near the pit (a). When they are hot, they are pushed into the pit with long sticks (b–d). Then leaves are placed over the hot stones, and bundles of vegetables and sections of butchered pig are piled on top (e–h). A pig carcass about to be added to the pit is seen on the left of the picture (f). When full, the pit is covered with leaves and sealed with dirt (i–l). From long bamboo containers, water is poured into the pit through the cover of dirt and leaves (m). This water produces steam when it reaches the hot stones at the bottom. Cooking is usually completed in about one to two hours. [a, g, m, Agakamatasa (Waieti), 1962; b, c, e, f, Kasokana, 1957; h, k, Wanitabe (Kagumuti), 1963]

FIGURE 35. TOPPING THE PIT. Bundles of vegetables are usually placed on top of the section of pig before the pit is covered. In addition to the many bundles of sweet potato, there are always several indigenous vegetables. Bundles of winged bean root (*piga*) are placed on top of bundles of sweet potato and next to a bundle of the popular thick-stemmed grass with a succulent core (*pitpit*) (**a**). Bundles of edible green leaves (*kumu*) are placed on top of bundles of sweet potato and winged bean pods (**b**). [Yagareba, 1967]

36–38). Many of the participants would leave once they had received their share, to divide and eat the food in the privacy of smaller groups (*figs. 39–41*), often taking the food back with them to their villages. Women who had received bundles of food divided and exchanged food among their close friends and children as the eating began.

Instead of a pit in the ground, an upright, hollow wooden cylinder was sometimes used to cook the food for a feast. More common in the past, these cooking cylinders were made from large tree trunk sections burned out by blowing on a coal placed on the part to be removed. Only a few hamlets still possessed these cooking cylinders in 1969. The cooking procedure was much the same as that for the pits, i.e.: Hot stones were carried with split-branch tongs and dropped into the bottom of the hollow cylinder; leaves and bundles of raw food were then placed on top (*fig. 42*).

Economic Patterns

Food production from small, shifting gardens was the foundation of the Fore economy. Hunting and gathering played an important but subsidiary role. Since climate did not permit food storage beyond a few days, food was produced for immediate consumption—not to be stored as surplus wealth: The Fore economy was one dependent on virtual daily harvesting.

Monetary units had not evolved among the Fore, and exchange of value was accomplished largely by exchange of food, although, among intimate peoples, there were also more personal exchanges, such as of affection, labor, personal items and tools. Food sharing was the clearest

FIGURE 37. COOKED SWEET POTATO AND PIG. Sweet potatoes and pig were the most significant foods at formal feasts. Pig was the basis for such feasts and was, therefore, the most important food. However, sweet potatoes were also always cooked in great abundance. A pile of cooked sweet potato, also containing taro and corn, awaits distribution (a). Sections of pig just removed from the pit will be divided among participants (b).

FIGURE 38. FOOD DIVISION. An assortment of food is parceled out for distribution to feast participants. Sometimes this can include a variety of foods. Cooked leaf vegetables are taken from a bundle to be added to a plate containing sweet potato, maize, beans, taro and pieces of cuscus (a). A plate of beans, sweet potato, taro, greens and cuscus is ready to be presented (b).

FIGURE 36. OPENING THE COOKING PIT AND DISTRIBUTING THE FOOD. When the food is thought to be sufficiently cooked, the cap of dirt and leaves is removed (a, b). Removing the cooked vegetables and sections of pig (c–f), the men apportion the food, first among themselves (g, h, i) and to the guests for whom the feast is celebrated. Then, aided by some of the children, they distribute bundles to the waiting women (j, k). The women, in turn, further divide the food among their children and exchange food gifts with friends and relatives (l, m, n). Uneaten food is carried to dwellings for later consumption.

FIGURE 39. PACKING FOOD TO CARRY HOME. More frequently in the past, guests at formal intervillage feasts did not eat at the feast site. Rather, they gathered their food together and carried it back to their hamlets to eat there in the privacy of their own close associates.

FIGURE 40. SHARING FOOD. Final food division took place as sharing within small groups of close associates, either at the site of the feast or after return to one's hamlet. Since these close associates were well in tune with one another's subtle indications of preference, exchange of food among them was informal and fluid.

FIGURE 41. EATING AT THE FEAST SITE. Eating begins as soon as the food is distributed, friends and relatives gathering in small groups. Traditionally men and women tended to eat in separate groups (row 1). But in the last few years this custom has been disappearing (row 2). [a, c, d, Agakamatasa; b, Waisa (Anati), 1963]

FIGURE 42. COOKING IN A HOLLOW WOODEN CYLINDER. Sometimes vegetables are cooked in a wooden cylinder instead of in a pit in the ground. The hot stones are placed in the bottom and the vegetables arranged on top. The cylinder is capped with banana leaves and dirt (a). The steam-cooked food is removed by hand when cooking is complete (b, c). Much more common earlier, this technique of cooking was rapidly fading during the 1960s. [Yagareba, 1968]

measure of cooperative relationship and community solidarity.

In the small Fore communities, sharing was informal and voluntary among friends and close associates. There was no attempt to quantify value to facilitate repayment. Obligation was based not on a concept of fixed value but rather on a sliding subjective scale based on ease of production, need and desire. Cooperative relationship entailed sharing work, material, tools and food according to an intimate understanding of the interests, desires and good will of one's associates and friends.

This system worked well among close associates, but it was hard to extend it to aliens because of the need for personal familiarity to work out the values involved. In order to solve this problem, the Fore modified their food-sharing practices, formalizing them so they could be extended to aliens as a gesture of good will and as a means to political rapprochement and social engagement. This was done by means of intergroup feasts, which were increasingly formal, with increasingly valued foods, as unfamiliarity or social distance increased.

Among more closely related groups, such as those in nearby associated hamlets, garden produce could provide the basis for cooperative food sharing on rather short notice at rather informal feasts (see fig. 28). More distantly associated peoples were sometimes the recipients of more prized foods: pig, andi nut, piga bean root or even a large catch of wild game. Such feasts were usually between groups already somewhat associated as a result of some previous joint activity or kinship connection. Some were held periodically as traditionally recurring celebrations.

At the base of the Fore economy was the sweet potato. It was not only the dietary staple, but it alone made the Fore protoagricultural way of life possible. It determined settlement patterns and, thus, influenced social and political organization.

Where alien and potentially antagonistic non-intimate groups began to have more contact with each other, the domestic pig became important as a means to exchange value and develop cooperative ties. Large catches of wild game and the piga bean root crop sometimes also met this need. Other garden produce was not suitable because such large quantities were needed to represent significant value. This imposed transport problems and the probability that the large quantities needed to have real value would rot before they could be consumed. Exchanges of labor and personal items were not well suited to initiate relations, since an established intimacy was required before their appropriateness could be properly gauged.

Thus it was the pig that was uniquely suited for

value exchange between the Highland agricultural peoples. They represented considerable value per unit, and the amount of labor needed to raise pigs was commonly understood. Furthermore, pigs provided a source of protein in a diet in which protein was not abundant. No other produce incorporated so much potential for exchanging good will among alien peoples.

The degree to which hunting and gathering occupied the attention of the Fore depended on the abundance of accessible wild lands. Where extensive forest lands remained, there was more hunting and gathering; but where agricultural activity had made serious inroads on the accessible forest lands, hunting and gathering became less important.[22] Sweet potato horticulture was the basic economic activity of all the Fore, and its requirements superseded those of hunting and gathering. Thus, the forests used for hunting and gathering slowly gave way, first to gardens and then to grasslands.[23] At the same time, domestic pig replaced wild pig and became an increasingly important means to develop and sustain friendly relations between alien groups.

By the time of contact, sweet potato was the foundation of the Fore economy, but domestic pig was the basis for intergroup economic exchange.

Chapter 4   Socioecological Change

The Fore moved their gardens and hamlets into the edge of the forest on the fringe of a much larger Eastern Highlands population. In many respects their practices and way of life were similar to these other groups, which were dispersed across the Highlands, speaking several different languages. Protoagriculture seems to have been an important molding factor for the Fore—one which also helps us to understand the socioecological development of the New Guinea Highlands.[24]

Like many of the other Highlands peoples, the Fore cleared new garden sites in the nearby virgin forest when soil in old gardens was exhausted. Grass sprang up in abandoned gardens. With the help of repeated burnings, these sites of past agriculture were ultimately replaced by permanent grassland. Because the soil in these grasslands was considered less productive, and, because they were harder to clear with stone axes and wooden digging sticks, they were not recultivated while virgin lands remained accessible. At lower altitudes they also harbored death adders.

This horticultural practice, together with its ecological result, laid the foundation for a proto-agricultural, socioecological evolution in the Eastern Highlands of New Guinea.

Impact of the Sweet Potato

There is substantial evidence that the sweet potato arrived in New Guinea only after European discovery of the Pacific—probably from America via the East Indies. How and when it reached and diffused across the New Guinea Highlands is un-known, but most contemporary evidence indicates that at least one major route was up the Markham River valley from the coast. It appears to have been in some Highlands regions for over 200 years, but it is just now being introduced into others.[25] The Fore appear to have had sweet potato for about a century; but it has only recently begun to replace taro as the staple in regions to the east of the Fore. Among the Simbari, southern Tairora, Awa and Genatei, sweet potato has replaced taro as the staple only within living memory. Throughout all regions taro plays some role in the ceremonial life, and older varieties are considered "men's crops," a possible indication of ancient importance.[26]

Because of the ease with which the sweet potato could be propagated in the Fore homeland, it became a crucial factor in the socioecological change affecting the Fore people. It grew well where other staples, such as taro, did not, particularly at the higher elevations comprising most of the Fore lands. It also produced greater crop yields.[27]

Thus, the sweet potato not only permitted the Fore horticulturalists to move their gardens and hamlets up into the extensive virgin lands between 5,500 and 8,000 feet, it also increased the carrying capacity of the land. This single crop not only permitted denser populations, but it made possible the steady movement of gardens and settlements into vast virgin regions at higher elevations. With it the Fore intruded into the original rainforest ecology of their present homeland (fig. 43).

Although new gardens were usually on the edge of the forest, there were always a few isolated gardens that invaded the forest more deeply (fig. 44).

FIGURE 43. HORTICULTURAL SETTLEMENT. The hamlet and its associated gardens are the basic living unit. Here such a unit has recently been carved out of the forest beyond the limits of an older, now uninhabited and deforested site. Grass and scrub growth have already begun to replace the first gardens. [Paiyanili hamlet of Yagareba, 1967]

FIGURE 44. INVASION OF THE FOREST. Unmarked by garden activity only two years ago, this tract of virgin forest has just begun to be exploited. As yet, only a few garden plots, marked by dead tree trunks, have been cut out of this tract of forest. [Yagareba, 1967]

Ecological Change

Wild grasses, typically *pitpit (Miscanthus floridulus)*, an early succession vegetation, and *kunai (Imperata cylindrica)*, the apparent climax cover, replaced abandoned garden and hamlet sites. Thus, as gardens and hamlets continued to advance into the original forest lands, trails of grassland were left to mark the passage of the Fore horticultural activity *(figs. 45, 46)*. This clearly visible path of ecological disturbance can be readily identified in aerial photographs *(fig. 47)*.[28]

In some abandoned regions, evidence of extensive contiguous gardening can still be seen checkerboarding the tracts of uninhabited grassland *(fig. 48)*.

In most areas, grassland boundaries remained remarkably stable *(fig. 49)*. In a few, usually wet areas with less sunlight, secondary scrub growth also emerged, usually in association with the grass *(fig. 50)*. Only in areas near the Lamari valley did bamboo thickets also occasionally replace gardens instead of *kunai* grass. This may represent a special condition in this region, which allowed bamboo planted near gardens to proliferate after the gardens were abandoned *(figs. 51, 52)*.

The widespread practice of burning grasslands seems to have helped to stabilize them. Where extensive burning was not practiced, scrub growth more often replaced old clearings.

Since the mid-1960s, the Australian government officials discouraged grassland burning. This has permitted regrowth of trees and bush in a few marginal regions *(fig. 53)*; but in most areas it has led to denser and taller growth of grass *(fig. 54)*.

The decrease in grassland burnings is recent, a direct result of Western government intervention. Before Western contact, high stands of grass and scrub growth facilitated ambush. For defensive reasons it was kept short by burning. Furthermore, the burning of grasslands was an effective aid to hunting grassland fauna: It exposed the eggs of ground-nesting birds for gathering. The Fore also seemed simply to enjoy burning grass. Even when defense and hunting were not the motives, men and boys often took advantage of dry periods to set fire to the grass beside trails as they walked along.

Thus, up to the mid-1960s, when government efforts to discourage burning began to take effect, the relation of habitation and settlement to deforestation was direct.

FIGURE 45. FINGERS OF GRASSLAND DISSECTING THE FOREST. In regions where agricultural activity has continued to make inroads into the forest, fingers of grassland may mark the paths it has taken. Above, three gardens, in various stages of clearing, occupy the end of the finger thrusting down the slope at the bottom center. [Awarosa, 1967]

FIGURE 46. THE CHANGING FORE LANDS. Vast stands of virgin rainforest cover much of the mountains that the Fore call their home, particularly at the higher elevations (a, b). Irregular clearings of varying size punctuate this rainforest, indicating present or past cultivation (a, b, c). Thick *kunai* grass usually takes the place of abandoned gardens and hamlet sites, often leaving an irregular path through the forest (b, c). In regions where gardening has gone on for a long time, or where population is greater, a more general breaking up of the forest may be seen (d, e). In some areas this has led to extensive deforestation, sometimes covering entire valleys (f). [a, Takai, 1967; b, Koventari, a settlement of Kamata people near Wanta in the Waisarampa River valley, 1967; c, Ilesa, 1967; d, Ai, 1967; e, f, Abomatasa, 1967]

ILESA

WANTA

YAGAREBA

FIGURE 47. HABITATION AND ECOLOGY. Looking south-ward across the South Fore region to the uninhabited lands beyond, this aerial photograph was taken by the U.S. Army for mapping a decade before the first government patrols entered the region. It reveals the pattern of deforestation that accompanied habitation up to that time. Solid light-grey areas are abandoned grasslands, dark areas are the uninhabited rainforest, and speckled and mottled regions are those of active residence and gardening. Most gardening activity, especially during the precontact period, invaded the forest lands centrifugally, leaving abandoned grass-lands in the center of an expanding population group. The tendency for Fore groups to segment and form new units is revealed here by the satellitelike clearings beyond the main clearings.

The two large, cleared areas (lower center left and upper center right) are the sites of origin of two dia-lectally distinct South Fore population groups (Atigina and Purosa). In the upper right corner are the sites of the recently established bilingual South Fore village of Paiti, adjacent to its Gimi-speaking neighbors. The smoke plume as well as the blackened area of grasslands somewhat above the smoke reveal the common practice of burning uninhabited grasslands. Some of the larger, cleared zones represent the fusion of previously sepa-rated clearings.

FIGURE 48. EVIDENCE OF OLD GARDEN SITES IN ABAN-DONED GRASSLAND. In some regions, as on this mountain-side adjacent to the North Fore, indentations in the ground mark the old sites of now-vanished garden fences and the trails that ran adjacent to them. Such evidence can be seen when the *kunai* grass is short, as after a major burning. Present villagers have no knowl-edge of these earlier gardens.

FIGURE 49. THE STABILITY OF GRASSLAND BOUNDARIES. More than a quarter of a century ago, the South Fore of Abomatasa, on the eastern slopes of Mt. Wanivinti, gave up exploiting the region pictured above. In the 25 years that separate these two pictures (**a,** 1943; **b,** 1968), these lands remained uninhabited, except for the ridge at the top center. The patterns formed by the boundaries of forest and grassland have remained very much the same. Only in areas adjacent to streams can some slight regeneration of forest be detected. It is possible that the stability of the boundaries seen here is related to some extent to the local custom of repeated burning of grasslands during dry spells.

FIGURE 50. FOREST REGENERATION I. Grassland does not always replace gardens. In a few wetter areas, as in the drainage fan above, particularly where micrometeorological conditions restrict daily sunshine, second-growth bush and small trees may also sprout along with the grass. Where repeated burning is practiced, this second-growth bush and trees are not likely to persist. [A mountain slope near Abomotasa, 1967]

FIGURE 51. BAMBOO THICKETS. In the Awarosa, Ilesa and Abomatasa regions of the South Fore, extensive bamboo thickets sometimes replace the forest instead of grassland. The conditions permitting this are not well understood. That these thickets tend to cluster in damper places or on hillsides receiving less direct sunlight, indicates that an optimum water condition helps them thrive. [Awarosa, 1967]

FIGURE 52. KUNAI GRASS VERSUS BAMBOO THICKETS AS CLIMAX VEGETATION. In the few regions where bamboo thickets also replace abandoned sites of agricultural activity, their different requirements make it possible for grassland to cover one side of a hill up to the crest and bamboo, the other side. In part this seems to be a result of more direct sunlight where the grass grows; but it is also possible that the sharp line at the top of this ridge represents where grassland fires burning up the slope stopped at the top. [Awarosa, 1967]

FIGURE 53. FOREST REGENERATION II. Since the early 1960s, in areas where government influence was strong, efforts to discourage the burning of grasslands have been successful. On some hillsides previously covered with mixed bush and grassland, the absence of frequent burnings in recently gardened areas appears to have permitted trees and bush to regenerate. [Aga, 1967]

FIGURE 54. TALLER GRASSLANDS. In some places the absence of repeated burnings since the early 1960s has left tracts of taller grasses, essentially without tree regrowth. The almost impenetrable tract of grassland seen on opposite page is an example of this development. Only a few planted banana trees, casuarina trees and an occasional sprouting wild tree marks this expanse of unburned grassland. [Ivaki, 1967]

Sociopolitical Change

It was undoubtedly by means of the same slash-and-burn horticulture practiced today that the earlier Fore protoagricultural groups advanced into the virgin forest that once covered their present homeland. Because the movement was into

new lands with new crops, an attitude of tolerance to innovation and free segmentation was advantageous. Whether this attitude developed as the Fore migrated into the new lands, or whether the Fore moved because they were already innovative and residentially unrestricted is unknown. Eventually, however, the lands began to fill up. Increasing population and decreasing availability of easily gardenable land obstructed the dispersive exploitation normally practiced. New social and political problems ensued. Warfare and the intergroup pig feasts became important concerns.

WARFARE: Three ecologically and demographically influenced phases can be associated with the development of warfare among the Fore:

Phase 1) *Abundant surrounding virgin land.* Small, isolated groups of protoagriculturalists made up of close and trusted associates diverged unhampered into the uninhabited surrounding forest lands. Fighting was rare.

Phase 2) *The beginnings of competition for land.* Previously diverging, somewhat alien peoples began converging on the same remaining stands of virgin forest. There were increasingly frequent episodes of confusion, anger and fighting. Conflict was characteristically by small raiding bands bent on redressing specific immediate grievances. There was an increase in migration to avoid conflict.

Phase 3) *The increasing rarity of new forest land.* Contiguous free segmentation was no longer feasible. An increase in sorcery suspicion and accusation narrowed social horizons. Untrusted persons were excluded from residental areas. Inter-hamlet attacks began to occur. Defined sociopolitical groupings began to develop. Alien groups joined in alliance to drive mutually objectionable impinging peoples away. More severe dispersion of populations occurred as migrations took segmenting groups to distant new lands across intervening groups and lands.

PIG FEASTS: Before Western contact, intergroup pig feasts had become an important means to cooperation and accommodation among semi-alien peoples in the more congested regions. Essential to the development of these politically motivated pig feasts were domestic pigs.

Where wild lands began to fill up with diverging sweet potato cultivators, wild pigs became more scarce as their forest ranges gave way to grasslands and as they were hunted more frequently. On the other hand, wild pigs were relatively common in the remote regions, especially where forests still extended into the lower valleys (e.g., Agakamatasa and Kasarai). In such regions, wild pigs were taken in hunting as often as two or three times a month. In contrast, they were rarely seen in the more heavily populated regions with a longer history of settlement. When asked, local informants in these areas said they all had been hunted out. The lower altitude forests, which were more suitable for the wild pigs, were virtually gone in these regions.

Although pig husbandry helped fill the void left by the disappearing wild pig, it also did much more: It yielded more pigs than were ever supplied by the hunt and also provided a dependable source of pigs—one not subject to the uncertainties of the hunt.

Raising pigs requires feeding them. Only people having a potential agricultural output in excess of their own needs can seriously entertain such thoughts. Fortunately, the sweet potato provided this potential at the same time that it brought about the decline of the wild pig. The sweet potato made pig raising possible as well as necessary.

The full dynamics of the diffusion of pig feasts across the Highlands is not known, nor is the origin of the idea. However, what seems to have happened in the Fore region was: first, the diffusion of the sweet potato into the previously virgin lands; second, population growth and a filling up of the lands;[29] third, the decline of wild pigs; fourth, increased pig raising; fifth, the use of pigs in feasts to solve the new political and social problems that also came with increasing congestion of the land.

The idea of pig-exchange feasts probably came into the Fore from their more populous neighbors to the north and northwest who had sweet potato earlier.[30]

To see the relationship of the pig feast to population in the Highlands, it is only necessary to review the ethnographic literature on pig feasts in relation to population density: As one moves northwestward from the Simbari (6/sq. mi.) to the South Fore (27/sq. mi.), the North Fore (54/sq. mi.), the Usurufa-Kamano (68/sq. mi.), the Bena-bena (82/sq. mi.), the Gahuku (83/sq. mi.), the Asaro (103/sq. mi) and the Chimbu (over 200/sq. mi.), the political importance and elaborateness of the pig-exchange feasts increases.

By the time of Western contact, two kinds of pig feasts were employed as means to peaceful intergroup accommodation:

Pig-gift feasts were a way of settling a wrong or repaying a debt. Their immediate effect was to

FIGURE 55. FORMAL INTERGROUP FEAST. Formal pig feasts are a traditional means of settling a condition of debt or dispute betweeen two groups and of sustaining political or defensive alliances. The guests for whom the feast is prepared may be armed, often keep to themselves while awaiting the cooking and frequently depart with the food without eating. Here, the guests are seated in the woods at the far left, while the hosts busy themselves with preparation and cooking. Such feasts are very serious affairs and represent one of the highest degrees of organization and planning existing among the Fore. [Awarosa, 1959]

defuse tension; their effectiveness stemmed from their obvious (and dramatic, from the Fore point of view) effort to make things right while at the same time, providing a means for social contact. They entailed the formal preparation and cooking of pigs by a host group for a group of "guests" who were, as often as not, armed and whose demeanor was usually that of righteous hostility and grudging acceptance. While awaiting completion of the cooking, most of these guests kept to themselves, away from the activity of their hosts (fig. 55); most left immediately after the presentation of the meat and other gifts.

Pig-exchange feasts were a further step toward political consolidation. They were traditionally recurring events between regional groups, where mutual gifts of meat were exchanged among two or more participating groups. Such feasts led to visiting rights, migration privileges and friendship among these groups. The dance and oratorical forms associated with these feasts, however, have remained those of conflict—an indication of their less amicable origin (fig. 56).

Pattern of Change

This historical reconstruction, based on contemporary evidence, shows that adoption of the sweet potato by the Fore set in motion a series of events that has been transforming their institutions and natural surroundings. As the consequences of this act unraveled, the Fore moved to virgin lands at higher altitudes; their population increased; natural surroundings changed; the economic arena narrowed; new patterns of social and political accommodation developed. Warfare and the development of intergroup pig feasts were major sociopolitical consequences of the change.

The South Fore had not moved as far down this socioecological evolutionary path as their neighbors to the north and northwest. South Fore populations were more sparse, and virgin lands were more accessible. Institutionalization of warfare was less advanced. Intergroup pig-exchange feasts were less elaborate. Regional political consolidations were not as significant.

Where there was plentiful surrounding virgin

land, the Fore communities expanded slowly and contiguously, almost centrifugally, ever outward into the edge of the forest. Only as adjacent virgin land resources were exhausted did migration become more discontiguous and more dramatically dispersive and did new sociopolitical practice come into existence.

Underlying this pattern of socioecological evolution was an interdependent chain of ecological, demographic and social developments deriving from the protoagricultural way of life. These developments determined population distribution, affected economic organization and influenced sociopolitical practice. They do not necessarily imply that such socioecological evolution could not have occurred without the sweet potato, or that a similar development could not have occurred with other crops earlier. What is obvious is that, in this case, the sweet potato provided the opportunity to exploit new lands, that egalitarian and group-segmenting practices met this challenge well and that the protoagricultural expansion was finally limited by the very practices that originally made it possible.

FIGURE 56. ANTAGONISTIC STANCES AT A PIG-EXCHANGE FEAST. The demeanor and behavior of celebrants at pig-exchange feasts frequently resembles that of conflict. Armed men assume stances of self-righteous indignation and provocation in a setting in which others accuse them of unfriendly or injurious behavior while arguing their own virtuous conduct and prowess. This 1967 pig-exchange feast was held by groups from Yagareba, Amora, Kume and Higitaru on a traditional ceremonial site in Kume village.

Chapter 5 Protoagricultural Movement

Penetrating a fringe pioneer region extending southward from a large deforested Eastern Highlands core, the Fore verged onto a vast region of exploited forest. The protoagricultural pattern spread outward from this core, and the mixing of two of its major offshoots in the Fore region can be seen by examining the patterns of ecological disturbance it caused and the genetic differences existing in the blood-group frequencies of the contemporary subgroups.

Like the Fore, the Eastern Highlands protoagriculturalists cleared new garden sites when the soil in the old gardens was exhausted. Abandoned garden sites became unproductive stable grasslands.

As long as plentiful virgin lands surrounded regional population clusters, a basic contiguous migration moved slowly outward into the surrounding virgin forest land (fig. 57). But where this process had begun to exhaust the exploitable adjacent land resources, as in an ecologically circumscribed region, this basic migratory movement altered and became discontiguous and more dispersive (fig. 58).

Because of the mountainous nature of the Eastern Highlands, many of the agriculturally exploitable regions were ecologically circumscribed in various ways by altitude barriers. However, what was an altitude barrier for one crop did not necessarily bar another.

Where taro was the staple, horticulture was restricted to altitudes below approximately 5,500 feet. As a result the taro protoagricultural movement was, for the most part, confined to river valleys (fig. 59) and sometimes to lower altitude "islands" of exploitable land. These taro lands varied in size and configuration. Introduction of the sweet potato changed and expanded these limits by raising the altitude limit for protoagricultural movement to approximately 8,000 feet.

Typically, a group settling new lands slowly expanded outward to the adjacent edge of the forest until, finally, the regional limits of exploit-

ability began to be reached. This inaugurated a period of increased conflict, causing increased desire among segmenting groups to migrate. Some began to migrate even across ecological barriers to completely new virgin valleys, often planting themselves afar essentially as clones. Such transplanted population segments would then expand by the basic contiguous segmenting process until increasing land pressure in the new region caused the cycle to repeat itself. It is this cyclic protoagricultural pattern of population spread that appears to have given rise to the present configuration of ecological change and the distribution of population in the Eastern Highlands.

Analysis of more than 1,000 aerial photographs of the Eastern Highlands region has revealed the location and size of grasslands and forest and made possible their mapping (map 8). Because the protoagricultural movement in the Eastern Highlands converted virgin rainforest to stable grassland, this map suggests probable routes of settlement based on the following assumptions:

1) Uninhabited grasslands indicate areas of past agricultural activity and settlement.

2) Larger regions of grassland have supported protoagricultural activity longer than smaller regions.

3) Discontiguous migration tends to move to the nearest exploitable virgin lands.

These assumptions are derived from examination of contemporary protoagricultural segmentation and gardening practices.

Genetic Distance

Steadily separating through dispersive segmentation, subgroups from original regions of settlement eventually became isolated from one another. Genetic differentiation occurred. With the help of Peter E. Kenmore, it has been possible to examine this differentiation through analysis of the blood-group genetic data reported by Sim-

FORE

Purosa

Kaza River

Lamari River

FIGURE 57. UNCONFINED PROTOAGRICULTURAL SPREAD. When surrounded by extensive virgin lands, the Eastern Highlands protoagriculturalists slowly moved their gardens and settlements into the retreating edge of the adjacent forest, leaving abandoned grasslands behind. Here, South Fore protoagriculturalists have expanded outward from the Purosa valley, ever widening the grasslands marking their persistent centrifugal resettlement into the edge of the surrounding forest. These South Fore represent a southern projection of the general Eastern Highlands protoagricultural movement where it penetrates a vast unexploited region. This 1943 aerial photograph, taken by the U.S. Army for mapping purposes, looks northwestward across part of this uninhabited region from the junction of the Lamari and Kaza Rivers—before the cultural isolation of this region was breached by Westerners.

FIGURE 58. NONCONTIGUOUS SETTLEMENT. When land resources in a given region become scarce, segmenting protoagriculturalists migrate to altogether new regions to carry on their way of life. These migrating groups form new expanding population groups marked by new expanding patches of grassland. In this 1943 aerial photograph, looking northward across the site of what was to become Okapa (approximately below the O in "FORE"), four such ecologically distinct Fore regions of population can be distinguished (Awande, Ibusa, Mage and Ofafina). Meeting them in this disappearing tract of rainforest are southward-segmenting groups of Kanite, Usurufa, Kamano and Keiagana. Words in upper case are names of linguistic groups; words in lower case are names of ecologically defined regions of population within the Fore linguistic group.

FIGURE 59. CONFINED PROTOAGRICULTURAL SPREAD. Confined by altitude limitations to the Lamari valley, the Tairora protoagriculturalists followed this valley downstream from an entry point in its headwaters.

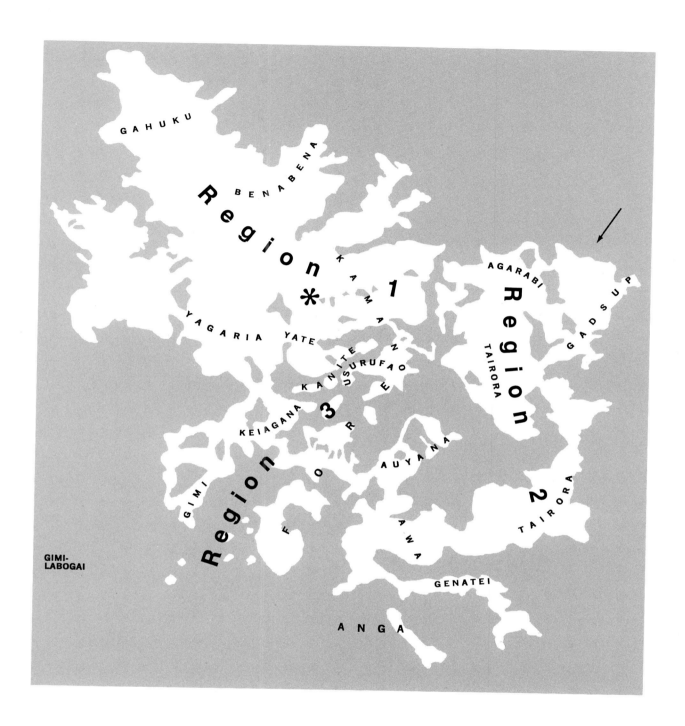

MAP 8. PROTOAGRICULTURAL SPREAD IN THE EASTERN HIGHLANDS. This map, plotted from aerial photographs taken in 1943, reveals the regions of anthropogenic grasslands (white areas) and virgin rainforest (dark areas). Gardening, as a major means to subsistence, appears to have entered the Eastern Highlands from the Markham valley through the Gadsup region (see arrow). Taro would have been the staple crop. The more recent sweet potato protoagricultural movement, into Region 3, appears to have originated in the Kamano region (see asterisk), probably emerging there when the taro growers exhausted the lower valleys and began to move into higher lands. The Pawaian group is very sparsely spread out below the bottom edge of this map.

	North Fore	South Fore	Gimi	Keiagana	Awa	Kamano	Kanite	Usurufa	Agarabi	Gadsup	Genatei	Gimi-Labogai	Pawaian	Tairora
South Fore	0.0589													
Gimi	0.0799	0.1245												
Keiagana	0.0738	0.1069	0.0605											
Awa	0.1092	0.0859	0.1700	0.1628										
Kamano	0.1252	0.1059	0.1774	0.1462	0.1612									
Kanite	0.1490	0.1489	0.1623	0.1644	0.2138	0.1551								
Usurufa	0.1826	0.1341	0.2046	0.1779	0.1965	0.1104	0.1105							
Agarabi	0.1196	0.1200	0.1345	0.1537	0.1691	0.1492	0.1412	0.1886						
Gadsup	0.1655	0.1673	0.2034	0.1635	0.1787	0.1723	0.1800	0.1678	0.2286					
Genatei	0.1067	0.0926	0.1542	0.1628	0.1429	0.1276	0.1071	0.1347	0.0890	0.2037				
Gimi-Labogai	0.1092	0.1230	0.0844	0.0815	0.1925	0.1422	0.1642	0.1857	0.1149	0.2159	0.1557			
Pawaian	0.1787	0.2248	0.1466	0.1632	0.2599	0.2232	0.2420	0.2913	0.1848	0.2597	0.2337	0.1566		
Tairora	0.1253	0.1318	0.1654	0.1298	0.1265	0.1776	0.1937	0.1888	0.2067	0.0765	0.1888	0.1916	0.2409	
Anga	0.1589	0.1682	0.1358	0.1426	0.2451	0.1534	0.1357	0.1782	0.1197	0.2401	0.1583	0.0830	0.1752	0.2381

mons et al. (1961, 1972), in relation to the ecological evidence.

Adopting methods described by Harpending and Jenkins (1973) (see also Friedlaender 1974), genetic distances were calculated between 14 Eastern Highlands linguistic groups. Focusing on nine alleles at three loci (ABO, MNS, Rh), the mean of frequencies of an allele among all the populations (weighted by the proportional contribution of each population sample to the total size of the sample) were taken as an approximation of the original population distribution. According to Wahlund's principle (see Cavalli-Sforza and Bodmer 1971, p. 397), the normalized variance of the entire sample is a measure of decreasing overall heterozygosity and thus an indication of the heterogeneity of populations under drift (see Crow and Kimura 1970, p. 327). Therefore the normalized covariance of any two subpopulations,

$$\frac{(p_i - \bar{p})(p_j - \bar{p})}{\bar{p}(1 - \bar{p})},$$

where $\bar{p}$ is the mean frequency of allele p and p_i and p_j are the frequencies in subpopulations i and j, is a measure of their genetic relationship. The normalized variance for one population,

$$\frac{(p_i - \bar{p})^2}{\bar{p}(1 - \bar{p})},$$

is a measure of that population's degree of inbreeding and drift. By averaging the matrices for all alleles, we obtained an overall variance-covariance relationship for all alleles and all populations. The formula suggested by Harpending and Jenkins (1973),

$$d = \text{Var pop}_i + \text{Var pop}_j - 2\text{coV pop}_{ij},$$

was used to obtain the genetic distance between each group and every other (table 2).

Principal-Components Analysis

A set of Eastern Highlands people, which fitted the theoretical model of genetic drift outward from a source population, was revealed among those Eastern Highlands linguistic groups known to have some ethnohistorical or linguistic affiliation. In order to show the overall genetic distance relationships among these groups, a principal-components analysis was constructed (map 9). Following Harpending's and Jenkins's (1973)

MAP 9. EASTERN HIGHLANDS LINGUISTIC GROUPS AC-
CORDING TO BLOOD-GROUP FREQUENCY SIMILARITIES. This
principal-components map shows the blood-group genetic relationships existing among the linguistic groups
of the Eastern Highlands. The two axes are scaled to
"imaginary" frequencies of the two most variable genes
obtained in the principal-components analysis. The
position of Kamano near the center of the map agrees
with the ecological hypothesis that a proto-Kamano
group was a major source of subpopulations that diverged both geographically and genetically into most of
the rest of the Eastern Highlands. On this map, the
Kamano group may appear closer to the Fore and
Kanite peoples than is actually the case for the
Kamano as a whole. This is because the Kamano blood
samples used in this study were taken from Kamano
living in the border region near the Fore and Kanite.
A more representative Kamano sample would probably
move this group closer to the intersection of the axes.
The genetic relationships indicated by this map are
consistent with the ecological evidence and support the
belief that an original protoagricultural population
diverged outward into the surrounding lands, according
to the pattern of ecological alteration seen in map 8.
The Agarabi and Pawaian, however, appear to be different stocks and not part of this major protoagricultural spread.

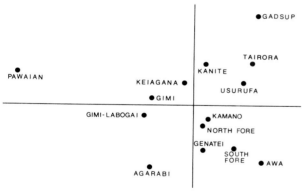

frequencies for the two most variable genes. The
axes can be interpreted as showing the frequencies
for the two most variable genes, the first axis being
the gene with the most variability. Because some
alleles in an area are much more variable than
others, most of the variability of the sample is
retained while still showing relationships clearly.

The Kamano linguistic group falls near the
center of this principal-components map. This suggests a proto-Kamano group as the major source of
the contemporary Eastern Highlands populations
displayed. The proximity of Kamano on this map
to Fore and Kanite may be due in part to the fact
that the blood samples used were taken from
Kamano living in the border regions near these
people. A more representative sample of Kamano
bloods might move them even closer to the intersection of the axes.

Keeping these considerations in mind, this
genetic map represents divergence of subpopulations through time over several generations. This
divergence is accomplished through dispersive
protoagricultural movement and the isolations
that follow. The genetic distribution is consistent
with the dynamics of protoagricultural movement
and with the ecological assumptions on which the
interpretation of map 8 is based.

Genetic Networks

In order to place the salient protoagricultural
expansion from the Kamano region in a larger
perspective and to show its relationship to an
earlier taro protoagricultural movement and the
possibility of prehorticultural populations in the
Eastern Highlands, a genetic network was constructed with the assistance of Dr. Stephen Wiesenfeld.[31] This convenient way to present the
larger picture graphically is constructed using the
least-squares method for minimizing the genetic
distance differences shown in the matrix. It allows
incorporation of all pairwise genetic distances into
a single diagram (see Kidd and Sgaramella-Zonta
1971).

A large number of possible networks may be
constructed from one set of genetic distances, even
from one least-squares solution. Even though the
similarity of the shortest networks obtained to the
one that corresponds best to the existing ecologi-

principal-components method, this map was constructed by taking the eigenvectors of the different
selected populations from the matrix, multiplying
each eigenvector by the square root of the corresponding eigenvalue, ranking the eigenvalues in
order of size and plotting the resulting factors in
a coordinate system, whose axes are the vectors of
the two largest eigenvalues.

In effect, this produces a table of all subpopulations, each with "imaginary" uncorrelated gene

cal, ethnohistorical and linguistic evidence suggests that shorter networks may be better networks, there is theoretically no way to select the best, or even to judge similarity, by reference to the genetic data alone. Only with reference to other evidence is it possible to select a "most probable" network.

Map 10 represents such a "most probable" network for 14 linguistic groups of the Eastern Highlands and a neighboring group in nearby Papua (the Pawaian). It was selected because of its shortness and its compatibility with the available geographic, ecological, ethnohistorical and linguistic evidence as well as the protoagricultural dynamics.

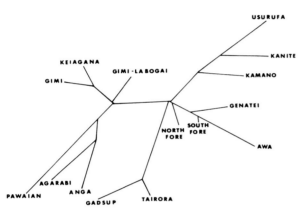

MAP 10. SALIENT GENETIC RELATIONSHIPS AMONG CONTEMPORARY HIGHLANDS LINGUISTIC GROUPS. This "most probable" genetic network relates 12 linguistic groups of the Eastern Highlands to three other groups just outside this region (Anga, Genatei and Pawaian). It is one of several possible constructions based on similarity of blood-group frequencies alone. It was selected because of its shortness and its compatibility with the available historical, linguistic, geographic and ecological evidence. The sampled groups fall into six major branches: 1) Kamano, Kanite, Usurufa; 2) North Fore, South Fore, Awa, Genatei; 3) Keiagana, Gimi, Gimi-Labogai; 4) Gadsup, Tairora; 5) Agarabi, Anga; and 6) Pawaian. If we consider the geographical, archaeological and ecological evidence in relation to these branches, three salient polar groups emerge: 1) Kamano-Kanite-Usurufa; 2) Gadsup-Tairora; and 3) Anga-Agarabi. Situated between these polar groups are two distinct hybridized groups: 1) Fore-Awa-Genatei; and 2) Keiagana-Gimi-Gimi-Labogai. Pawaian, a group outside the Eastern Highlands, has no strong genetic relationship to any Eastern Highlands groups.

Protoagricultural Migration and Population Distribution in the Eastern Highlands

Most simply viewed, the ecological alteration of the Eastern Highlands, seen in relation to differences in blood-group frequencies among its present regional populations, suggests a proto-Kamano group as the major source of the present inhabitants—an apparent consequence of a strong sweet potato-based protoagricultural movement originating in that region. A second important source seems to have been a proto-Gadsup group, a taro-growing, protoagricultural people who advanced most clearly down the Lamari valley, but who may also have been one early source of the proto-Kamano peoples. A still earlier, but sparsely settled aboriginal population, which did not cut down the forest to make gardens, appears to have been partly displaced and partly absorbed by these protoagricultural movements.

Most likely, cultivation was first practiced in the Eastern Highlands by the proto-Gadsup—a people who were either representative of an agricultural movement coming up the Markham valley or who obtained taro and knowledge of cultivation from these neighbors. In all the Eastern Highlands, it is the Gadsup region that verges most conveniently on the edge of the upper Markham valley, making its people the most probable beneficiaries of the diffusion of agricultural people or techniques from that region.[32] The greater antiquity of cultivation in this region is also suggested by the evidence that the proto-Gadsup must have originally been taro, not sweet potato growers. Taro was probably an earlier staple by several hundred years. Areas where it could be grown (i.e.: below about 5,500 feet) are now covered by extensive tracts of short *kunai* grass, an indication of intensive cultivation and burning for several centuries (thus, before introduction of sweet potato).[33] Furthermore, in the southernmost extension of the Gadsup-Tairora movement, sweet potato has only replaced taro as the staple within living memory. What this evidence suggests is that an early taro protoagricultural movement down the Lamari valley from the Gadsup region was overtaken by a more recent movement of sweet potato from the northwest.[34]

Both archaeological and genetic evidence indicate that a distinct aboriginal people already occupied widely spread parts of the Eastern Highlands before the arrival of the taro or sweet potato cultivators. These earlier people did not remove the forest as they made their living, and they left carved stone mortars and stone club heads to mark their activities.

At the time of contact, the genetically distinct Anga were still making and using the same kind of stone club heads found archaeologically across the rest of the Highlands. No other groups had any use or knowledge of them. When found in the gardens, they were attributed to ancient spirits. The Anga also showed a close genetic similarity to a few other widely separated regional groups (Gimi-Labogai and Agarabi).[35] They are, therefore, the most likely contemporary representatives of the early aboriginal occupants of the Eastern Highlands. However, the Awa, with no close genetic similarity to any groups but its immediate neighbors, may have descended from another, less widespread early group.

Many of the Anga-like aboriginal groups appear to have been absorbed by the more numerous and more economically advanced protoagriculturalists. The Gimi-Labogai, Gimi and Kanite, for example, show a clear genetic relationship to an Anga-like stock. The Kamano are also related to a lesser degree, as are most of the remaining groups in Region 3 (Keiagana and Fore). The Agarabi, as representatives of the early aboriginal population, also show a distinct genetic relationship to the Gimi, Fore and Genatei. The Gimi-Labogai, as representatives, show a relationship to Fore, Gimi and Keiagana. This situation is most easily explained by hybridization of an earlier aboriginal population with the invading protoagriculturalists. Populations in Region 3 show this hybridization most clearly.

The taro movement, stemming from the Gadsup region, remained distinct throughout most of Region 2. The genetic correlates of this movement are obscure in Region 1, but widespread short *kunai* grasslands below about 5,500 feet there indicate an early intensive taro agriculture in this region also. The contemporary genetic situation is probably the result of protoagricultural invaders mixing with aboriginal groups already there. Further strengthening the effect of the aboriginal

genetic contribution to Region 1 could be that some of the aboriginal groups had adopted taro growing before the Group 2 migrants reached their lands. This would have left them more numerous, more viable and already in possession of the taro growing lands. This may also be the reason the aboriginal Agarabi maintained their genetic distinctiveness in the face of the taro movement. Similar smaller groups in Region 1 may have been absorbed.

There is also a possibility that the greater genetic distinctiveness of Region 1 was, in part, due to the rapid genetic drift that can occur in very small populations. If the group that first adopted sweet potato as their staple was such a group when it expanded with sweet potato, it would have skewed the overall Region 1 population toward its particular genetic makeup.

Whatever the cause of the genetic character of the original sweet potato cultivators, the impact of their expansion was more clearly traceable because of it.

The direction of the sweet potato movement into the new lands of Region 3 is more clearly demonstrable, presumably because there were no sizeable populations there to mix with the invaders. In regions where there were already taro growers in the lower valleys, the regional genetic impact of the sweet potato movement would have been less marked; it would have been tempered by the genetic pool already there.

In some taro growing regions, the idea of sweet potato cultivation was adopted before other migrating groups could move in. This allowed the original population to move up into the sweet potato-exploitable lands, essentially preempting them. This appears to have been what kept Region 2 genetically distinct, even though sweet potato eventually replaced taro as the staple there too.

The overall genetic relationships resulting from this kind of movement are revealed by a principal-components analysis, while the genetic distinctiveness of the separate basic populations can be seen more clearly in the diverging arms of a genetic network *(see maps 8–10)*.

To hypothesize: Before the protoagricultural invasions of the Eastern Highlands, there was a sparse but widely distributed Anga-like aboriginal population scattered through the forested mountains. These people, primarily hunter-gatherers, were absorbed (some may have been displaced) by the advancing protoagriculturalists. The initial protoagricultural movement was with taro, out of the Gadsup region; the second, later movement expanded out of the Kamano region with sweet potato. The Agarabi were essentially bypassed, possibly because they were sufficiently warlike as to discourage the early bands of taro growers, or, because they also had adopted taro cultivation and had already moved into their taro-exploitable lands before the Gadsup-like migrants reached them. The movement out of the Gadsup, however, was the one that preempted the remaining lands.

Later, in Region 1, one of the taro growing groups, which had been altered genetically over time by genetic drift and hybridization, adopted sweet potato as its dietary staple. With its new crop, this group was able to expand into the vast abutting virgin lands above the altitude limit of taro cultivation. In some areas, these advancing segmentees appear to have mingled with the earlier taro growers by moving into the higher lands above and around them. However, these sweet potato growers were able to move and diverge more freely into the previously unexploited lands of Region 3.

In Region 2, the idea of sweet potato growing appears to have entered before sweet potato growing segmentees from Region 1 reached it. This enabled the indigenous residents to preempt the higher lands around them, making them less attractive to immigrants from Region 1. Thus they maintained their genetic distinctiveness.

This combination of ecological and genetic evidence suggests that an early protoagricultural movement based on a taro staple introduced from the Markham River valley, moved across the upper valleys of the Ramu River headwaters and continued down the Lamari River valley from the north. Another branch went west, between the Kratke and Bismarck ranges, taking advantage of the Dunantina and Benabena River valleys (see map 1). In these western valleys, perhaps in response to increasing land pressure, sweet potato was adopted as the dietary staple. Unlike taro, which did not grow well above about 5,500 feet, sweet potato grew satisfactorily up to about 8,000 feet. Its adoption thus opened the extensive higher regions of the Eastern Highlands to protoagricultural exploitation. With it, the former taro growers ascended the edges of their valleys, following the edge of the forest into the higher lands beyond. Behind them they left broad valleys of short *kunai* grassland to mark their earlier regions of exhaustive taro cultivation.

Movement into the Fore Region

To the southeast in Region 3 lay the higher unexploited Fore region—between two major populations: the taro growers of the Lamari valley and the northwestern groups, which had adopted sweet potato. From 448 aerial photographs taken before contact showing the Fore region, it has been possible to chart the configuration of grasslands (*map 11*) and define regions of population ecologically (*table 3*). Blood-group frequency similarities among these ecologically defined populations and some of their neighboring linguistic groups (*table 4; map 12*) suggest the major routes by which protoagricultural peoples entered the Fore region.

Very little of the Fore lands were low enough to support a taro-dependent people. When sweet potato was finally introduced, the taro movement had only proceeded into the lower Puburamba River valley and along the adjacent lower Lamari

TABLE 3. ECOLOGICALLY DEFINED REGIONS OF SETTLEMENT

Region	Census units
Aga	Aga
	Keiakasa
	Yagusa
Agakamatasa	Agakamatasa
Atigina	Amora
	Higataru
	Kalu
	Kamira
	Kanigitasa
	Kume
	Mentilasa
	Waisa
	Wanikanto
	Wanitabe
	Wanta
	Yagareba

Region	Census units	Region	Census units
Awande	Awande	Okasa	Ilafo
Ibusa	Emesa		Kasokana
	Etesesa		Okasa
	Ibusa	Paigatasa	Paigatasa
	Ibusa-Moke		Tunuku
	Kagu	Paiti	Paiti
	Keyanosa	Purosa	Ai
	Opoiyanti		Ivaki
Ifufurapa	Intamatasa		Ketabi
	Kasarai		Mugaiamuti
	Orie		Purosa-Takai
	Takari		Takai
	Umasa		Urai
	Weya	Wantokabarosa	Anumpa
Ilesa	Abomatasa		Kasogu
	Awarosa		Kasoru
	Ilesa		Mage
Kabuye	Amusi		Moke
	Aneiga		Pusarasa
	Kabuye	Yasubi	Kaga
	Oma-Kasoru		Kamata
Ofafina	Famia		Keiakasa
	Kalu		Miarasa
	Tiarana		Tamogavisa
			Yasubi
			Yasu-Tunuku

TABLE 4. GENETIC DISTANCES BETWEEN FORE REGIONAL GROUPS AND SELECTED LINGUISTIC GROUPS

	Okasa	AWA	Ilesa	Paigatasa	Paiti	Wantokabarosa	Ibusa	KEIAGANA	GIMI	Purosa	TAIRORA	Yasubi
AWA	0.1013	0.										
Ilesa	0.0925	0.1359										
Paigatasa	0.1696	0.2024	0.2132									
Paiti	0.2270	0.1971	0.1647	0.2681								
Wantokabarosa	0.1197	0.1107	0.1152	0.2250	0.2271							
Ibusa	0.0972	0.1548	0.1146	0.1110	0.1937	0.1732						
KEIAGANA	0.0968	0.1629	0.1091	0.1526	0.2283	0.1236	0.0999					
GIMI	0.1036	0.1789	0.1024	0.1715	0.2428	0.1304	0.1107	0.0605				
Purosa	0.1784	0.1228	0.1842	0.2372	0.1546	0.1760	0.2001	0.2021	0.2325			
TAIRORA	0.1284	0.1276	0.1352	0.2292	0.2283	0.0973	0.1734	0.1298	0.1654	0.1815		
Yasubi	0.0919	0.0979	0.0926	0.2170	0.1993	0.0801	0.1528	0.1275	0.1217	0.1502	0.1441	
Atigina	0.1383	0.1241	0.1561	0.1764	0.1489	0.1784	0.1371	0.1571	0.1901	0.0776	0.1751	0.1441

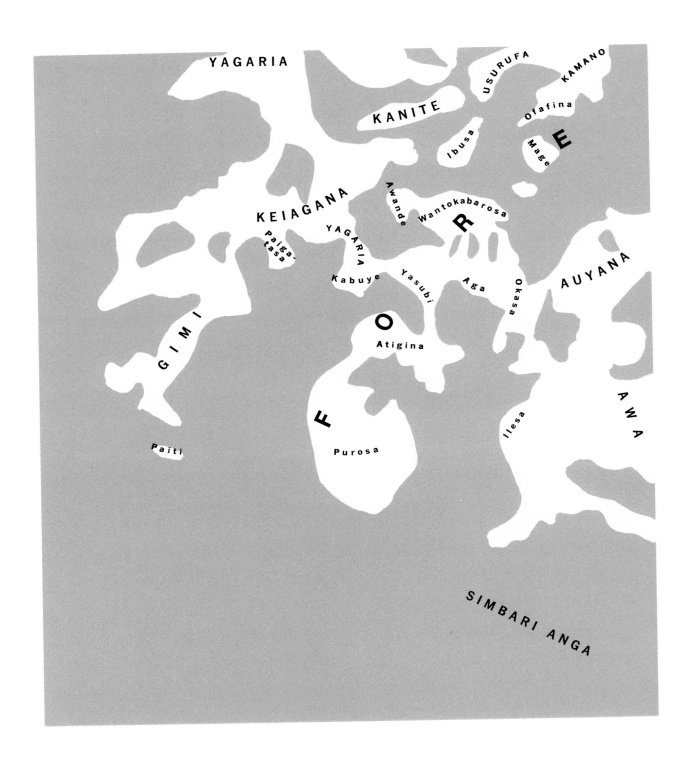

YAGARIA

KANITE

USURUFA

KAMANO

Ofafina

Ibusa

Mage

E

KEIAGANA

Awande

Wantokabarosa

Paiga, tasa

YAGARIA

R

Kabuye

Yasubi

Aga

Okasa

AUYANA

GIMI

O

Atigina

A W A

F

Ilesa

Paiti

Purosa

SIMBARI ANGA

MAP 11. DEFORESTED REGIONS OF THE FORE HOMELAND. The configuration of deforestation in and around the Fore region not only indicates the routes by which protoagricultural peoples moved into the region, but it also suggests a classification of the Fore population by ecologically defined regions of settlement. These regions are labeled in smaller type; surrounding linguistic groups are in larger type.

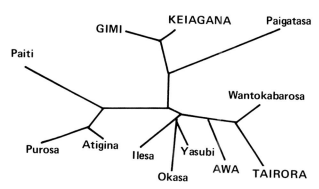

MAP 12. GENETIC RELATIONSHIPS AMONG FORE REGIONAL POPULATIONS AND ADJACENT LINGUISTIC GROUPS. Two distinctly separated outside populations lead genetically into the Fore populations along the two major paths of ecological disturbance (cf. map 11). Emerging from a juncture of these two movements, a branch leads into the South Fore region (Paiti, Purosa, Atigina), suggesting a merging of the two original mainstreams in the populating of this region.

slopes. Those areas of the Waisarampa and Kaza River valleys that could have supported taro growers had not been reached.

That taro, not sweet potato, caused the extensive grasslands that exist below 5,500 feet in the Puburamba and Lamari valleys is indicated by the short *kunai* grass covering these regions. Robbins (1963) has shown that several hundred years may be required for short grassland to develop as a consequence of horticultural intervention. The patterns of ecological opportunity provided by the often rugged and dissected Highlands channeled movement. Ideally, the protoagricultural dynamics leads to centrifugal expansion outward from a central core, and, where ecological barriers were minimal, this pattern of expansion characterized the Fore (see fig. 57). However, the rugged terrain of most of the Fore region tended to create corridors and pools of economic opportunity through and into which the protoagriculturalists flowed (fig. 60).

The first gardening populations to enter the Fore lands would have been from the Lamari valley (fig. 61). The moderate altitudes of the lower Puburamba valley of the North Fore and the western fringes of the Lamari in the South Fore were low enough to support a taro-based economy. However, this would have to have remained confined

to these regions until infiltrating groups from the northwest introduced sweet potato.

Among the Fore, child-handling and rearing practices produced explorative and innovative individuals (see Chapter 8). Informally organized in an egalitarian society and lacking binding sociopolitical ties, the Fore moved easily in search of new opportunity in new lands. An absence of formal territorial boundaries or sociopolitical obligations made it easy for segmenting groups to ally with alien groups and to settle with or near them. When the segmenting groups of sweet potato growers descended into the Puburamba valley, they interdigitated and mixed with the taro growers who had advanced upward from the Lamari valley.

To these people, they would have demonstrated the advantages of sweet potato cultivation. Together they advanced into the higher regions of the South Fore lands.

Protoagricultural advance was not always precisely contiguous. Sometimes, groups jumped a short distance past the edge of the forest to establish a new island of expanding population (fig. 62). Sometimes ecological barriers had to be jumped (fig. 63).

Many of the discontiguously segmenting groups that had leap-frogged ahead to new opportunities were eventually reabsorbed by the more general expansion.

Sometimes segmenting groups bridged ecological barriers that turned the others elsewhere. Origins

FIGURE 60. CHANNELS OF ECOLOGICAL EXPLOITATION. The protoagricultural movement into and through the lands of the Fore followed paths of economic opportunity. Etched by grasslands, the Puburamba River valley marks the site of the earliest protoagricultural penetration. Breaching a ridge above Yasubi, segmenting groups moved into the headwaters of the Waisaramba River to create the Atigina region. Expanding onward into the headwaters of the Kaza River to the south, these sweet potato growers deforested the Purosa valley and sent offshoots into the virgin lands beyond. Meanwhile segmentees moved up the mountainsides from the Lamari valley to form the Ilesa region. Auyana represents an independent movement from the Lamari valley into that region. Gimi appears to be a southward extension of a proto-Keiagana people. This picture looks southward from a point just above Okapa in the Wantokabarosa area.

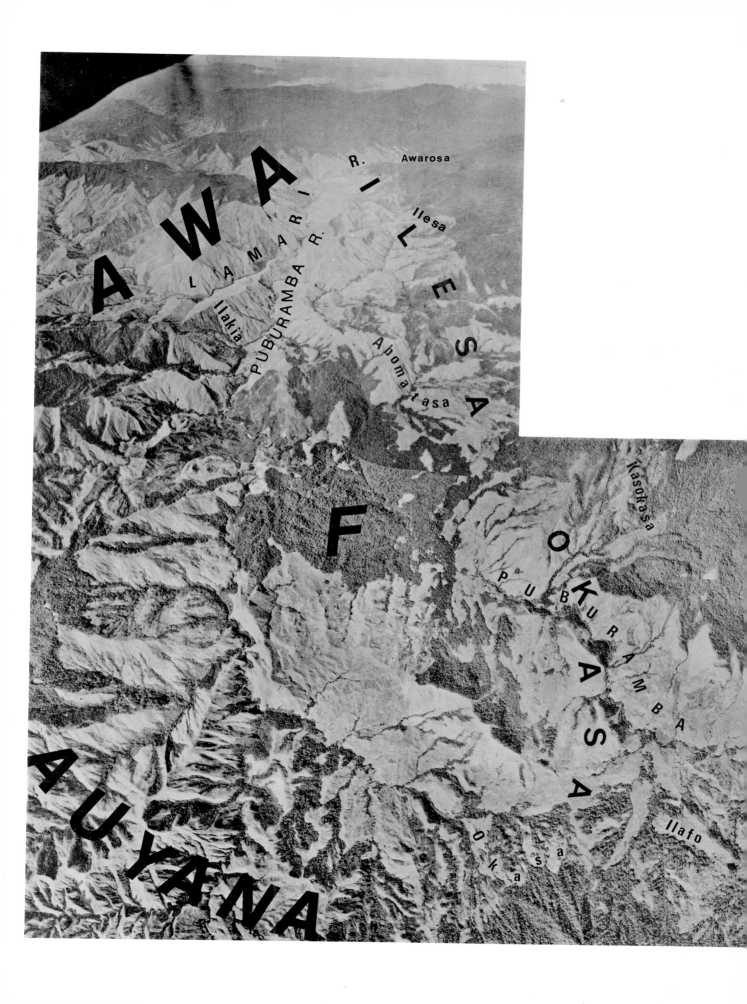

A W A - I L E S A

Awarosa

Ilesa

LAMARI R.

PUBURAMBA R.

Ilakia

Abomatasa

F

AUYANA

Kasokasa

O

P U B U K U R A M B A

K
A
S
A

O

O
k
a
s
a

Ilafo

FIGURE 60. CHANNELS OF ECOLOGICAL EXPLOITATION. The protoagricultural movement into and through the lands of the Fore followed paths of economic opportunity. Etched by grasslands, the Puburamba River valley marks the site of the earliest protoagricultural penetration. Breaching a ridge above Yasubi, segmenting groups moved into the headwaters of the Waisaramba River to create the Atigina region. Expanding onward into the headwaters of the Kaza River to the south, these sweet potato growers deforested the Purosa valley and sent offshoots into the virgin lands beyond. Meanwhile segmentees moved up the mountainsides from the Lamari valley to form the Ilesa region. Auyana represents an independent movement from the Lamari valley into that region. Gimi appears to be a southward extension of a proto-Keiagana people. This picture looks southward from a point just above Okapa in the Wantokabarosa area.

FIGURE 61. THE TARO ROUTE INTO THE FORE LANDS. Both ecological and genetic evidence indicate a major early movement of taro growers from the Lamari valley into the lower Puburamba valley—a movement paralleled by ones into the Auyana and Awa regions. Picture **a** looks westward up the Lamari valley from a point just west of the confluence of the Lamari and Puburamba Rivers. It shows the ecologically confined path by which the early protoagriculturalists moved toward the Fore lands. Picture **b** looks eastward up the Puburamba River from the Lamari-Puburamba confluence.

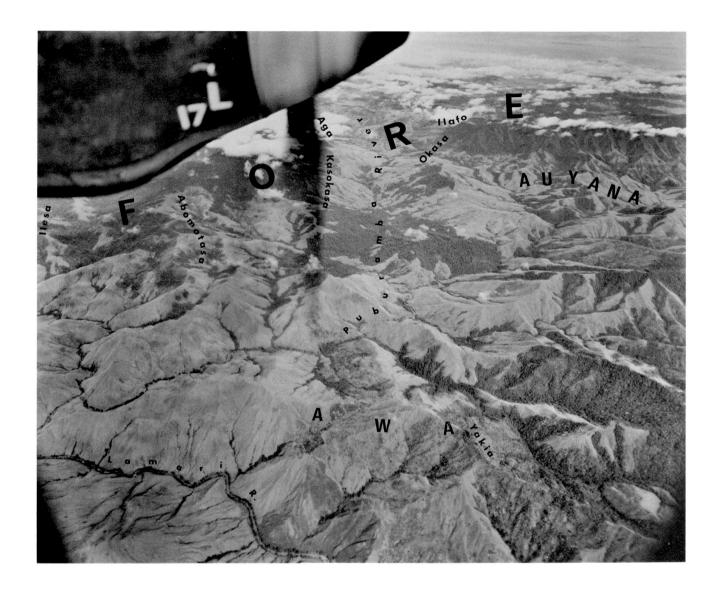

It shows the route followed by the Lamari valley proto-agriculturalists as they entered the Fore and Auyana regions. The pine forest "island" in the center of the lower Puburamba valley was not suitable for making gardens and has remained the only unexploited forest land in the lower valley. By the time of Western contact, the great Lamari valley grassland had become uninhabited except along its upper edges, near the remaining forest land. Names of linguistic groups are in large type. Regional population clusters ("villages") are in small type.

WAISA

FIGURE 62. MARGINALLY DISCONTIGUOUS MIGRATION. The Waisa region of population is the result of groups recently settling across a narrow intervening segment of forest to establish themselves somewhat beyond the edge of the Ivingoi grassland, the origin site of the Atigina populations.

FIGURE 63. DISCONTIGUOUS MIGRATION AND INTERDIGITATION. Established in the virgin forest beyond the protoagricultural core of the Purosa valley are several distinct regions of South Fore population, each marked by a growing core of grassland. Most of these jumped the high west ridge of the Purosa valley to establish gardens in the more productive lower western slopes (Orie, Weya and Umasa). A group from the Gimi linguistic group (Emo) has begun to interdigitate with nearby Fore groups. Similarly, South Fore settling Paiti now mingle with adjacent Gimi villagers. Eteve, a group usually attributed to Gimi because they now speak Gimi more than Fore and because they are culturally like the Gimi, originally broke away from Ketabi (Eteve is the Gimi way of saying Ketabi).

of such groups cannot be identified by examining ecological continuities. Here we need other kinds of evidence—ethnohistorical, linguistic and genetic.

Unfortunately, the shallowness of historical recollection among Eastern Highlands peoples leaves little ethnohistorical evidence with which to work, and the ease with which these small groups change language makes linguistic evidence unreliable. In this situation, genetic evidence can be quite helpful.

Similarities in blood-group frequencies *(map 13; table 5)* suggest distinct discontiguous migrations: 1) Aga people from the Keiagana region across intervening North Fore; 2) the distant Genatei linguistic group from the South Fore across the entire linguistic group of the Awa *(see fig. 61)*; 3) Mugaiamuti from the Puburamba valley after contact with Keiagana-like peoples; and 4) Agakamatasa from both the Atigina region and the Awa linguistic group.

Ethnohistorical accounts confirm the Aga and Genatei movements, and linguistic affinities support the Genatei-Fore connection. However, the Aga people have lost the Keiagana language and culture and are presently indistinguishable from North Fore. A lack of ethnohistorical confirmation for the Awa connection to the recently settled Agakamatasa is puzzling. (Aerial photographs show only virgin forest there as late as 1943.) But there are clear accounts of groups having come from a surprising number and variety of other places: Mugaiamuti, Wanitabe, Ivaki, Ilesa, Okasa, Ai, Waisa, Takai and even Gimi-speaking Au'uwaiyi.

In addition to the major protoagricultural source of the present Fore population, remnants of an earlier aboriginal population are suggested by the genetic analysis of the 14 Eastern Highlands linguistic groups examined *(see table 1; maps 9 and 10)*. An Anga-like genetic character is detectable in several, quite separated protoagricultural linguistic groups now occupying the southern regions of the Eastern Highlands. Indeed, some fringe groups are distinctly Anga-like, and Anga-like stone clubheads are found archaeologically in gardens throughout this region. Present populations have neither names nor use for them.

The Gimi-Labogai, Gimi and Kanite show the clearest genetic relationship to this Anga-like ab-

MAP 13. DISCONTIGUOUS MIGRATIONS REVEALED BY GENETIC EVIDENCE. This genetic network reveals populations separated from their parent groups by ecological or demographic discontinuities. One (Aga) represents a group that jumped along the edge of an existing ecological continuity past intervening groups. Another (Genatei) jumped over a region of severe ecological disturbance and an entire intervening linguistic group (Awa). Paiti and Paigatasa are separated from their sources by unexploited virgin lands, as is Agakamatasa, with its more complex origins. Mugaiamuti may represent an early jump across virgin lands, which have subsequently begun to fill up. Dotted lines indicate the genetic affiliations of these discontiguously settled regions. Solid lines connect groups having contiguous ecological and genetic connections. There is a remarkable congruence between this genetic network and the actual geographical distribution of these groups. Only Mugaiamuti is distinctly "out of place."

FIGURE 64. THE NORTHWESTERN SWEET POTATO ROUTE INTO THE FORE LANDS. A direct ecological connection to the Fore via the Yagaria and Keiagana regions marks this protoagricultural route into the Fore region. A distantly segmenting Yagaria group that moved entirely across the Keiagana is responsible for the small Yagaria region seen between the Keiagana and South Fore region of Kabuye. In 1957 this group spoke the Yagaria language; by 1963 it was speaking Fore. Distantly segmenting groups from Keiagana also settled the now-Fore-speaking regional group of Aga. Similar segmenting groups stemming from the Keiagana eventually reached the Purosa valley region with their original genetic character somewhat changed. Others helped form the present populations of Awande and Ibusa. This picture looks southeastward from a point over the Keiagana-Yagaria boundary, across the Keiagana to the Fore region. The path through the Keiagana to the Fore is clearly traceable through the ecological change that is left in the wake of gardening.

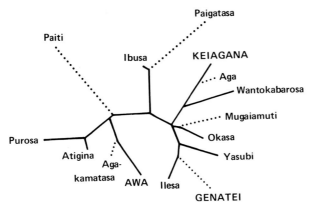

TABLE 5. GENETIC DISTANCES AMONG SELECTED FORE REGIONAL GROUPS

	Okasa	AWA	Ilesa	Paigatasa	Paiti	Wantokabarosa	Ibusa	KEIAGANA	Purosa	Yasubi	Atigina	GENATEI	Mugaiamuti	Agakamatasa
AWA	0.1013													
Ilesa	0.0925	0.1359												
Paigatasa	0.1696	0.2024	0.2132											
Paiti	0.2170	0.1971	0.1647	0.2681										
Wantokabarosa	0.1197	0.1107	0.1152	0.2250	0.2271									
Ibusa	0.0972	0.1548	0.1146	0.1110	0.1937	0.1732								
KEIAGANA	0.0968	0.1629	0.1091	0.1526	0.2283	0.1236	0.0999							
Purosa	0.1784	0.1228	0.1842	0.2372	0.1546	0.1760	0.2001	0.2021						
Yasubi	0.0919	0.0979	0.0926	0.2170	0.1993	0.0801	0.1528	0.1275	0.1502					
Atigina	0.1383	0.1241	0.1561	0.1764	0.1489	0.1784	0.1371	0.1571	0.0776	0.1441				
GENATEI	0.1076	0.1425	0.0901	0.2420	0.1708	0.1648	0.1501	0.1628	0.1725	0.0996	0.1475			
Yagusa	0.1091	0.1669	0.0857	0.1781	0.2175	0.1086	0.1112	0.0483	0.2126	0.1188	0.1766	0.1575		
Mugaiamuti	0.0820	0.1178	0.0891	0.1950	0.1823	0.1201	0.1170	0.0941	0.1532	0.1176	0.1202	0.1271	0.1068	
Agakamatasa	0.1071	0.0723	0.1289	0.1652	0.1719	0.1293	0.1244	0.1480	0.1149	0.0919	0.0955	0.1317	0.1516	0.1321

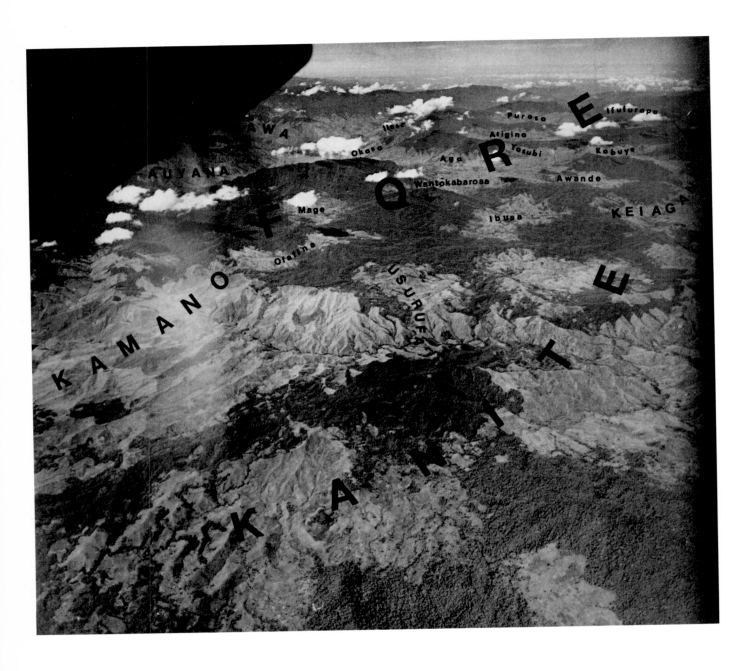

Labels on the image: AWA, AUYANA, Itoer, Okasa, Purosa, Ifufurapa, Atigina, Yasubi, Kabuye, Aga, Wentokabarosa, Awande, Mage, KEIAGA, Ibusa, Ofafina, KAMANO, FORE, USURUFA, KANITE

FIGURE 65. THE NORTHERN SWEET POTATO ROUTE INTO THE FORE LANDS. Segmenting groups from the Kamano region interdigitated with aboriginal populations in this region creating the contemporary Yate, Kanite, Usurufa and Fore groups. A direct line of ecological continuity joins the northern Fore region of Ofafina with a southern extension of Kamano speakers.

FIGURE 66. LOWER VALLEY GRASSLANDS OF THE FORE. The unbroken tracts of short grassland in the Fore region are all below 5,500 feet. Here, just above the confluence of the Puburamba and Lamari Rivers, trees sprout only along the edges of watercourses. In this now completely uninhabited region, the ancestors of the present Fore probably grew taro.

118

original stock; but the Kamano, Keiagana and Fore also appear to have been affected. This earlier population, absorbed by the protoagricultural migrations, must have been made up of rather widely scattered small bands of hunter-gatherers.

SUMMARY: In the larger perspective, the Fore lands appear to have been populated by two major protoagricultural influxes: a taro-based movement from the Lamari valley *(see fig. 61)* and a sweet potato movement entering from the northwest *(fig. 64)*. A less dramatic flow of sweet potato growers appears to have entered directly from the Kamano region to the north *(fig. 65)*.

As these movements expanded across the Fore homeland, they appear to have encountered and absorbed some elements of an Anga-like aboriginal population, probably hunter-gatherers. The major movements met in the Puburamba River valley, moving in from opposite ends. As they exploited its virgin resources, they interdigitated, mixed and moved on to more distant regions, particularly to the south *(map 14)*. Other groups moved directly from the unbroken grasslands of the lower Lamari valley *(fig. 66)* to the edge of the forested higher elevations overlooking it *(fig. 67)*.

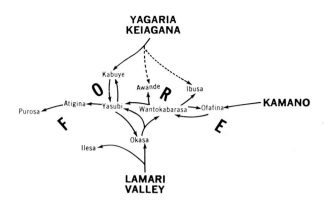

MAP 14. PROTOAGRICULTURAL ROUTES INTO THE FORE REGION. One taro and two sweet potato movements entered the Fore region. Taro people advanced up the Puburamba valley from the great Lamari River valley. Until they adopted sweet potato, they were restricted to the lower valley. Later, two sweet potato movements entered the Fore lands across the high mountains in the north and northwest. The movement from the Keiagana-Yagaria region appears to have been stronger. However, the Kamano movement is also distinctly traceable genetically and ecologically. These movements met in the upper Puburamba valley and mixed as they spread outward from this region, particularly to the south.

FIGURE 67. MOVING UP FROM THE LAMARI VALLEY. Perched above the unbroken grasslands of the Lamari River valley, dispersed hamlets and gardens of Ilesa follow routes of economic opportunity up the slopes of Mt. Tamiloa. The full range of ecological change is visible: virgin forest, gardens and hamlets, mixed cover, permanent tracts of grassland. The extensive deforestation of the lower Lamari valley is apparently the result of an exhaustive taro cultivation practiced there before the introduction of the sweet potato.

Chapter 6   Friends, Neighbors and Communities

Consistent with a protoagricultural situation that differed somewhat from north to south, a loose, informal sociopolitical organization had evolved among the Fore, which facilitated digressive adaptation to new economic opportunity. In the south, a pioneer environment surrounded by extensive tracts of uninhabited virgin forest permitted a slow, contiguous dispersion of communities. In the north, decreasing virgin land opportunities fostered a more dramatically dispersive resettlement, as segmenting groups more often went further afield in quest of new virgin lands.

Channeled by the dissected Highlands topography, these conditions gave rise to a distinctively protoagricultural demographic situation, which stamped its requirements on the sociopolitical system. As segmenting groups expanded into new regions, relations among the diverging communities took shape in association with a dispersive, opportunistic pursuit of economic advantage. These relations could not be rigid or formal without obstructing this basic pursuit.

Regions of Population

Several large, distinguishable regions of population marked the Fore lands (map 15). They comprised a central, uninhabited grassland with population clusters dispersed along the circumference. The configuration of these regions was governed by the economic opportunities provided by the surrounding virgin forest.

The Fore did not give much thought to these larger regions. They did not give them formal, generally recognized names; nor did they consider themselves either territorially or politically affiliated with such regions. The residents of these regions did not organize against those of another. Rather, the warfare that broke out from time to time among the Fore was typically among the smaller communities, usually within a region.

Coleman, the first patrol officer at Okapa, made the first attempt to define these regions. Using Coleman's data, Gajdusek, Zigas and Baker (1961) mapped them for use in their medical studies. However, the Western convention of formal "boundaries" was foreign to the way the Fore viewed and moved within their geography, and these first attempts did not reflect the indigenous situation accurately.

Once identified, these regions of population were variously defined by the early Western observers. Gajdusek, Zigas and Baker (1961) called them "tribal groups." Berndt (1962) spoke of them as "districts." Glasse (1962) suggested they might be related to phratry social organization. More recently, Gajdusek (1970) thought they might reflect past political consolidations that may have developed around "big men" during past times of warfare. This variety of approaches to understanding these regions reflects their ambiguous sociopolitical nature.

The protoagricultural model shows that these regions are largely the result of pioneer horticultural expansion in topographically channeled regions of economic opportunity. To refer to them as "tribal groups" may have been a useful Western convenience for officials who needed an identificatory handle to pursue their own work more effectively, but it did not accurately reflect the indigenous situation. "District" is more correct, but because it is more abstract, it succeeds by not having to come to grips with the sociopolitical issue. "Phratry" indicates an awareness of an agnatic orientation among the Fore, but it fails in the larger sense because there were no clear tribal or clan identities that corresponded to these regions.

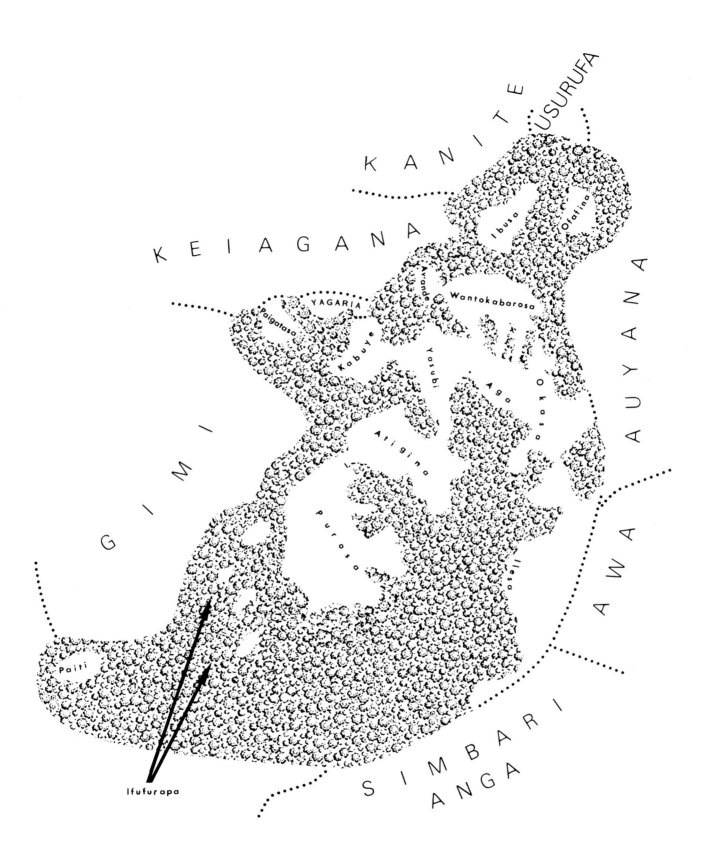

To consider them the result of past warfare alliance verges on the fanciful.

The difficulty in achieving a sociopolitically valid definition of the regions of population seems to stem from the lack of need to be concerned about regional territoriality among protoagricultural people.

The geographical identifications now used are those imposed by the early government officials. However, as the needs of Western administration are quite different from those of protoagriculturalists, they do not correspond very well to the way the Fore viewed their regional geography. It does not matter that the names used were provided by Fore informants; they were used in a non-Fore way.

In the Fore society such names were neither formal nor fixed; nor was it expected that everyone would use the same names. Words and names were communicational expedients, often tailored at the time to fit the problem or question at hand. As with ethnodescriptions of anything, they reflected interests and needs that emanated from a way of life. The Fore way of life required that such interests emanate from individuals; there were no abstract interests, such as those possessed by states or regions, nor were there collective interests such as those that inhere in established political leaders. Identifications, thus, emerged from discourse and corresponded to an individual's interests and views.

It took me a while to learn this, and when I first began moving about the Fore lands, it surprised me, for example, to discover that most of the residents of the Ifufurapa, Wantokabarosa and Kamikina regions did not know them by these names. I considered the possibility that the officials who had identified and mapped these regions had been arbitrary. But, after attempts to find out the "real names," I discovered there simply weren't any formally established regional names. Ifufurapans, for example, frequently cited "Purosa" when pressed to name a large affiliation or region to which they belonged. This was not, as I eventually learned, because they felt any sense of belonging to a "Purosa" region or people, but because they had learned that Westerners were happier if they could relate to some such geographical identification already known to them. In this case the nearest site of distinct Western activity was Purosa, where there was a census site, aid station, mission and road terminus. Others cited "Ivingoi," a core region from which many of the Ifufurapan settlements had originated, where there was another census site, agricultural demonstration project, government rest house and anthropologist's station. Still others cited "Pamousa," and others "Asafina." A few years later "Umasa" was cited, after it had become the road terminus and was the site of a new-style consolidated village on the government census site, next to the government rest house. Many individuals still could give no more than the name of their own smaller population clusters.

Population Clusters

All regions of population contained smaller population clusters. Although boundaries were hard to pin down, the clusters often had a center discrete enough to provide the basis for the establishment of census units by the early patrol officers. However, as there were no barriers to crosscultural resettlement or residence, these communities tended to interdigitate socially and territorially. Anyone's individual social, economic or territorial connections could extend across other clusters in a variety of ways, depending on the strength of the associated individual friendships. This precluded sociopolitical or territorial exclusiveness on the cluster level and made it difficult to define clusters geographically or politically. Dispersive group segmentation practices of the Fore played an important role in sustaining this sociopolitical diffuseness, as did the

MAP 15. REGIONS OF POPULATION WITHIN THE FORE. Following river valleys and natural topographic configurations, the centrifugal expansion of the protoagricultural Fore was patterned by their natural surroundings. These regions of population are marked by a central uninhabited grassland with gardens and hamlets on the edge of the forest. Small regions are probably the result of expansion from a single origin site. Larger regions may be the result of several expanding groups coming together and removing the forest, which once stood between them.

lack of a concept of formal membership in territorially based groups.

The way Fore spoke of the clusters reflected this diffuseness: Smaller clusters would, for a time, be spoken of as part of a larger one by some observers but not others. Some hamlets would be said to belong to one cluster by some Fore but to another by others. Even members of the same hamlet did not always claim affiliation with the same population cluster or necessarily use the same names when referring to them. Obviously, a good bit of this confusion was a result of the ease with which Fore moved around and formed new associations. This made it possible for individuals in a population cluster to start focusing their social or economic activities in another cluster without committing the others in their "home" cluster to the same affiliation or jeopardizing their affiliation to that cluster.

The names of population clusters were clearer and better known than those of the larger regions of population of which they were a part. But the names for these clusters still possessed the same somewhat flexible character.[36] Typically small migrating groups settling or visiting others were at first identified by their old names, but they could lose these identifications as they became socioeconomically integrated with their new neighbors. However, if they continued to maintain a separate settlement, their old names tended to stick (see footnote 36).

In the ultimate analysis, it was probably not useful or meaningful for Fore to identify themselves or their associates by regional or political names. Personal social and economic ties defined one's loyalties—not a territorial affiliation—and dispersive resettlement made it difficult to link these to named territories or groups.

Despite the problem of assigning names to the Fore lands and people, population clusters still possessed a sociopolitical character. This derives from the fact that Fore tended to settle near their childhood friends and associates. Thus friends tended to be neighbors, and socioeconomic ties among these neighbors defined de facto associations, whether named precisely or not. These associations were somewhat epiphenomenal and could not be formally defined either politically or geographically; because of the protoagricultural segmenting practices of the Fore, they could readily change membership and boundaries.

Hamlets

The least territorially ambiguous population group in the Fore was the hamlet (fig. 68). Its territorial limits were clearly visible, and its members were all fraternal and in close association. Yet because the Fore freely segmented to take advantage of new land opportunities, hamlets were not permanent. Locations and memberships were prone to change, even for this basic demographic unit.

Fore land tenure practices abetted such flexibility. With rights to specific plots of land limited to those actually benefiting from them by virtue of their own labor, lands not being actively used for gardening or residence were open to use by others. In areas already inhabited, such use was usually limited to individuals who were associated with (a) member(s) of the extant population. But it was relatively easy to form this kind of association, particularly in neighboring groups where some people would already be known. Personal rapport was the essential requirement for land use in occupied regions. In uninhabited regions, simple occupation sufficed.

Hamlets were named for the particular ground on which they were situated, not usually for the people who settled them. When a site was abandoned, its name stayed with the site (although old names could be forgotten). Sometimes a relocated hamlet would continue to be known by its old name, at least by some people (see footnote 36).

Compatibility and individual preference brought hamlet-mates together. Without formal ties, common names or political leaders to bind them together, sociopolitical identity, even on the hamlet level, remained a partially articulated affair—an epiphenomenal, fluctuating aspect of an everchanging, aterritorial, dispersive network of personal affiliation embodying common economic, social and political interests.

Even though these networks could extend haphazardly through a variety of hamlets and regions, individual liaisons were more likely in neighboring regions. This is what provided the regional sociopolitical character that existed and made it possible for the early patrol officers to begin to identify populations territorially. These liaisons were strongest on the hamlet level, less strong on the cluster level and weakest on the regional level.

The rather undefinable character of the warfare

was a consequence of this type of sociopolitical organization. Although most of one's close associates were neighbors, it was not uncommon for the respective members of a hamlet to have many out-of-hamlet associates of different degrees of camaraderie in different places. Members of some hamlets could trace their affiliations not only to other hamlets in their own region, but also to other population clusters afar. This created a situation in which there were individuals who would not join their hamlet-mates during warfare because of their close association with individuals in the "enemy" hamlets. It explains why these "neutrals" could move freely across the lines of hostility, even during times of battle.

Demographic Organization

Of the six levels of Fore population organization (see table 6), three were significant sociopolitically: 1) hamlets; 2) interhamlet affinity groups; 3) population clusters.

TABLE 6: CLASSIFICATION OF THE FORE POPULATION DISTRIBUTION AT THE TIME OF CONTACT

Grouping	Characteristics	Names of identified units
LINGUISTIC GROUP	Unnamed. Not politically significant.	
DIALECT GROUP	The names are not necessarily accepted by all the speakers of any dialect. Not politically significant.	Atigina, Pamousa (Purosa), Ibusa, Ilesa.
REGION OF POPULATION	No fixed or formal names. Not politically significant.	Ofafina, Ibusa, Wantakabarosa, Aga, Okasa, Kamikina, Atigina, Ilesa, Purosa, Ifufurapa, Asafina.
POPULATION CLUSTER	Territorially based, but with ambiguous boundaries. Tend toward internal political unity, but exclusive internal allegiance not expected. Not territorially exclusive. Not fully united socially or politically.	Agayagusa, Anumpa, Awande, Emesa, Etesesa, Famia, Ibusa, Ibusa-Moke, Ilafo, Kagu, Kalu, Kasogu, Kasokana, Kasoru, Keiakasa, Keyonosa, Mage, Ai, Amora, Amusi, Awarosa, Higitaru, Ilesa, Intamatasa, Ivaki, Kabuye, Kaga, Kalu, Kamata, Kamira, Kanigitasa, Kasarai, Keiakasa, Ketabi, Kume, Mentilasa, Miarasa, Mugaiamuti, Oma-Kasoru, Orie, Paigatasa, Paiti, Purosa-Takai, Takai, Takari, Tamogavisa, Tunuku, Umasa, Urai, Waisa, Wanikanto, Wanitabe, Wanta, Weya, Yagareba, Yasubi, Yasu-Tunuku, Abonai, Nosuguri, Onuri, Yanaraisa, Orasa, Ibunarasa, Azapinti.
INTERHAMLET AFFINITY GROUP	Unnamed. Not possible to enumerate. Informal, unbounded, changing and not territorially based. The focus of political activity.	(no names)
HAMLET	Basic social unit. Semistable membership. Impermanent sites. Names usually change when sites change.	(several hundred such units)

FIGURE 68. TYPICAL HAMLET SITE (above). The only territorially focused Fore sociopolitical entity was the hamlet. Outward from these clearly visible sociopolitical units, affiliations ramified unpredictably. These hamlets were not permanent, however, nor were their memberships fully stable. Hamlets were not only the result of segmentation, but they were susceptible to it. Here, a relatively newly formed hamlet of the Yasubi population cluster has formed from segmenting groups from two other hamlets; an even more recent arrival has started to build a house next to those already inhabited.

RESIDENTIAL DISPERSION (opposite). Although hamlets were the clearest definable residential unit, the freely segmenting Fore people continually eroded the geographical integrity of even this basic unit. Individuals or small groups leave established hamlets to build new houses on new sites of interest. Friends may join them there with additional houses, thus establishing a new hamlet. Some build single houses, somewhat removed from a hamlet proper, maintaining a moderate isolation. Sometimes an entire hamlet will move away as new hamlets are formed in an adjacent region. In this way, hamlets begin to dot the regions that have been inhabited longer. Even rather small, isolated hamlets are subject to this basic protoagricultural schismatic process.

Although social and economic interaction was centered in hamlets, it also extended through more widely dispersed groups of individuals. For lack of an appropriate established name, I refer here to these larger, more diffuse groups as *interhamlet affinity groups*. These hard-to-identify, loosely ramifying associations extended across several hamlets. For the most part they were a consequence of old hamlet-mates staying in touch after segmentation; but they also absorbed new friends and associates. Because members of these affinity groups could reside for a while in one hamlet and then in another, it was not always clear when an individual belonged to a particular hamlet or to one of the interhamlet affinity groups extending into that hamlet.

The larger, geographically centered *population clusters* contained several associated hamlets, and they usually harbored extensions of a number of interhamlet affinity groups, without being very congruent with any. Like the interhamlet affinity groups, population clusters were nondiscrete, interlocking and sociopolitically fluid. However, unlike these affinity groups, they typically extended outward from an identifiable territorial core. The cores were usually unambiguous; but it was not so clear when the peripheral extensions were too vague to constitute a solid sociopolitical link. The situation was particularly murky where different segmenting peoples were moving into the same region. This fading at the edges of population clusters made it difficult to define them with any degree of precision.

The larger *regions of population* had no sociopolitical status in and of themselves. They were simply the regions where the protoagricultural dispersion characteristic of population clusters had set their ecological imprint on the land. They could usually be identified ecologically in aerial photographs but were not so easily defined otherwise.

The *dialect groups* were also ecologically distinct and identifiable in aerial photographs. Although they were recognized by most Fore, there was not full agreement on their number, names or boundaries. They had virtually no political or social function or importance, beyond that accruing to people who speak the same way.

The still larger Fore *linguistic group* was not named, not defined, not recognized and of little sociopolitical significance.

Segmentation, Dispersal and Mobility

At the time of contact, the Fore did not travel much beyond the lands of friends and associates, except under very pressing circumstances. However, within and adjacent to the Fore region there was a degree of mobility somewhat in excess of what would be expected of a protoagricultural people. This condition was sufficiently noteworthy that all the early observers commented on it.[37] Nearly everyone had friends, kinsmen or associates in other villages, and they found ways to go back and forth, using their own trails or those of friendly peoples. At any time, in any village, "visitors" could be found. Some were in temporary and even semipermanent residence with their "hosts" *(map 16)*. Group migrations to join distant people were not uncommon.[38]

This mobility was a clear outgrowth of the Fore practice of free segmentation, although the extensive dispersal evident at the time of contact seemed also to be related to a particularly severe recent "time of troubles." Land pressure had increased in many parts of the Fore, and kuru had aggravated the sorcery problem. Both of these accelerated dispersion. Mobility increased with dispersion.

This was most acute in places where land pressure was the greatest. In the less congested southern population clusters (e.g., Kasarai, Urai, Umasa and Agakamatasa), contiguous segmentation was usually preferred to distant migration to unfamiliar lands.[39]

In other parts of the Fore, population congestion had more severely limited the availability of new land, and neighboring groups began to expand into one another. This development forced basic changes in the customary protoagricultural practice of unrestricted contiguous segmentation. Once the land had become congested, further segmentation had to be either noncontiguous or by means of forceful occupation of desired lands by armed might. Recultivation of old lands was a difficult third possibility, and one that could only provide temporary relief (i.e., until continued population growth and degradation of land resources exhausted this remedy). At the time of contact, all of these alternatives were being pursued in various degrees.

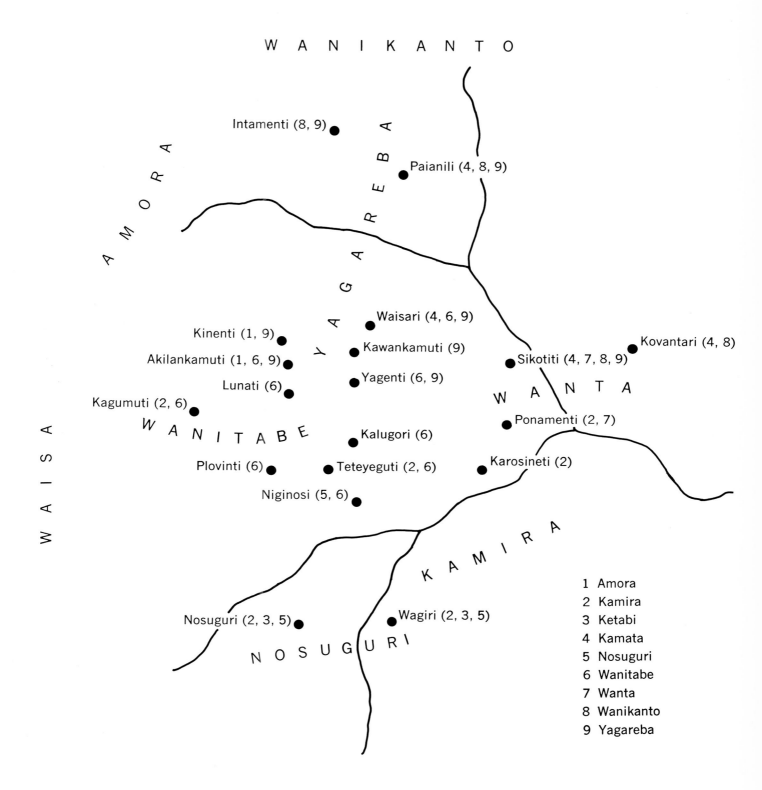

WANIKANTO

AMORA

YAGAREBA

Intamenti (8, 9) ●

Paianili (4, 8, 9) ●

WAISA

Waisari (4, 6, 9) ●

Kinenti (1, 9) ●

Akilankamuti (1, 6, 9) ●

Kawankamuti (9) ●

Kovantari (4, 8) ●

Sikotiti (4, 7, 8, 9) ●

Lunati (6) ●

Yagenti (6, 9) ●

WANTA

Kagumuti (2, 6) ●

WANITABE

Ponamenti (2, 7) ●

Kalugori (6) ●

Plovinti (6) ●

Teteyeguti (2, 6) ●

Karosineti (2) ●

Niginosi (5, 6) ●

KAMIRA

1 Amora
2 Kamira
3 Ketabi
4 Kamata
5 Nosuguri
6 Wanitabe
7 Wanta
8 Wanikanto
9 Yagareba

Nosuguri (2, 3, 5) ●

Wagiri (2, 3, 5) ●

NOSUGURI

MAP 16. MIXED AFFILIATIONS. Because of dispersal and mobility, individuals with quite different population cluster affiliations have come to settle in the same hamlets. The above hamlets, situated in the upper Waisarampa River valley, are shown with regional origins claimed by their residents.

The shift to noncontiguous migration unavoidably entailed kindred dispersal; conflict undoubtedly accelerated it. But I do not completely agree with Glasse (1962) that defeat in war was the main reason for dispersal, although it was certainly one of several as Glasse states.[40] Much of the movement of people about the Fore region was undertaken to avoid warfare and other social problems stemming from congestion. In fact, the typical way of coping with unpleasant social situations and the threat of conflict was to move away. Usually, this was temporary, but in cases where exacerbating conditions persisted, it became permanent. Fore were accustomed to relatively unrestricted segmentation as their traditional means of pursing opportunity. Very little change in this practice was necessary to utilize it also as a means to escape social difficulty. Land tenure was loose, and abandoning old lands, a normal practice. As drastic a force as defeat was not necessary to cause migration; the threat of conflict, fear of sorcery, unfavorable economic conditions or preconflict conditions were as important as actual defeat.

The development of extended interhamlet affinity groups seems to have been a direct consequence of the dispersal of associates. Childhood association created strong bonds of trust and understanding, which were not easily severed. Thus, dispersal of old friends created a desire to travel and visit. Friends and childhood associates were also those to whom one turned for support and assistance in times of trouble or need; they could usually be counted on to provide refuge or a place of alternative residence.[41]

Thus, the greater the dispersal, the greater became interregional fraternization and travel. This, in turn, extended the interhamlet affinity groups more widely. Where groups were sparsely settled, associative bonds tended to keep kindreds localized; but, when pressing demographic conditions forced more dispersive resettlement, increased mobility and interregional liaison followed.

Linguistic, cultural and blood-group differences have shown the degree to which the present Fore regions of habitation have been the beneficiaries of immigration from other places.[42]

The degree of mobility noted at contact may have been relatively recent. Undoubtedly greater demand made on the land resources by the increasing population was partly responsible. However, the increased fear of sorcery caused by the near epidemic occurrence of kuru may be responsible for the full extent of this rather dramatic dispersal.

Whatever the cause, delocalization was the result. It led the Fore from their earlier, relatively isolated regional clusters to an emerging, more interregional body tied together with geographically dispersed networks of personal affiliation. The delocalization also wrought changes in the population organization: As old friends dispersed more widely, interregional networks began to develop. Residential possibilities increased, and the sociopolitical arena became larger.

Polylocality

I define polylocality as a practice permitting individuals or small groups to take up alternative residence at will, unrestricted by formal kinship responsibilities, exclusive community loyalties or legal barriers to resettlement. Polylocality is advantageous in a protoagricultural situation but disruptive in settled agricultural societies where laws and codified practices establish exclusive control of lands by individuals, kinship groups or corporations. It is easier to exercise in regions with plentiful new lands or where the carrying capacity of the land is significantly greater than the demand being made. Informal social segmentation to exploit environmental opportunities is one manifestation of polylocality. Extended visits with old hamlet-mates in their new locations, and interhamlet affinity groups are others.

By the time of contact with the West, dispersal, mobility and residential flexibility were pronounced. It was not unusual for the different members of the same hamlet to have close out-of-hamlet associates from quite different groups. Personal affiliation could extend to several different, even distant, regional population clusters. Such associations abetted further residential dispersal. By the time of Western contact, individuals born in Yagareba, for example, were living in at least 10 other population clusters, including one speaking another language.

Because availability of free lands varied from one part of the Fore region to another, their polylocality was manifested in two ways:

1) Local polylocality in which unrestricted re-settlement into new lands by simple outward diffusion dispersed kindreds into adjacent regions.

2) Extensive polylocality in which far-reaching resettlement privileges with friends or associates living in widely separated communities led to widespread mobility.

Local polylocality was a natural consequence of the protoagricultural situation. It also established a basis on which increasingly disjunctive migration could readily develop into extensive polylocality, increased mobility, widely spread intercommunity ties and interregional visiting. The impetus to resettlement in both types of polylocality was the desire for better gardens, well being and social compatibility.

Affiliative Kinship and Informal Adoption

Affiliative kinship played an important part in Fore social organization. Social and economic ties not defined by descent led to an affiliative kinship, which was as strong as biological kinship. Genealogical priorities were not paramount; propinquity and preference also played important roles in the formation of kindreds. One could move to another group and be accepted as a full member simply by participating in the daily activities as a close friend.

Kinship terms were applied as readily to affiliates as to consanguines, and behavior was a more specific indicator of relationship than descent (although they often coincided). Those who helped each other in common social or economic endeavors could become kinsmen.[43] They were not hindered by any sense of formally belonging to a family or descent group. Thus, kinship transfer (adoption) was relatively easy; it was only necessary to integrate one's activities more fully with those of other associates. Sometimes this only required moving; segmentation and polylocality were generative conditions for affiliative kinship. Although males and females were free to move among the associates of their hamlet-mates, males were much more active in this, and only males moved on to unrelated people.[44]

Aside from the restrictions on the freedom of females, pursuit of preference among the Fore included associates and place of residence. Children learned to be polylocal, like their parents. For example, when rapport or mutual attraction developed between a child and a new acquaintance, he was free to remain with his new friend. Neither formal transfer of responsibilty nor any legal sense of custody was involved. It was simply the practice of polylocality by the child according to the adult model.[45]

The adoptive relationship could be either with an adult or with a group of age-mates—usually age-mates for boys and adults for girls. Adoption across distant villages was more likely to follow from a rapport established between a youngster and an adult, typically as one or the other was passing through for trade, visiting a distant associate or more recently, working as a patrol carrier for Europeans.[46]

The degree to which afamilial residence may occur in the South Fore is indicated by a survey I made in 1967–68. Of a random sampling of 176 South Fore living in 24 hamlets in Yagareba, Wanitabe, Amora, Waisa, Agakamatasa, Wanta and Kamira, I found 54 residents who were unable to establish a genetic nuclear family relationship with any other resident of their hamlet. In at least 18 more, the relationships were ambiguous and could have been fictive.

Unconcern for lineal kinship was prerequisite to this kind of distribution. Without such unconcern it is unlikely that polylocality would have developed to this extent. To be able to settle in another community and not be a second-class member because of imperfect kinship abetted flexible resettlement.

Affiliative relationships dominated Fore kinship thinking. To learn the biological genetic links, it was often necessary to convene a number of old friends. Adding to the difficulty was the failure of the Fore to distinguish linguistically true parentage from adoptive. Thus, identities of true mothers, fathers and kinsmen were more likely to become obscured over time. To obtain true identities of biological parents was not always easy. To be sure of other blood kinsmen was even more difficult.

In my attempts to obtain genealogies for an investigation of kuru epidemiology, I repeatedly encountered these problems. It was always necessary to make clear that the natal connection was the information desired. A close bond existed between a mother and the child she had nursed. This was usually remembered if the mother had not died when the child was still very young. An aid to determining true motherhood was, therefore, knowing from whom the child had nursed. However, this approach was not foolproof, and to be certain of true motherhood, it was better to ask from whose vagina a child had come. To get a final answer on this sometimes required calling in several older people for consultation. Particularly in the case of an older person, whose mother had been dead for a long time, the subject would have difficulty in remembering her name. Among boys, the mother tie diminished after they ceased living in the women's house, after the age of about five or six years. However, in the case of girls, the bond remained strong through continued daily association until the time of marriage. Children usually knew the names of their true mothers; adults remembered less frequently.

Affiliative kinship, informal adoption and polylocality seemed to go together. Dispersal and mobility undoubtedly increased the impact of these practices. The focusing of socioeconomic activity and residence in hamlet units, rather than in family units, in itself tended to obscure direct familial ties and replace them with community associations.

Protopatriliny

At the time of contact, the South Fore did not resort to descent principles to formalize their social or political groups or to sustain solidarity. Specific ancestry and birth were not required for (and they did not bar) full membership in any group, nor did they confer higher status or special benefits in any situation. Occasionally, patrifiliation was cited in defense of an inheritance claim to an established, productive garden. However, claimants to such lands usually cited the work they had contributed to the gardens in association with the deceased owner, or their close cooperative economic association with him, rather than kinship alone. The right to make use of unused land in partially settled new areas usually required an affiliative (not

patrifiliative) connection with someone already active in the vicinity. In one's home region such connections were abundant; in uninhabited regions they were not required.

In the absense of a common descent requirement in Fore social, residential or cooperative groups, or in the obtaining of land use or residence privileges, affiliation (sustained by voluntary social and economic interaction) became the cornerstone of Fore sociopolitical unity. The patrilineal character of communities that did exist was largely the result of childhood sibling association, not formal descent principles.

However, the beginnings of a descent orientation may have begun to emerge in the North Fore. R. Berndt (1955, 1962) held that North Fore social structure was somewhat patrilineal, like that of their Kamano, Usurufa and Yate neighbors to the north.[47] However, in order to evaluate this statement properly, it is important to recognize that Berndt examined all of these groups as a collective Eastern Highlands unit, in an effort to define a general Eastern Highlands type of society. The patrilineal patterns seen among the Kamano and Usurufa (see C. Berndt 1953) may not exist so strongly in the North Fore. It may be significant that when Berndt does restrict his comments on social organization specifically to the North Fore, he speaks of nongenealogically defined groups and "coresidence" as important organizing principles.[48] Except for this, it is not possible to determine from Berndt's writings precisely how the North Fore social organization differed from that of its northern neighbors. He made no observations among the South Fore, whose departure from the patrilineal model of the north would have been more obvious.

My own observation is that the North Fore were more patrilineally oriented than the more sparsely populated South Fore but less patrilineally inclined than the more densely populated Kamano and Usurufa to the north.[49] Possibly there is a relationship between land pressure and patriliny and that therefore both became greater as one moved north and northwest.

Meggitt's (1965) hypothesis relating agnatic interest to pressure on land resources seems to be borne out among the Fore and their Kamano and Usurufa neighbors. But his hypothesis does not sufficiently explain why the South Fore, with plentiful new lands surrounding them, still possessed patrilineal bias in the membership of their population clusters, even though they did not concern themselves with descent principles.[50]

I suggest that a combination of two factors may be responsible for the de facto, but not de jure, patrilineal aspect of the South Fore population clusters:

1) *A custom entering from other regions:* The ecological evidence indicates that an earlier proto-agricultural period with taro was coming to an end before the introduction of sweet potato. This raises the possibility that the pre-sweet potato Fore may have responded, during this period, to the greater land pressure by organizing themselves more patrilineally. This view is supported by the vestigial character of the Fore interest in preserving sites for ancestor spirits and in the status of the cordyline plant as a symbol of the male generative and unity principle.

2) *An accidental result of other practices:* Patrilocal residential practice could provide a patrilineal character to the demographic structure, as contiguous protoagricultural expansion in land-rich regions proceeded. A de facto male descent character would develop as males resettled in the vicinity of their natal community and females married out to other communities. In such a situation, descent would not have to be formally traced through the male line in order to sustain a patrilineallike demographic structure. However, because of the absence of the patrilineal principle and because inheritance was not governed by descent principles, we cannot speak of this situation accurately as patrilineal. Yet, because it provides a ready basis on which patrilineal social principles could emerge, we may speak of it as protopatrilineal.

The ecological evidence suggests that land pressure increased in the Fore during the end of their taro period. The adoption of the sweet potato reversed this situation. By the time of Western contact, land pressure was again beginning to appear across much of the Fore. Possibly the Fore became interested in patrilineal principles at the end of the taro period, lost this interest with the adoption of sweet potato, and again became interested when land pressure began to appear in the north.

This model would explain why interest in descent is so absent among the Fore, even though there is a de facto patrilineal bias in their population clusters. In land-rich areas there was no reason to invoke lineage to secure land, indeed such practice would interfere with the kind of free segmentation that so well suited the protoagricultural situation.

Social Cohesion

Instead of a formal hierarchy to govern social and political activity, the Fore had developed a system based on interpersonal compatibility and cooperation among close associates. Social cohesion, particularly where Fore residential clusters were widely separated, was based on rapport, not principle. Within each Fore residential grouping, whether a single hamlet or a cluster of hamlets, a familiarity and intimacy developed in the course of long-term daily association. Growing up together and having common economic objectives strengthened this ingroup social focus and made formal social organization less needed.

Informal affinity groups, not formal kinship or territorial groups, were the Fore means to cooperative activity. Individual Fore associated with those persons whose company they enjoyed most. Formal accountability or relationship did not enter into this system, except in the case of marriage: Women were discouraged from leaving their husbands by a formal marriage agreement and feast, which had to be paid back in the event of separation. Still, even with this restriction, wives could make extended visits to friends in other villages when they felt the need.

The movement of men and boys was freer. They pursued economic opportunity through social segmentation. They would build new hamlets any time they wanted to try a new place or a new set of associates. This freedom to move to be with more congenial people kept residential groups relatively free of internal friction and promoted internal harmony within communities.

Living with trusted intimates made it possible for cooperative endeavors to be based on friendship and mutual regard. Interpersonal attraction, common feeling and mutual understanding brought these Fore individuals together in cooperative informal groups.

Within such groups there was an informal sharing of materials, affection, food and labor among intimately associated individuals. These were extended as a personal gesture, not to fulfill a formal social obligation. Since personal affection, not obligation or etiquette, sustained cooperative endeavors, subtle behavior, more often than spoken requests, communicated need or interest and provided the basis for participatory activity. Mutual understanding was such that these were usually evident without discussion. Close comrades were gratified by common efforts and quickly responded to each other's aspirations. Failure to respond to subtle behavioral cues was a mark of estrangement among the Fore. A direct request would be open recognition of alienation.

Two opposed forces determined the pattern of Fore social organization:

1) Cooperative association with trusted intimates was the basis for the Fore social cohesiveness. Growing up together in the Fore milieu appears to have been particularly instrumental in creating a close and enduring bond of understanding and regard. This bond was not easily ruptured.

2) The Fore were territorially digressive, explorative and socially innovative—traits consistent with their protoagricultural way of life.

The combination of these two somewhat antithetic forces contributed to a relatively harmonious social dispersiveness, which provided stability and flexibility. In the protoagricultural setting they interacted so as to enable the Fore to take advantage of open frontiers and new opportunities, while maintaining an appropriate social cohesion.

The sustained, somewhat fluid cohesiveness that resulted from the advance into new lands required a compatible social organization. Only in regions where lands began to fill up and population clusters began to expand into one another, did such traits begin to lead to social confusion, community dispersal and a need for a new system.

Chapter 7 **Expressions of Emotion**

Culture, as the selectively patterned realization of basic human potential according to the social and physical parameters of a milieu, may modify subcortically programmed expressions of emotion. These neurophysiological "universals" may be common to all men, regardless of difference in culture and background, as Darwin (1872) thought, but, at least in part, culture seems to pattern their expression.

The protoagricultural way of life of the Fore patterned their expression and recognition of basic human emotion in keeping with the requirements of their social organization. This patterning of human response emerged in the growing child as his central nervous system was programmed by the various social and physical experiences provided by the Fore milieu. Statistical analysis of Fore responses to a standardized set of photographs of the facial expressions reflecting basic emotional states may be compared to responses of individuals in other cultures, so as to reveal their culturally specific view. The differences in response suggest how social organization in the protoagricultural situation acts to modify and stereotype the Fore responses to basic expression of human emotion.

This study grew out of earlier work by Tomkins, Ekman and Friesen on recognition of facial affect by Westernized college students (Tomkins 1962, 1963; Tomkins and McCarter 1964; Ekman and Friesen 1969a,b) and by Ekman, Sorenson and Friesen on pancultural elements in the expression of emotion (Ekman, Sorenson and Friesen 1969; Sorenson 1973).

At the time of this fieldwork, in 1967–68, many Fore were in daily contact with Western government officers, missionaries and scientists (and their families). These Fore had had a chance to learn the facial expressions of emotion displayed by Westerners. But there were also Fore who had remained apart from these Westernizing influences. Some had remained in their old-style isolated hamlets and had not had an opportunity to become very acquainted with Westerners and their facial expressions. These individuals met the requirement of *visual isolation* [i.e., insufficient direct experience with outsiders (or their pictorial media) to have become familiar with their facial expressions].

The different degrees of acculturation reached by the Fore made it possible to divide them into three groups: most acculturated, less acculturated and least acculturated.

The set of photographs used was standardized by Ekman and Friesen, who used pictures drawn largely from Sylvan S. Tomkins's work defining *primary affect states*. Seven basic emotions were represented: happiness, fear, anger, surprise, sadness, disgust and contempt. This set of pictures was selected from more than 3,000 affect photographs taken by Edward Gollub in association with S. Tomkins, on the basis of high agreement among American college students on the emotion expressed *(fig. 69)*.

Two basic sampling strategies were devised. Both required native responses to the set of stimulus photographs:

METHOD I was adapted from a technique first used by Dashiell (1927) and modified by Izard (1971). On the basis of knowledge of Fore culture, short stories were devised to portray a particular emotional state in relation to an aspect of typical Fore life. For example, theft or deliberate injury to someone's pig would be certain to cause anger. Thus, the story connoting anger was about a man whose pigs had been injured by another. The subject was asked to point to a picture, out of a set of two or three, which showed how the owner of the pig felt. No verbal response was required. This

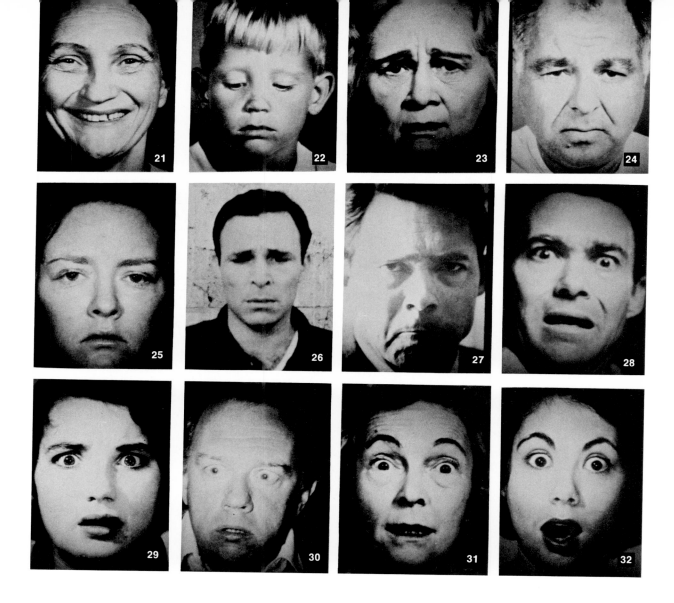

seemed to be an easier task than having the Fore respond with a spoken answer.

The outstanding weaknesses of this technique were the difficulties of: 1) devising stories in an alien culture that were sure to reflect unambiguously the emotions we had in mind; and 2) controlling the testing situation.

Neither Ekman nor Friesen, who participated in this part of the study, knew Melanesian-Pidgen or Fore. My own Melanesian-Pidgen was good; but I was not up to following native discourse or making myself understood in Fore beyond the simplest messages. Therefore, for the least acculturated Fore we had to rely on Fore translator-assistants to explain the task and to relate the stimulus stories. We were not able to monitor this communication.

In view of the Fore communicational conventions, it was likely that at least some responses were

FIGURE 69. THE FACIAL EXPRESSIONS OF EMOTION. With the affects displayed having been defined by high statistical agreement among American college students, these photographs, primarily taken by Edward Gollub for Sylvan Tomkins, were shown to non-Western subjects in New Guinea and Borneo in an attempt to see if they agreed with Westernized peoples on the affect displayed. In this study we limited ourselves to the following affects: Happiness (1–4, 21), sadness (5–8, 22–26), anger (9–12, 27), fear (13, 14, 28–30), surprise (15, 17, 31, 32), disgust (18, 19), contempt (20).

influenced by feedback between translator and subject. The Fore, even those trying to be most Western, could not be expected to have internalized our Western concepts of a testing situation sufficiently to avoid "leaking" information. The suggestion that free exchange of information was "cheating" was quite incomprehensible to the Fore and alien to their view of language as an element of cooperative interaction among close associates.

The best we could do was to impress our assistants continually with the importance of not discussing the pictures with the subjects, and particularly, not telling them which pictures to select or suggesting key features for which to watch. The effect of our cautions could not be determined.

METHOD 2 was a less ambiguous testing procedure, but it triggered communicational dissonances. We showed a set of photographs of facial expressions of emotion, one at a time, to individual subjects. Only the subject, I and a single Fore assistant who had worked closely with me for several years were present during the testing. The Fore assistant explained the task to the subject in the Fore language before the testing began. I showed the pictures, one after the other, and waited for the subject to give the affect term he thought best described the expression in the picture. Responses were in the Fore language. The Fore assistant remained silent while the pictures were being shown. He was positioned so that he could not see the pictures.

The subject responded to each picture with a single affect term in his own language. When terms I did not know were given, I asked for a translation from my Fore assistant. If they were new affect terms I had not heard before, they were added to my list of terms. When the response was not an affect term (e.g., "she is just looking," "he is ugly," "he is stupid," etc.), an affect term was requested. This worked well in the majority of cases.

The advantage of Method 2 was that it reduced the translator's influence on the subject's responses considerably. The translator did not even see what pictures were being shown and remained silent during the testing. He was present only to explain the task to the subject and occasionally to explain the meaning of a novel response or new word to me. The weakness of this method, however, was that it required a spoken response among a people who were not familiar with question-and-answer discourse as a means of communication. Among traditional Fore, direct questions were usually considered hostile provocations; answers were not usually expected.

The results of Methods 1 and 2 are presented in tables 7 and 8.

The greatest difficulty stemmed from the need for formal interview sessions involving question and answer in a society in which the interrogative style of discourse had not evolved.

In the face of the need to respond to the interrogative procedure, many displayed uncertainty, hesitation and confusion. Some were completely tongue-tied; others trembled and perspired profusely or looked wildly about. The least acculturated were most afflicted; they often seemed bewildered, even fearful, in the face of the kind of interrogative communication that Westerners take so much for granted.

This confusion and nervousness was a direct consequence of employing communication practices of Western culture to Fore who were threatened by it. As discussed earlier, question-and-answer discourse had not evolved among the Fore, apparently due to its inappropriateness in a society based on close personal familiarity and intimacy. In this society direct questions were an unmistakable sign of alienation and provocation.

In order to gather data from these New Guinea subjects, there was a major cultural gap to be bridged. The style of interpersonal communication among the intimately associated Fore differed so markedly from the Western style that unfamiliar interviewing dissonances occurred, which were hard to cope with or evaluate.

Fortunately the problem was partially ameliorated by the eagerness with which the economically opportunistic Fore people were ready to change their activities and beliefs according to the Western model. Both native assistants and subjects were generally very eager to do things in the Western way. This greatly aided our attempts to communicate, because the will was so pronounced, even in the face of our rather rude, provocative question-and-answer challenges.

This caused other kinds of difficulties: Like other things Western, our pictures and procedures were the subject of considerable interest and active discussion by the behaviorally alert Fore. They were quick to seize on the subtlest cues for an indication of how they should respond and react. This undoubtedly skewed our results, particularly those of Method 1, toward ideas of appropriateness developed by both the translator-assistants

TABLE 7: RESPONSES TO PICTURES OF FACIAL AFFECT BY 189 FORE ADULTS AND 130 FORE CHILDREN *(Method 1)*

Emotion connoted by story	ADULTS		CHILDREN (prepubescent)	
	Percent of correct choices	Incorrect choices by frequency	Percent of correct choices	Incorrect choices by frequency
HAPPINESS	92	sadness, anger, disgust, fear, surprise	92	sadness, anger, disgust, surprise
SADNESS	79	anger, disgust, fear, surprise, happiness	81	anger, disgust, fear, surprise
ANGER	84	sadness, disgust, fear, surprise	90	sadness
DISGUST/ CONTEMPT	81	sadness, surprise	85	sadness
FEAR	80	sadness, disgust, happiness, surprise	93	sadness, anger, disgust

TABLE 8: RESPONSES TO PICTURES OF FACIAL AFFECT BY 100 FORE SUBJECTS *(Method 2)*

Emotion seen in picture	GROUP A (most contact)		GROUP B (less contact)		GROUP C (least contact)	
	Pidgen language	Fore language	Pidgen language	Fore language	Pidgen language	Fore language
HAPPINESS	99 h	82 h	92 h	67 h 18 an	87 h	60 h
FEAR	46 f 31 an	54 f 25 an	37 f 21 an	30 f 20 an	36 h 33 f	23 f *
DISGUST	38 d 21 pa	39 d 21 pa	41 an 23 pa	24 h 22 c	26 h 22 an	23 h *
ANGER	56 an 22 f	50 an 25 f	56 an 16 f	49 an 29 c	51 an 25 h	48 an *
SURPRISE	38 su 30 f	45 f 21 an	34 an 28 su	31 f 27 h	33 su 33 an	31 h 26 su
CONTEMPT	29 an 21 sa	36 an 29 c	40 d 27 an	28 c 26 an	33 an 25 d	27 an *
SADNESS	55 sa 23 an	56 an *	37 sa 27 an	57 an 13 f	42 an 26 h	53 an *

Group A: Experienced at least one year of government or mission schooling; spoke Melanesian-Pidgen well and dressed in Western shorts.

Group B: Had lived away from the Fore region on a government station, mission station or plantation for more than 4 months; wore cloth; spoke moderate Melanesian-Pidgen; and had not had more than one year of mission schooling.

Group C: Had not left the Fore region for more than brief visits of a few days; never worked for Westerners; spoke little, if any Melanesian-Pidgen; wore traditional dress.

h-happiness, f-fear, an-anger, d-disgust, pa-pain, su-surprise, sa-sadness, c-contempt

*no clear second mode

FIGURE 70. A FORE EXPRESSION OF ANGER. Under the conditions of Fore social organization, the expression of anger is often like that of sadness. This expression of anger posed by a Fore native was shown to other Fore natives who agreed that it represented anger. Only a few said it was sadness. No one thought it was anything else.

and the Fore subjects. We must assume that the somewhat Westernized veneer of the two partially English-speaking, school-boy assistants, employed during Method 1, is reflected to some degree in those results.

That pictures of Caucasians were used to elicit responses from visually isolated non-Caucasian peoples also caused uncertainty. Some of the more

haphazard responses may have been due to the strangeness of the pictures among people who had seen few Caucasians. Among the subjects least familiar with Westerners, these pictures often caused consternation, laughter and animated discussion.

The most striking result was that the Fore saw anger more often than did Westernized subjects, particularly in the pictures representing sadness or fear (fig. 70).

We can begin to understand these atypical responses when we consider them in relation to the kind of social organization possessed by the Fore. Recognition of the socially disruptive and schismatic aspects of anger was less escapable where relations were based somewhat precariously on personal rapport. Informal and dispersive, Fore group structure was more vulnerable to anger than are more formal and stable social organizations. The affiliative social organization possessed by the Fore led logically to a situation in which sadness and fear may more frequently be associated with anger.

We need only to consider those areas of our own society in which personal rapport is a vital component of a relationship: The expression of anger between lovers ruptures such rapport. Perhaps it should not be so surprising that anger developing in such a context may have elements of sadness and that expressions of sadness among lovers are sometimes interpreted as anger. Similarly anger developing between a mother and child may also trigger elements of sadness.

Because the Fore society is so informal and intimately organized, its members would be more broadly susceptible to such consequences of anger than would people in societies in which relationship and responsibility are stabilized by more formalized kinship requirements and enforced codified obligation.

In loosely organized societies, where formally established patterns of human relations are lacking, anger would also be more likely to engender existential fear. Again we may look into our own culture to find situations in which a dependent's anger against those who nurture him and on whom he depends may be mingled with fear. This shows up most clearly where security and well-being depend on bonds of personal understanding and trust. Anger is a serious threat to these kinds of relationships; it not only threatens one's sense of social identity, but it also undermines his sense of the future. Thus a condition of existential fear may emerge when anger threatens valued human relations that are anchored only by personal trust and affection.

Social structure and economic order among the Fore were highly dependent on such bonds. Consequently anger, even incipient anger, was a serious matter, something to be forestalled if possible. Since recognition must precede efforts to forestall, it is reasonable to expect recognition of even traces of anger to be well developed.

Fear may also be more readily triggered by occurrences of anger in the loosely organized way of life. This could explain why the least acculturated Fore exhibited fear and trembling in the face of questions. Our procedures must have appeared provocative and hostile to them, the circumstances must have seemed somewhat Inquisitorial.

In societies like our own, where group structure is stabilized by formally established customs and codes of responsibility, the power of anger to provoke existential crisis would be much less. Expressions of anger would less frequently trigger despair and fear of the sort to which groups with less firmly established social organization would be susceptible.

It is more likely that the Fore responses reflect a special sensitivity to subtle expressions of anger, and possibly pre-anger. It would be reasonable to expect this in communities in which the social organization would be quite seriously threatened by anger. Irrevocable termination of valued relationships could be brought on rather easily. Thus, the Fore had good reason to be specially attuned to perceiving traces of anger, which in other kinds of societies could more safely be ignored.

We must consider the possibility, therefore, that our Fore respondents directed their attention more often to subtle anger components in the facial expressions shown in our pictures of Westerners. Perhaps they noticed the subtle expressions reflecting our aggressive-competitive social system—possibly facial consequences of the repressed anger, backbiting and gossip that occur in more competitive social systems. These components could be disregarded by Westernized respondents as constants; but a more anger-vulnerable people would pay more attention to them.

Chapter 8 **Growing Up**

Because of his more complex, more programmable nervous system, man is more able than other living species to respond and adapt to the new opportunities and challenges provided by a changing world. He does this through modification of his habitual patterns of behavior. When the new patterns become part of an established way of life and are passed to subsequent generations, they can be said to mark "way-stations" in the ongoing process of human adaptation and evolution.

The Fore occupied such a way-station, possibly as a last representative of a once widespread protoagricultural way of life. Hence their patterns of adaptation and behavior not only tell us something about a hitherto poorly known form of human culture, but they also provide insight into the larger question of human cultural evolution in the world. By examining how these patterns are transmitted to growing children, we may discover aspects of basic human potential different from those seen in our own culture.

Transmission of culturally specific patterns of behavior has to take place as the growing child's central nervous system interacts with his milieu. Different milieu provide dissimilar typical situations, which can expose the infant or young child to different languages of sensory input, different patterns of emotional organization and different foci of perception and cognition. Divergent practices involving such basic human experiences as touch, kiss, caress and embrace; smell, taste, nursing and feeding; sound, voice, story and myth; gesture, rhythm, music and dance; and manners, morals, etiquette and kinship may each direct human development along divergent paths in which different aspects of basic human potentials are realized.

Theoretical Considerations

We members of a modern, expansive and technological "wired" culture, tend to be aware of the fact of differences in child handling and rearing throughout the world. Some of our eminent scholars—Mead, Whiting and Erikson, to name a few—have also provided increased insight into childhood in other cultures by making it the subject of scholarly inquiry.

Still, even with this worldly sophistication, it remains quite difficult to appreciate or to understand the dynamics of human behavior development in alien cultures. It may be easy to recognize the fact of difference and to talk about it. However, it is not so easy to go beyond a simple description of the differences phrased in the concepts of one's own culture.

Deeper appreciation is obscured by cognitive barriers. We are all enculturated beings and embody, therefore, culturally specific patterns of awareness and understanding. Culturally bestowed ideas of value screen our sensory input and structure our cognitive appreciation. We recognize, conceptualize and express in terms of the precepts, categories and habits bequeathed by our own culture. We perceive and talk about what we encounter in other cultures through the colored spectacles of our own culture.

Such barriers are not easy to transcend, and anthropologists are as subject to them as anyone else. With the possible exception of feral man, we are all products of enculturation. We all live in our way-stations of human development, and the observations we might make of other ways of life are culturally bound to our own way of life.

In an attempt to work with data extending beyond these cultural limits, I turned to making film records of events of Fore childhood as they occurred in day-to-day life. Although such records had to be made selectively according to my culturally programmed intellect and awareness, they also captured undifferentiated, unselected information from the original event. Like a fossil, the film record preserves primary data of the past event and can be distinguished from other kinds of records by this quality. Furthermore, like other kinds of fossils, film records remain available to permit reexamination from new points of view and perspectives, thereby facilitating discoveries beyond earlier habits of awareness.

Film is able to capture and preserve information beyond that perceived by its human wielders. Although human beings select the subject to be photographed and cameras make it possible, it is the film that actually takes the picture. Because of this, film preserves data not only of what is "seen" or "selected" by the culturally programmed mind of the observer, but also what is not. Even when the camera is picked up, pointed and turned on and off according to a cameraman's particular interests and concepts of appropriateness, it also gathers information interstitial to and beyond the cameraman's interests and awarenesses. It can produce, therefore, a deeper record of events than is possible by relying on human perceptive and descriptive abilities. As a means of gathering visual data, it extends beyond the cultural barrier, beyond the individual's personal or cultural screen. Data collection that relies on transcription of only that which has been perceived and transcribed by a human observer does not extend so far.

In earlier studies of human behavior, visual records have proved valuable, in some cases critical. The use of film to discover and demonstrate culturally specific patterns of behavior on Bali by Mead and her colleagues clearly showed the value of visual data in anthropological inquiry. More recently, Birdwhistell's discovery of subtle, visible components in communication from film records showed that film was indispensable in detailed analyses of human interaction. This was further supported by Hall's demonstration of cultural difference in nonverbal human interaction. Lomax's study of patterns of human movement in dance and work, and their relation to social and economic evolution would not have been possible without access to a growing body of anthropological films containing retrievable data not necessarily sought or recognized by their filmers.

Recently much has been made of the fact that filming is selective, therefore not objective, not scientific and not suitable as a data source. This view underestimates the degree to which human interest and selectivity underlie all human inquiry, systematic or spontaneous, scientific or humanistic. We would have little scholarship or scientific knowledge, perhaps none, if we forbade human interest and selective observation as important components of scholarship.

An advantage of film inquiry over other types of inquiry is that visual records, even when selectively made, also contain the interstitial, peripheral and contextual data in which the phenomena selected for study are immersed. Such records, examined by scholars moved by their selective interests, facilitate original and validative inquiry in a number of ways:

1) Discovery of information not previously noticed becomes possible.

2) Like any preserved specimen, film records possess information permitting reexamination and substantiation of findings.

3) Such records can be prepared so as to reveal biases, which may have influenced the selection of information.

4) They provide information, which can be reexamined when new knowledge leads to new questions.

5) They preserve details and relationships too subtle, fleeting or complex to be detected in the real time of daily life or under the demanding conditions provided by fieldwork in other cultures.

6) They advance us a step toward providing "unacculturated" data when dealing with other ways of life and culture.

7) They permit examination of an event or episode in relation to its antecedents, consequences and existential context.

Even though analysis of what is seen in research film records proceeds according to concepts of significance emerging from one's own culture, it is of considerable advantage to be able repeatedly to refer to data that extends beyond these limitations, applying personal predilections and creative intuitions during peak periods or at leisure, unconstrained by the problems of fieldwork and the ideas that may have been in mind at the time of field-work. To thus be able to take advantage of hunches, partially formulated ideas, intuitions, shifts in interest and whatever momentary insights that may develop at different times, expands the potential of research and facilitates development of cumulative insight and understanding.

In order to exploit these scholarly potentials of film better for my studies of child behavior and human development among the Fore, I systematized the use of film, developing a research film theory and methodology. These research films represent my first attempt to take advantage of the scholarly potential of film records in a major study of child behavior and human development in another culture. (See Appendix 1 for details on theoretical background and methodology.)

Still cameras were used to capture data on items, locations, positions, context, accoutrement and expression, including that which could not be observed or considered in detail under the pressure of fieldwork. Similarly, motion picture cameras were used to gather information on patterns and subtleties of process and development in Fore behavior and social interaction.

Fieldwork Procedures

A great wealth of visual information emanates from all natural events, and any attempt to obtain a "complete" record would be a fruitless pursuit of an unachievable fantasy. Many more than thousands of "channels" would be needed to show "all" micro and macro views of everything from all angles and perspectives. Fortunately, just as paleontological fossils do not have to present a complete record of every individual biological entity that has ever existed to be useful in the development of knowledge about the evolution of biological form, neither do "film fossils" of human behavior have to provide a record of every moment of life in a culture to provide useful information on the development of human behavioral patterns. It is only necessary to obtain a useful sample. One needn't try to film everything.

Initially the sampling strategy took shape somewhat intuitively, as a combination of three approaches: 1) opportunistic sampling; 2) programmed sampling; and 3) digressive search. (See Appendix 1 for details.)

Employing a mix of these filming strategies, I divided the study of child behavior and development among the Fore into three phases (fig. 71): 1) initial fieldwork and collection of visual data as research films; 2) analysis of research film records to discover culturally specific patterns of child activity, behavior, handling and socialization; 3) new fieldwork to test the hypotheses formed.

PHASE 1: Because so little was known about Fore behavioral patterns in advance and because there was behavioral diversity across the Fore territory, I emphasized opportunistic sampling and digressive search in my early filming. What programmed sampling there was was very general: simply to shoot whatever child behavior and social interaction I saw.

Initially, I tried to develop a randomness in sampling; but it proved quite difficult to move randomly in the rainforest environment, and there were cultural barriers as well, which made it harder to film in some locales (e.g.: women's houses). The digressive search was an attempt at randomness that remained semirandom.

So that the novel effect of my presence would not be too disruptive to the daily patterns of life, I chose two South Fore communities (Waisa and Yagareba) as sites for concentration. In these places my presence came to be accepted as an everyday affair—not a special event.

My subject of interest (child behavior) was also fortuitous in that infants and toddlers were seldom interested in my presence or behavior unless it was very close and directly affected their specific activities and interests of the moment. It also worked to my advantage that I was in the Fore region to investigate the epidemiology of the disease, kuru. This made my interest in social behavior less obvious.

I was also lucky, in 1963–64, that most Fore were not yet familiar with cameras; there was no posing. Furthermore, the Fore use of eye contact to signal interest in social engagement and aversion of eye contact to break social contact worked to my benefit. Looking into my cameras effectively broke off and precluded social interaction with Fore individuals while I was filming. The Fore soon treated my photographic activities very casually, probably because no ostensible effect could be attributed to them.

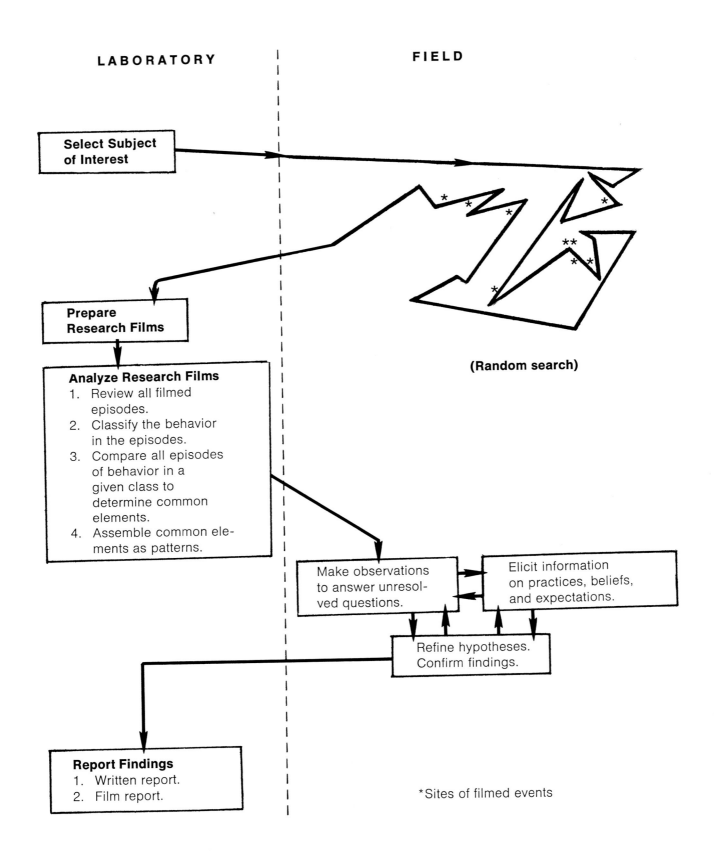

LABORATORY   FIELD

Select Subject
of Interest

Prepare
Research Films

(Random search)

Analyze Research Films
1. Review all filmed
   episodes.
2. Classify the behavior
   in the episodes.
3. Compare all episodes
   of behavior in a
   given class to
   determine common
   elements.
4. Assemble common ele-
   ments as patterns.

Make observations
to answer unresol-
ved questions.

Elicit information
on practices, beliefs,
and expectations.

Refine hypotheses.
Confirm findings.

Report Findings
1. Written report.
2. Film report.

*Sites of filmed events

FIGURE 71. MODEL OF RESEARCH PROCEDURE USED.

I had come to the Fore with two motion picture cameras, two still cameras and 40,000 feet of film on my first visit. *(See Appendix 2 for abstracts of the films.)* I began to film immediately, even before I learned anything about what I was filming.

Roaming the Fore lands and moving somewhat haphazardly from one site to another, I conducted the digressive search for child behavior. A simple rule governed my use of the camera: When I had it with me and whenever children were seen engaged in any kind of activity, I pointed the camera and let it run until either the film ran out, the activity ceased or I feared to use too much film on something that seemed repetitious. Dramatic and aesthetic considerations did not affect this filming rule; nor did a poor camera location or disadvantageous lighting keep me from filming an event.

Sometimes, my filming activity attracted the attention of those being filmed; other times it did not. This did not alter my approach to filming. I felt that how attention was manifested in relation to me and my activities was also of interest and would be useful. For example, much of the data I accumulated on fear reactions of babies and toddlers was during my encounters with them on first visits to their hamlets. It was my close presence that caused the fear among these children who were very unaccustomed to seeing individuals they had not known all their lives.

I never asked to have any activity repeated in order to film it better; nor did I ask to have specific acts performed in order to film them.

By relying on my cameras to provide me with the behavioral data I needed, I did not have to discuss behavioral matters formally with the Fore, during my 1963–64 fieldwork. This I felt was advantageous in that I was able to obtain data on the *actual* behavior, rather than on the *idealized* view the Fore would have of their own activities. Furthermore, reliance on cameras made it easier to avoid the problem of my Fore hosts being disconcerted by too obvious and intrusive an interest in their activities by a stranger. By relying on the camera, I was able to limit my usual inquiries to those that might be expected of anyone new anywhere; ie., where I was and what was going on around me. This information was appended to the film record. Inquiries about behavior seen came later, during Phase 3 of the study. Because the movies taken during Phase 1 were to provide data for later analysis, I had only to prepare the film record as a research document, which could be re-

peatedly reexamined without loss or disorganization of the data. To facilitate this, I kept a record of time, place and circumstances of event filmed.

Phase 2 of the study was analysis of the film record. When the job of assembling the research films was complete *(see Appendix 1 for method)*, analysis began. All films were searched for episodes of infant handling, nursing, physical activity, affectionate expression, exploratory behavior, aggressiveness, response to aggression, deference patterns, disposal of body wastes, instruction, learning, peer interaction, expressions of anger and sharing—all categories of behavior of interest to members of Western culture. Obviously many other categories of behavior are also of interest, but these were the ones I chose as lending themselves to a manageable elaboration of cultural patterns and styles of Fore behavior. Because I still had my film record, this decision did not foreclose future examination of other categories.

For some categories I had many events, for others, only a few. All sequences falling into any one of the selected categories were viewed and compared; a norm was hypothesized on the basis of commonness, absence of contradictory behavioral events and analysis of reactions of others present. In many cases, sequences were observed in slow motion and stop frame (in order to detect fleeting or subtle movements or expressions). The still photograph record was also searched for incidents falling into the categories of analysis. From repeated examination of these data, patterns were postulated. If, for example, I could find no cases showing the breast being denied the child for nursing, I tentatively assumed that one of the features of the Fore pattern of nursing was the availability of the breast according to the desires of the child. Similarly, if in all the sequences of aggressive behavior by young children, I could find none where older children or adults became angry or retaliated when attacked, I assumed that the pattern of relation of elder to younger children was that of friendly tolerance to aggressive impulses.

In some categories of behavior, there were very few examples to examine. There was only one event of a toddler defecating in public. However, since this was in the middle of a hamlet yard at the time of a community feast, I made my deduction on the basis of the reactions of the people present (as well as on my own recollection of similar events I had witnessed, which I was unable to film). Because no one seemed surprised or disconcerted, and because mother and an older sibling good humoredly cleaned up as the toddler repeated his discharges first in one place and then in another, I tentatively assumed that the pattern of toilet training was permissive—even from this single filmed episode. All such assumptions were subjected to field verification during return fieldwork.

In this manner, the initial patterns, styles and modes of typical Fore child-related behavior were hypothesized.

PHASE 3 was the return to the field during which the validity of the results of research film analysis was subjected to further inquiry. Observation was selective now, not randomized as before; informants were questioned. I deliberately searched for exceptions to my tentative findings when they did not correspond with what we would normally expect in our own culture. For example, I made a special effort to look for incidents of aggressive behavior among children. I tried to find instances of older children insisting on precedence over younger. I asked men, women and children about the behavioral patterns I had postulated from the film analysis and whether such behavior was ever thought to be unusual, peculiar or intolerable. I also asked about possible exceptions to the behavioral norms I had postulated. New information was checked against further observation; more questions were asked as long as contradictions remained. Unsubstantiated hypotheses were discarded; uncontradicted hypotheses were accepted. In some cases new information led to additional findings; but, usually more precise formulations emerged. In nearly all cases, the findings derived from analysis of the research films were substantiated.

Because such behavioral patterns manifest themselves through time, they can be reported more effectively in a motion picture report than is possible by narrative or selected still photographs. I have, therefore, used my findings as the basis for the assembly of a research report film titled *Growing Up As a Fore*. Typical sequences of each category of behavior studied were assembled in an attempt to display the culturally specific patterns of Fore child development and socialization more coherently. Now part of the National Research Film Collection of the Smithsonian Institution, *Growing Up As a Fore* will remain permanently available for scholarly examination. In this chapter, selected sequences of frames from this film and special assemblages of still photographs are employed to present the same findings.

These photographic assemblages are accompanied by a short summary of each of the basic patterns discovered. This combination is designed to demonstrate the culturally specific expression of each category of behavior examined more efficiently than is possible using words or pictures alone. In Chapter 10 there is a discussion of the implications of the Fore style of protoagricultural childhood in relation to the rather spectacular cultural change experienced by the Fore after Western contact.

The rather lavish degree of physical contact provided to infants and young children appears to be crucial in the patterning of Fore social and behavioral development. The spinning out of the effects of this hitherto poorly studied type of early experiential input runs like a unifying thread through Fore childhood, tying it to their protoagricultural way of life.

A second crucial thread running from infancy through childhood was the unrestricted manner in which exploratory activity and pursuit of interest were left to the initiative of the child.

We repeatedly see the importance of these two threads, extensive human physical contact on the one hand and freedom to explore and pursue individual predilection on the other, in the behavioral development of growing Fore children and in the fashioning of the Fore protoagricultural personality. The typical response of elders to the interests, desires and aggressive impulses of the child reflects these threads, as does the warm deference of older children to their younger associates. The manner by which toddlers and young children acquire the knowledge and skills enabling them to become economically viable and recognizable Fore adults can also be seen as related to them, as is the way in which the Fore young enter their world of peers and develop habits of interactive and cooperative behavior. These culturally patterned behavioral underpinnings underlie the type of nursing and feeding behavior characteristic of the Fore, and they play a crucial role in reintroducing this pattern to each new generation. They foster the development of the important prelinguistic, tactile communication seen between infants and their caretakers—a previously unstudied way of bringing young babies into social communicative interaction with those around them at a very early age. The early acquisition of this communicative skill circumvents much of the kind of infant frustration often seen in other cultures.

These early basic childhood experiences seem to engender a confidence and realistic self-reliance permitting independent experimental and inquisitive probings of surroundings at the discretion of the young growing child. The ability to explore the characteristics of potentially dangerous elements, such as knives and fire, without being hurt or seriously injured, seems to emerge naturally from Fore infant handling practices, which occur in a milieu of close human physical proximity and tactile interaction. The manner of contact between younger and older children reflects this, as does their manner of resolving conflicting objectives. The emergence of cooperative behavior among informal aggregations of age-mates stems from these, as does development of the voluntary associations of adults, which so effectively exploit the economic opportunities provided by their protoagricultural surroundings.

Handling the Young Child

Infants and toddlers were kept in almost continuous bodily contact with their mothers or her close associates, often on the laps or under the arms of their caretakers (fig. 72). The lap of the seated mother was the center of activity for infants, and they spent most of their time there, often at play with their own bodies or those of their mothers. From the vantage point of close and uninterrupted physical contact with their caretakers, the young Fore children became aware of the world around them, while their physical needs, such as sleeping, nursing and stimulation, were satisfied without obstacle, almost without notice.

Carrying of the very young infant was often by net bag (bilum), where he could lie in an almost fetal position against the back of his mother; he was also carried under her arm. An older infant or toddler was normally carried straddling her hip, and he continued to rest and sleep, as he felt the need, against his mother's body or on her lap (fig. 73). He was not put aside even when she was otherwise occupied, as when food was being prepared or she had heavy loads to carry.

Older children participated more and more in the carrying and handling of young children as they grew older (figs. 74, 75). These caretakers were not assigned, but rather, their role developed from a mutual attraction established between themselves and the young child. The infants or toddlers could reject one older associate in favor of another, (fig. 76), and as a result, they were accustomed to being in the hands of individuals whose presence they preferred. They quickly learned to assume part of the responsibility for remaining mounted on the backs of their preferred older comrades as they were carried about (fig. 77).

Nursing

Nursing was on impulse. The breast was always uncovered and always available for nourishment, nursing satisfaction or play. Infants and toddlers were expected to take advantage of it, according to their needs or pleasure (fig. 78). Considerable freedom was permitted to tug, pull and manipulate the breast (fig. 79). The reaction to breast biting was usually surprise and momentary withdrawal of the breast, followed immediately by affectionate playfulness with the annoyed child (fig. 80). This usually dispelled his pique or dismay.

Weaning typically took place gradually, as the child grew older and began to take greater interest in the other activities and foods provided by his environment. Often his quest for this supplementary nourishment was in a manner similar to the way he would seek his mother's milk (fig. 81). By the age of four or five, weaning was usually complete, although occasional returns to the breast occurred. In special circumstances, such as the impending birth of a sibling, or in case of terminal illnesses such as kuru, mothers would speed weaning by applying unsavory substances to their breasts. But this was not a frequent practice, and mothers typically shunned forced weaning. More often, Fore mothers who were faced with an impending second child preferred to allow their older child to continue nursing after the birth of his younger sibling (see fig. 78). Two children could share the mother's milk. Women who feared they would not have enough milk to satisfy more than one youngster, sometimes refrained from intercourse for several years rather than be faced with the need to wean a child abruptly.

FIGURE 72. HOLDING THE YOUNG CHILD. The most salient feature of early Fore childhood was the degree to which infants were kept with the mother or one of her close associates. They were rarely put down or out of actual physical contact with an habitual associate. There was always someone to hold or carry them. Usually it was the mother who held and carried the small infant; but as he grew older she shared this activity with other individuals of her social circle. Older children, in particular, participated in the holding and carrying of the young child. Small babies were often carried in net bags (*bilums*) padded with bark and leaves against the backs of their mothers (**a, b**), but they were also frequently carried under their mother's arms. As the infants grew, they were also carried on their mothers' hips (**c, d, e**). Older children who participated in the care and handling of toddlers frequently carried them on their hips (**f–j**), but they more often carried them on their backs (**k, l**), which

adults did not. When the toddlers were not being carried, they were kept on the laps of their mothers or one of her close associates (**m–p**). They were not put aside for sleeping or while their mothers or other caretakers were otherwise engaged.

FIGURE 73. RESTING AND SLEEPING. Fore infants and toddlers were not put aside for resting or sleeping. Their naps were taken on the laps of their caretakers, even when they were occupied with tasks. The child could cease nursing for a nap and awake with the breast still at hand. Even after the birth of a second child, a toddler wishing to sleep against his mother was not put off. Here, a mother peels a sweet potato as her child sleeps in a typical fashion on her lap (**a**); a young boy has just dozed off after nursing (**b**); a toddler and her infant sister sleep against the body of their mother (**c**).

FIGURE 74. PARTICIPATION OF OLDER CHILDREN IN THE CARE AND HANDLING OF INFANTS I. Older children, usually of the mother's household or that of one of her close friends, joined in the care and handling of their younger associates. They did not do this against the wishes of the infant, but rather, when he desired their company. Frequently, they carried their young charge about the hamlet or garden as they went about their play or other activities. Such introductions to the world about him were often appreciated by the infant, who quickly learned to take much of the responsibility for clinging to the back of his young caretaker-mentor. Here, the young girl carries an infant as she investigates interesting activities and companions. At first, she squats to watch the cutting of fence posts; then, she gets up to join friends a short distance away. Note that she does not put the infant down on the ground even when she is squatting, but rather she slides him around her side and onto her knees. This is typical of the kind of contact infants and toddlers came to expect of even their mobile child caretakers.

154

FIGURE 75. PARTICIPATION OF OLDER CHILDREN IN THE CARE AND HANDLING OF INFANTS II. Older children participated more in the handling and care of older infants and even carried them about after they were able to walk. Such association between infants and older children was mutually satisfying, it not being the custom of the Fore to remain in an association that was not satisfying. Caretakers were not assigned by parents but developed out of reciprocal attraction between the infant and the older child. As a result of this situation, each party tended to be in tune with the moods and interests of the other. Often this was only to maintain a comfortable position from which to survey the passing world; but it could also be to communicate interests. A sagging youngster would indicate that he needed help in securing a better hold (a, b). The typical manner of doing this was by bending down and shuffling the child up (a-c, e-f). The way in which an infant was shifted from the back of his caretaker to her lap, as seen in the preceeding figure, can be seen here in closer detail (h-j).

FIGURE 76. CHOICE OF OLDER ASSOCIATES BY THE YOUNG CHILD. The wishes of the young child were an important factor in determining his association with older persons. He usually had a choice of several persons to be with; and older children often courted the interest and attention of their younger hamlet-mates. But such overtures could be rejected in favor of someone else. Here, the older boy has made tactile overtures to the toddler (a), who rejects them in order to lean against his mother as she cooks potatoes in hot coals. The older boy departs with the standard Fore nonverbal signal of agreeable acquiescence to the desires of a friend (i.e.: a light tap with the hand on the other's body) (c, d).

FIGURE 77. INFANT GRASP AND BALANCE. The special requirements of being carried about made Fore toddlers particularly adept in coordinating their grasp and balance so that they could stay on when their caretakers negotiated difficult trails (a) or cavorted in play (b).

FIGURE 78. NURSING. Considerable freedom is permitted to the infant or young child in the satisfaction of his nursing desires. The child may nurse whenever he likes from a variety of positions, playing with and manipulating the breasts or holding the breast in his mouth without sucking. This free access to nourishment and nursing satisfaction is facilitated by the habitual close physical contact normally existing between mother and child.

FIGURE 79. GRASPING AND MANIPULATION OF THE BREAST. The breasts of mothers are among the earliest things to attract the interest of the child. As he begins to grow older, this familiar source of nourishment and satisfaction is also a source of physical diversion as the child's coordination and physical ability increase. This leads, at times, to rather vigorous play and manipulation of the breasts.

FIGURE 80. MANAGEMENT OF BREAST BITING. The typical reaction of a mother whose breast is bitten by her
teething child is usually momentary withdrawal. This
often antagonizes the child, who is not accustomed to
such treatment, and a frequent reaction is to strike out

in anger. Such acts of discontent and retaliation are
typically sidetracked by affection, play, hugging, kissing and caressing, followed by renewed access to the
breast. Here, the mother has just been bitten and has
withdrawn her breast as the sequence starts.

FIGURE 81. WEANING. Weaning occurred gradually, usually over a course of years. An infant's caretakers would provide bits of softened sweet potato or other foods from their extended fingers, which the infant often approached as if he were approaching his mother's breast for nursing (a, b, c). He may also use this technique to feed himself (d, e).

Attention and Affection Provided to the Young

A considerable amount of attention and physical affection was lavished on infants and toddlers by their associates (*figs. 82, 83*). Sibling rivalry was almost impossible to detect, as much of the daily pleasure enjoyed by older and young siblings was that derived from affectionate play with each other. The demands for attention and affectionate contact by an infant or toddler were usually welcomed and virtually always tolerated by older associates, who often sought the diversion and enjoyment such contact provided. Older children, in particular, often responded with generous physical and oral affection; and their play with their young hamlet-mates frequently included considerable caressing, kissing and hugging (*fig. 84*).

FIGURE 82. ATTENTION FOCUSED ON INFANTS. Fore children enjoyed seductive play with their younger associates sufficiently to make them the centers of attention frequently. The pictured episode represents a typical clustering of adults and older children about an infant. The boy on the right attempts to evoke the interested attention of the infant by physical stimulation. The girl, opposite, participates in this encounter, ultimately inducing the child to exercise momentary preference for her. This attracts the young boy on the right to move even closer to the infant.

FIGURE 83. AFFECTIONATE CARE OF INFANTS AND TOD-
DLERS BY OLDER CHILDREN. Infants and toddlers were
the recipients of considerable affectionate attention by
their older hamlet-mates, who often sought opportunities to fondle and hug them. Often, this was simply
part of the holding and caretaking activity during
which episodes like those illustrated here repeatedly
occurred.

163

FIGURE 84. AFFECTION AND INQUIRY. From close contact with caretakers who provided him with the physical stimulation and affection he desired, the young child was also exposed to their activities and interests. Here, hugging and kissing is followed by play with a pig bladder, with close attention given by the infant to the activity of his caretaker.

Inquiry and Exploratory Behavior

The developing Fore child encountered the world from the sanctuary of his mother's body or one of her close associates. As his ability to exercise preference grew, he was permitted to seek his interests insofar as his physical capabilities and anxieties permitted. Initially, his interests were related to his desire for the nourishment, warmth and stimulation provided by his mother's body; these were generously available to whatever extent he was able to make use of them, including, influencing the mother by his own behavior. As his awarness increased, his interests broadened to the things his mother did, his attention focused on the objects and materials she used and on her associates and their activities *(fig. 85).*

As toddlerhood approached, the young child's interest in things around him increased, and he began to explore. This was done at his own initiative and initially involved short excursions to nearby objects that attracted his attention *(fig. 86).* Soon his excursions were extended to the entire hamlet or garden *(fig. 87).* Such explorations followed the individual child's predilections, and he was free to explore and play with those objects or materials he found about him, without interference and with minimal supervision. This included

FIGURE 85. INQUIRY. From the vantage point of close physical contact with his caretakers, the young child viewed the world around him and began to investigate and explore the materials and objects at hand. Most often these were what was of interest and concern to his caretakers, and thus, the young child was in contact with activities and materials of importance to his socioeconomic welfare quite early.

FIGURE 86. EXPLORATORY ACTIVITY I. Commensurate with their physical abilities, toddlers begin to make brief exploratory excursions to nearby objects that attracted their attention. At first, these were only short sorties out from the accustomed physical proximity of a caretaker. Here, a toddler is attracted by a bit of debris a short distance from his mother. After examining this, he moves a short distance further to investigate similar objects.

FIGURE 87. EXPLORATORY ACTIVITY II. As the child continued to mature, his excursions extended further and lasted longer. The hamlet and its houses and the nearby gardens became arenas of inquiry and exploration. Here, a young lad wanders off from his mother. He first investigates an axe head lying on the ground (a) and, then enters and looks about the nearby house (b); he approaches another child (c, d) and returns to his mother (e), only to depart again to watch activities of his mother's associates seated nearby (f).

sharp or potentially dangerous objects such as knives, machetes and axes *(figs. 88–90)*.

During this early exploratory activity, toddlers also began to test their own capabilities and began to imitate the activities of others. For example, it was not uncommon for Fore toddlers to make their early attempts to walk by themselves, without encouragement or attention from others *(fig. 91)*.

The early pattern of exploratory activity included frequent returns to the mother. She served as the home base, the bastion of security but not as a director or overseer of activities. Although she would occasionally give her youngster encouragement in things he would have liked to do except for uncertainty or shyness, and, although she was ready to assist with minor needs brought to her, rarely did she attempt to control or direct his activities, interests or quests. She did not participate in his explorations or play, nor did she go to him or try to be with him on his jaunts. Her child could be away whenever he wanted, but when he was away, he was, essentially, on his own until he returned. He could however, depend on his caretakers to remain accessible and not drift away, while he was independently occupied.

FIGURE 88. EXPLORATORY ACTIVITY III. A child on an exploratory excursion was essentially on his own. His activities were not supervised or directed by his caretakers; he was relatively free to investigate whatever he felt confident enough to handle. Thus, he was not prevented from picking up and playing with potentially dangerous objects such as axes and knives. Children were only rarely hurt by such play objects.

FIGURE 89. ACCESS TO KNIVES I. A generally practiced deference to the desires of the young in the choice of caretakers also governed his choice of play objects. He was allowed to investigate and handle knives and other potentially dangerous objects when he desired; he could use knives to examine the properties of other objects. Fore children frequently took advantage of this

freedom to hold and use knives (**a, b, c**). Even toddlers who grabbed at knives being used by their mothers were not denied the right to interrupt their mother's work to examine her tools and materials (**b, c**).

FIGURE 90. ACCESS TO KNIVES II. Children expected to make use of the tools and materials of their adult associates and were indulged in this expectation. As a result, use of knives was common, particularly for exploratory activities and play. In this series of pictures, a child makes use of his father's knife to experiment with and test the materials his father is using to plait a *pitpit* wall for a new house. Finally the youngster picks up a machete belonging to me for more vigorous "examination" of the *pitpit* stems.

FIGURE 91. SPONTANEOUS EXERCISE OF DEVELOPING PHYSICAL CAPABILITIES. Frequently young children began to test their own developing neuromuscular and coordinating abilities while on their exploratory excursions. Here, a toddler experiments with his ability to walk erect, as he explores the territory a few meters away from his caretaker.

FIGURE 92. FEAR I. When on an exploratory excursion, if a child became frightened, he returned to his mother. She was always available for comfort and refuge; but she did not usually go to the aid of her youngster unless there was serious danger. Rather the child was expected to return by himself when he became afraid or desired to be near her. Here, my arrival with the large motion picture camera frightened this youngster who was investigating a part of the garden a short distance from her mother and her friends. Her mother does not move from the place where she is gardening. Rather, she sympathetically beckons him while at the same time being amused by his fright.

Fear

At times of uncertainty, anxiety or fear, the young Fore children sought closer contact with their caretakers who were always available to provide security through close body contact. Caretakers did not, however, go to "rescue" their children when they were not with them; instead, it was up to each child to return to the security of personal association when he felt the need. Even though he was not protectively watched over, his caretakers did not usually move so far that he would have difficulty getting back to them in the event he wanted to. Thus, a child on one of his exploratory excursions was always able to return, not much more than the distance he had ventured, to the sanctuary of the body of a close associate *(figs. 92–94)*. Furthermore, the child could exercise preference in his choice of security figures *(fig. 95)*. Both adults and older children were virtually always available to allay the anxiety that might arise in their younger associates *(figs. 96, 97)*.

FIGURE 93. FEAR II. This is another example of a child who was frightened by my arrival with the camera while she was away from her mother in the garden. Although I happened to come between this child and her mother, she ran toward and past me in an effort to get to her mother as quickly as possible.

FIGURE 94. FEAR III. This sequence shows the effect of close contact with the mother on fright. A young boy with his bow and arrow had joined some older boys. My arrival frightened him, and he ran to his mother. My closer approach frightened him further; but, although I did not move back, closer contact with his mother assuaged his anxiety.

FIGURE 95. THE EXERCISE OF PREFERENCE IN SEEKING SECURITY. Any of the child's several habitual caretakers (i.e. those people belonging to his mother's circle of close associates) could be sought for comfort and refuge in times of anxiety. It was the child's prerogative to pick whom he preferred to be with for security as well as for pleasure. In this sequence, a child, fearful of my arrival, turns to one of his caretaker-associates who begins to lift him up in the customary way. When he notices a preferred possibility, he breaks a hand loose to gesture to her and begins to make a lunge toward her. However, a glance back at me frightens him sufficiently to abandon this course and to grasp again at his early choice. The other girl does what adults would but very rarely do, that is, she runs to the child, as she beckons him and picks him up in the customary fashion. Note the amusement of both older girls and how similar it is to the amusement shown toward other types of "childlike" behavior.

FIGURE 96. OLDER PERSONS AS SECURITY FIGURES. Older persons are always available for refuge and are the principal means of providing a sense of security to children who are otherwise unsure of themselves or frightened. Here, a frightened infant closes his eyes and closely leans into his mother (a); an apprehensive young girl surveys her surroundings from within the arms and legs of her mother who is making a net bag (b); a toddler, worried about my presence, moves close to her mother, taking her breast in her mouth without sucking (c); a toddler, crying from fear, clutches her father (d); a toddler wanting to examine my activities more closely crouches behind and holds one of his older caretakers (e); a young girl holds the wrist and hand of her father as she examines my activities (f).

FIGURE 97. CHILDREN AS SECURITY FIGURES. Tactile association with older children, even those slightly older, as well as adults, may be sought during periods of anxiety or uncertainty. A toddler, fearful of my presence, nestles against an older girl and closes his eyes (a); another toddler holds tightly to his brother for the same reason (b); a young girl holds the finger of an older boy while watching the activities of a medical patrol in her village (c); two small children who were on the edge of the hamlet away from older associates cling to each other as I come upon them; both had looked frantically about for other older persons to whom to run; but seeing no one else the smaller ran to the older who held him in much the same way he himself would have been held by an older associate (d).

Distress

When the child was in distress, he could withdraw to express his grief or discontent by himself. He could cry and have tantrums by himself, if he did not want comfort and contact with any of the available individuals around him *(fig. 98)*. But when he desired solace and close human contact, it was available. Affection and concern were not forced on a child, but rather, they were available for him when he wanted them. The disgruntled child was neither shunned nor given special attention. It was not the practice of the Fore to withdraw security to show dissatisfaction with a child or to punish him. Nor would they inconvenience themselves by efforts to pay special attention.

FIGURE 98. ATTENTION TO CRYING CHILDREN. The Fore did not normally give special attention or consideration to their crying infants, or even to those having tantrums. If the crying child desired close physical contact or food, he was treated with the same tolerance as if he had not been crying. Access to human comforting required the child to seek it. Although such comfort was virtually never denied when sought, it was almost never extended to a child not seeking it. Here, a Fore infant having a tantrum is virtually ignored by the people around him; only another child of about the same age looks on curiously (**a**). A crying child sits behind his mother; she makes no move or gesture toward him (**b**). A crying boy is held by the man sought during his distress (**c**).

Toilet Training

Although disposal of body wastes was a matter of great concern to adult Fore because of their use in sorcery, toilet training was not imposed. In fact, the term toilet training is not really appropriate to the Fore way of dealing with the matter. Restrictive measures were not taken, nor was a program of control imposed. A toddler could repeatedly defecate in the hamlet yard, even during a feast, without being chastised or subjected to overt signs of displeasure *(fig. 99)*. The mother and other close associates would scurry about to clean up and usually did so good-naturedly, often treating the matter with amusement. They did not attempt to discourage the youngster from such "errors." As the child grew older, he began to adopt the scrupulous community practices governing excretion by modeling his practices on those of the older children with whom he associated, who often treated "errors" in behavior as a cause for amusement. Such amusement tended to cause embarrassed reflection in the older toddlers and served as a major mechanism for molding child behavior in Fore society. Thus, as children grew older, they adopted the social consensus of their associates by emulating the behavior of older children and by responding to mild shame caused by the affectionate amusement of their older hamlet associates to their peccadillos and immature actions *(fig. 100)*.

FIGURE 99. TOILET TRAINING. Toilet training was not imposed or coerced, in spite of the care with which adult Fore disposed of all traces of their fecal matter for fear it would be used in sorcery. Here, a toddler repeatedly defecates in the middle of the hamlet yard, where a feast is also going on. His mother and sister scurry about to clean up while the toddler repeatedly defecates in new places. He is not chastised, nor is there any attempt to discourage him. His sister shows the amusement characteristic of Fore older children when their young associates behave immaturely, even while she cleans up after him. The toddler alternates his interest in the activity going on and the appearance of his feces.

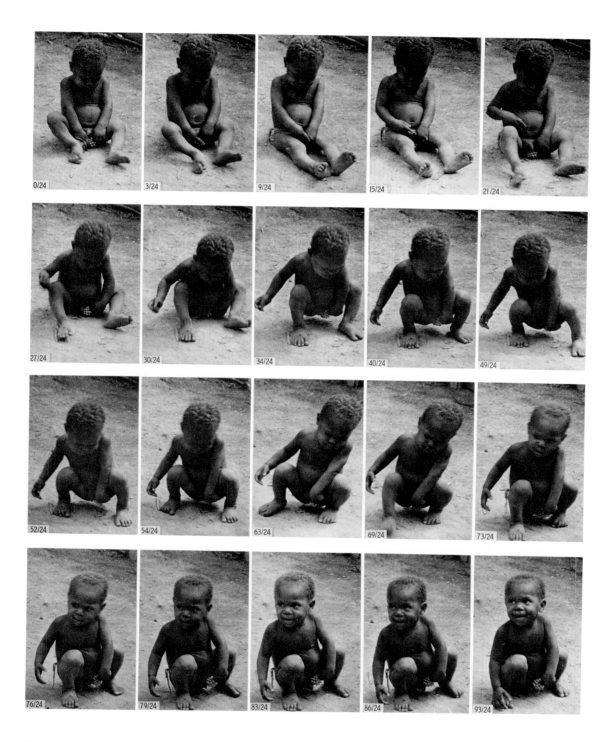

FIGURE 100. THE EFFECT OF AMUSEMENT ON THE BEHAVIOR OF A TODDLER. The amusement of others over his activities could embarrass a toddler and modify his behavior, consistent with his developing ability to gauge the effect of his behavior on others. In this sequence, a toddler was pushing a bunch of berries against his genitalia and anus until a nearby man showed amusement and remarked about the activity that caused it.

Tolerance of Child Aggressiveness

Aggressive acts by toddlers and young children were considered natural, and no attempt was made to chastise or punish them, nor was anger or marked displeasure usually shown. Instead, interested, affectionate amusement was the typical reaction of older children and adults to socially aggressive or hostile actions of the young children (figs. 101-105) . When, for example, adults or older children were the subject of attack by younger children, they usually received it affectionately or without notice. If the attack became painful, they would usually move away or try to divert or distract the young child by affectionate playfulness or engaging him in other interests (figs. 102–104). The older children and adults normally regarded such incidents as amusing diversion rather than annoyances. The young child was not instructed in the error of his ways, nor was his behavior thought reprehensible. Similar aggressive acts toward young age-mates were discouraged, but again, not by sign of annoyance or by punishment but typically, by diversionary playful activity (fig. 105).

FIGURE 101. CHILD AGGRESSION I. Adults generally ignored the aggressive impulses directed at them by young children. Displeasure was sometimes shown, but repressive actions and expressions of anger were very rare. Typically, adults received minor attacks without notice. No attempt was made to instruct the aggressor in the error of his ways, nor was such behavior thought reprehensible. In fact, aggressiveness was not considered correctable, but rather, a natural and expected characteristic of children up to about six years of age. Here, a young girl hits her mother from the rear with a stick she has picked up. The mother simply brushes this off without attention to the girl and continues her previous activity. The girl then throws the stick at another woman and walks away.

FIGURE 102. CHILD AGGRESSION II. When older children were the subject of attack by young children, they typically received it with amusement and affection. If the attack became painful, they sometimes moved away, but more often, they tried to divert the young child from his aggressive intents by affectionate playfulness or engaging him in other interests. The older children usually regarded such incidents as an amusing diversion rather than as an annoyance. They did not chastise or reproach the young child, nor were attempts made to discourage such behavior. Here, a toddler picks up a stick and throws it at a young girl who, laughing, picks up the stick and throws it away, while her associate of about the same age beckons the toddler with the standard Fore gesture of affectionate invitation. The toddler, seduced by this gesture, moves to her to be picked up.

FIGURE 103. CHILD AGGRESSION III. A toddler throws a piece of sugar cane at an older associate. The older child amusedly picks up the sugar cane, and inviting the toddler to him, caresses him and inspects his genitals. The toddler remains with him as a preferred caretaker.

FIGURE 104. CHILD AGGRESSION IV. A toddler attacks an older associate who, preoccupied by poking the ground with a stick, ignores the attack. A third child, quickly joined by a fourth, moves in to playfully distract the toddler, who soon becomes the focus of a gentle affectionate play. This play attracts further participants and results, finally, in the kind of circle of interacting young age-mates that commonly develops around foci of stimulating or interesting activity in Fore villages.

FIGURE 105. CHILD AGGRESSION V. When the young children directed their aggressive acts toward their young
age-mates, they were interrupted by elders who attempted to divert the attacker and to assuage any
distress that may have been caused by him. Here, a
toddler strikes another toddler with a stick and then
throws the stick away. The stick is recovered by an
older boy who brings it to the "attackee" for inspection
before discarding it. The "attackee" recovers the stick
and throws it toward his attacker. Another boy rushes
in and presents the stick for inspection to the new "attackee" and then, throws it away. Amusement accom-
panies the activities of these older boys as they sidetrack
the aggressive peccadillos of their younger hamlet-mates.
As a result of this kind of protective activity, fights do
not erupt among youngsters who are still in their
aggressive stage.

Deference to the Desires of the Young

Young children accepted as a natural condition of life the readiness of their older hamlet-mates to help with difficulties. If, for example, a child picked up a piece of sugar cane while moving about, he could bring it to one of his older close associates to soften it with his stronger teeth, so that he could chew it (fig. 106). Or, if he was not sure how to use something, his older associates were available for explanation (fig. 107).

Deference to the young also extended to use of objects for play. When more than one child desired the same object, the youngest usually prevailed (figs. 108, 109). Older children were not usually nonplussed by the demands of their younger hamlet-mates and typically treated them with sympathy, amusement and helpfulness. Even slightly older children usually deferred without annoyance or ill will, and they often participated in helping the younger satisfy his desire (fig. 109).

Young children took what food they liked from that available (figs. 110–112). They were expected to reject gifts of food not fully to their liking and demand and receive choicer bits. Those older hamlet-mates who seemed most sympathetic and helpful were those with whom the child would tend to associate himself. Such association often determined the use of kinship terms.

FIGURE 106. DEFERENCE TO THE DESIRES OF THE YOUNG I. When on his exploratory excursions, if the child discovered something he wanted help in interpreting or using, he could return to his mother or any one of his caretakers for assistance. This was usually quickly forthcoming, even if it meant interrupting other pursuits. Here, a young girl has picked up a piece of sugar cane in the course of her exploration of the hamlet. Her teeth are not yet strong enough to chew it, and she brings it to her mother to soften it for her.

FIGURE 107. DEFERENCE TO THE DESIRES OF THE YOUNG II. Young children expected their older associates to show them things they did not understand or to assist them with the difficulties they brought to them. The manner of this instruction was a direct outgrowth of the manner by which younger children sought and obtained comfort and satisfaction from their caretakers. This sequence developed as a result of my having given candy to the children of this hamlet. The younger boy, not knowing what it was or how to use it, brings it to one of his older mates, who does not notice him until he is grasped in the typical fashion, which signals the desire to be lifted and comforted. The older boy then lifts him up and demonstrates how to eat the candy.

FIGURE 108. DEFERENCE TO THE DESIRES OF THE YOUNG III. Deference to the young also extended to use of objects for play. Older children usually deferred to younger children when they both wanted the same thing. A younger and an older boy want to swing on the same vine. The older boy has already deferred once to the younger. But when the younger boy completes the swinging, he keeps the vine for yet another turn merely by insisting. Although such behavior would be unusual among Western children, it is commonplace among the Fore.

FIGURE 109. DEFERENCE TO THE DESIRES OF THE YOUNG
IV. Three boys of different ages want to swing on the same vine. The insistent desire of the youngest is deferred to without ill feeling or a sense of annoyance on the part of the older boys (**a, b, c**). The slightly older boy even tries to assist his younger associate to get on the vine (**d, e**). Not succeeding in this, he happily backs off and sits down to wait (**f, g, h**) while the other fumbles about for a while. Finally, he returns, with the consent of his young colleague, to take him for a swing (**i**).

FIGURE 110. DEFERENCE TO THE DESIRES OF THE YOUNG V. The virtually unlimited access enjoyed by children to their mother's milk was, as they matured, carried over to other foods and governed the development of their feeding habits. This may have been an important factor leading to the deference to the desires of the young practiced with regard to other matters. Young children could demand and receive food that interested them, even that about to be eaten by others. Here, a toddler is attracted by the cooked *pitpit,* which a friend of his mother is peeling. He reaches for it (**a, b, c**), but is not satisfied with the small piece he gets (**d**). Frustrated, he reaches for a larger piece, which is just being peeled (**e**). He takes this new piece back to examine (**f, g, h**), and finally shares it with an older associate (**i**).

Play and Games

Most older children considered the playful company of younger children an enjoyable diversion, and, as a result younger children were often companions, in play, to older children. This pattern of relationship began while the Fore were infants and toddlers, a time when they were the subject of considerable affectionate and seductive physical play by their older hamlet-mates (fig. 113). As the youngsters matured, their older associates continued this somewhat solicitous enjoyment of close association with their younger colleagues and often participated in their explorations (fig. 114). Physical contact continued to characterize much of their activity together, even including biting play (figs. 115, 116).

Before Western contact, formal games (i.e., games with definite rules or specific performance objectives) were not a significant part of Fore childhood. Traditionally, the Fore children improvised their play, although this has changed somewhat since the introduction of marbles and soccer by missionaries and government officers. Typically, they utilized the materials, objects and persons in their surroundings. Ad hoc performance objectives were sometimes improvised, as when sliding down a muddy slope on a palm stalk, cooking or shooting arrows at objects thrown onto the ground or at birds in a hunt. However, rather than seeking to best an opponent, much of this play took on the character of exploratory inquiry into reactions and capabilities.

In games and play, the child tended to develop pleasurable strategies by which to approach and deal with the people and products of the surrounding world in a mutually satisfactory way. It was relatively easy for children of disparate ages to play together in the absence of competitive pressures requiring specialized performance to achieve formal goals.

Up to about the age of seven years, the activities of both boys and girls were much the same. Older girls spent more of their time playing in the gardens and hamlet yards, often with infants and toddlers. They did not explore much beyond these arenas, and they confined their interests predominantly to the social and horticultural activity going on in the women's circle and to participation in food handling and preparation (fig. 117).

Boys, on the other hand, ranged much more widely in their explorations of their material and geographical surrounding. They were much more likely to investigate objects and substances of their environment that were not salient aspects of the general Fore economic activity. Much of their time was spent in hunting and gathering, as well as in more boisterous physical play (fig. 118). In contrast to girls, who were more subdued and coquettish in their play, boys spent more time in chasing, rough-and-tumble frolicking and moving rather freely about the adjacent lands with their agemates. But both boys and girls tended to play games of inquiry, physical gratification and social encounter, and both made use of the materials and persons of their environments, according to their individual interests and capabilities without competitive jockeying.

FIGURE 111. FREE ACCESS TO FOOD. As toddlers matured and became mobile, they were permitted relatively unrestricted access to whatever food was accessible. They could freely sample, pick up and carry away any food they encountered in their excursions about the hamlets and gardens. Here, a young lad has picked up several pieces of sugar cane and is carrying them off.

FIGURE 112. CASUAL EATING. The relatively unrestricted freedom of children to pursue interests and preferences extended to eating. They could eat whenever they liked, taking food from their houses or gardens, or sharing that being eaten by friends and relatives. Frequently such snacks were eaten during the course of play or other activities. Here, a group of small girls plays while nibbling on ears of maize (a); a young boy idly chews a piece of sugar cane (b); another removes the skin from a baked sweet potato (c); a toddler sucks a piece of sugar cane while held in his mother's arms (d); another holds a sweet potato he has picked up (e); a child casually nibbles pieces of raw meat and blood clots from a pig being butchered (f).

191

FIGURE 113. PHYSICAL PLAY INVOLVING YOUNGER AND OLDER CHILDREN. As toddlers matured and spent less of their time being held by or sitting with their older caretakers, they did not cease to be the recipients of playful, affectionate attention from the older children they knew. Here, a young boy and an older associate walk together and begin to frolic. Note that this more active physical contact is not dissimilar to that seen between younger children and their caretakers. It is still characterized by gentle contact and enfolding, rather than force; and it involves delicate interplay rather than imposition or dominance. Such encounters frequently attracted nearby children. Two boys come to join the play (h, k). The kind of physical affection developing between younger and older children could also influence the manner of play between older age-mates. The two older boys embrace (i). Although three of the boys who are finally involved in this episode are older than the fourth, the youngest is not rejected or intimidated by the increasing number of frolicking older boys. In part, this is due to their activity being at least partially focused on the youngest member, and, in part, to the character of the play being gentle and sensual rather than forceful or aggressive.

FIGURE 114. ASSOCIATION OF YOUNGER WITH OLDER CHILDREN. The association of young children with the older children continued after infancy and toddlerhood and affected much of their continuing childhood experience. Older children continued to enjoy gratifying, observing and touching their younger cohorts and leading them to new experiences. Their younger associates not only enjoyed the attention provided by their older colleagues but relied on their example for behavioral experiments and for security as they approached their surroundings. This collection of photographs illustrates the development of the relationship between older and younger children. Infants and toddlers are carried about by older children (a–d); a girl helps her young friend across a fence (e); a toddler explores the physical and dynamic characteristics of a pole with the participation of an older girl (f); a toddler tests the springing characteristics of a limb with the help of her female caretaker and playmate (g); a toddler approaches an older boy for tactile play (h); an infant engages in manipulative play and touching with an older girl (i); a toddler's excited interest in nearby activity is made possible by his secure association with two confident girls who enjoy leading him to new experience (j); a young lad and his older boyfriend set off to explore land adjacent to their hamlet (k).

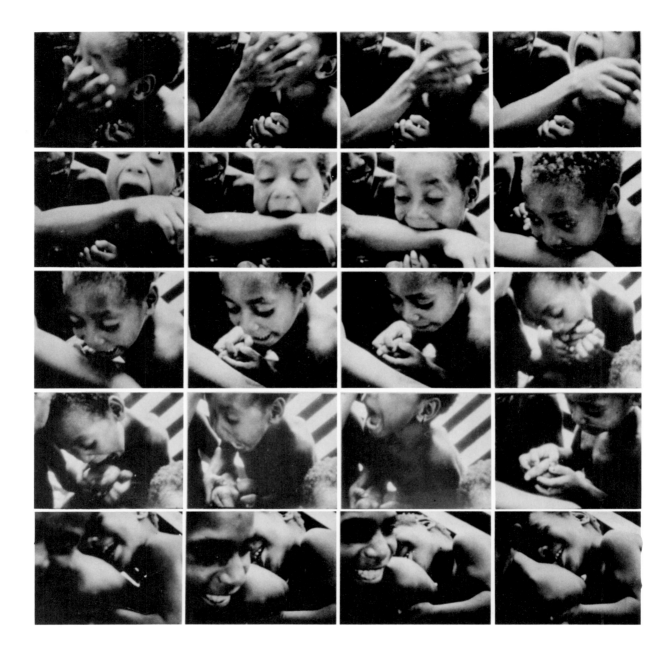

FIGURE 115. BITING PLAY I. Biting play was not uncommon among Fore children and represented a broader phenomenon of orality in play among Fore children. Sometimes younger children were encouraged and instructed in biting by older children. Such biting was considered an expression of affection; it was not uncommon to hear a child say that he wanted to bite someone because he loved him. This is compatible with one of the warm greetings in which a close friend might say he would like to eat the other. The practice of familial cannibalism by the Fore may also be related to this aspect of orality. An often-stated reason for eating their own close dead relatives was the desire to preserve within themselves traces of their lost loved ones. Here, two brothers engaged in an oral play invited by the older.

FIGURE 116. BITING PLAY II. An older cousin introduces a toddler to the pleasures of biting by lightly biting his hand and, then presenting his own hand for biting. The toddler reciprocates by extending his hand again for biting.

FIGURE 117. TYPICAL ACTIVITIES OF GIRLS. The activities and experiences of male and female infants and toddlers were essentially the same. Only after about the age of six or seven did differences begin to become important. Unlike their male counterparts, girls continued to spend most of their time in the hamlets or gardens after this age, where they tended to occupy themselves with food and its production and preparation, and in grooming each other and caring for the domestic pigs. In this sequence, girls attend their younger associates (a, b); associate with the women and other girls of their circle in the garden (c); participate in cultivation (d); carry thatching material back to the hamlet (e); experiment with food preparation (f); participate in cooking (g) play with a baby pig (h); idly scratch a sweet potato in the garden (i); pull burrs from a pig (j, k, l); and groom a friend (m, n, o).

FIGURE 118. TYPICAL ACTIVITIES OF BOYS. Older boys were both more active in their play and less bounded. They experimented more broadly with the materials and objects of their general environment and did so in a broader arena. They tended to divorce themselves more from the company of adults and to roam and live as peer groups, while girls tended to remain with the adult women. Here, boys slide down a muddy slope in their hamlet on a piece of split wood (a); pull each other about on a sled improvised from bunches of long grass (b); roll tethered coconuts down a hill (c); throw bits of debris at each other (d); swing on a vine (e); wrestle (f); blow up a pig's bladder (g); shoot *pitpit* grass stems at each other (h, i, j); play shooting games (k); hunt (l); and gather wild food (m).

Learning

Skills and social behavior were generally learned through observation, experimental participation and exploratory play *(figs. 119, 120)*. There was no formal instruction, nor was behavior coerced. Rather, learning took place cumulatively while playing about the older members of the community, and inquiring into those things that were of interest. For example, if butchering was underway, even toddlers could explore and manipulate the carcass, using whatever implements they could find. The participation of the young in the more purposeful activities of the older children and adults was generally motivated by simple desires for exploratory and associative activity *(fig. 121)*, without regard to the productive objectives. As children grew older, their participation in such activities came to be more and more directed toward the general social objective underlying the activity *(figs. 121–124)*.

A large part of the skills and behavior learned by Fore children also came from imitating older children during the course of daily contact and play. If, for example, an older boy climbed a vine, a younger would tend to copy his movements in an attempt to do likewise. Social behavior was also modified when affectionate amusement was shown over childlike behavior.

FIGURE 119. LEARNING I. Most of the knowledge, skills and many of the traits of behavior and social response were learned in the course of day-to-day living. Children were not formally instructed or directed in this learning, nor was their behavior coerced. Rather, they learned while playing about working adults or other children and experimenting on their own terms with the materials and activities at hand. Here, two youngsters play near their mothers who are making tapa cloth. As these young children sit idly with each other, one picks up a stick and casually strikes the tapa cape they are sitting on, a direct reflection of the activity of the nearby women. This is not at the suggestion of the women; nor is it an attempt to actually make tapa. Rather, it is a spontaneous re-creation of the activity preoccupying the women.

FIGURE 120. LEARNING II. A Fore child enjoyed abundant opportunity to observe at close range the activities of his mother (or caretaker), because of the sustained physical proximity between them—a situation ideally suited to kinesthetic learning. The lack of restraints placed on their exploratory behavior allowed children to pursue preference and, thus, gradually extend their interests, inquiries and experiments into the larger arena of their hamlet and village. As they grew older, these initially exploratory activities began to dovetail more and more with the socioeconomic objectives of their hamlet-mates. Here, a toddler, in typical close physical association with his mother, engrosses himself in her preparation of *pitpit* for cooking (**a, b**); another watches his mother cut pork (**c**); a child explores the thoracic cavity and jaw of a pig as it is being butchered (**d–g**); a toddler plays with a sweet potato while his mother prepares food for a feast (**h**); three children closely watch and participate as a male adult of their hamlet butchers a pig (**i, j**).

FIGURE 121. LEARNING III. Girls were not instructed in the art of gardening. Rather, while they were young, they began to play about the garden, often modeling their activities on those of their older associates. Eventually, this initially nonproductive (and, often, even destructive) activity began more and more to resemble the productive activity that sustained gardening as the basis of the Fore way of life. Two girls play somewhat randomly in a sweet potato garden with a digging stick, showing the results of their activity to each other (a, b, c); a young boy watches as a girl from his hamlet piles grass for burning (d); an older girl and her younger associate gather harvested sweet potatoes, the younger girl emulating the activity of the older (e); a girl effectively wields a spade in garden clearing (f).

FIGURE 122. LEARNING IV. The playful experimenting and exploratory inquiry of children led them to familiarity with the materials, tools and activities of their hamlet-mates. As this familiarity increased, their activity

began, almost unconsciously, to dovetail more and more with the life-sustaining activities and interests of their older hamlet-mates. Thus, prescribed method or technique did not govern Fore socioeconomic behavior as much as the ability and skill one informally acquired in exploratory inquiry and in interaction with one's associates toward common benefit. Here, a toddler plays with a stick amid adult associates, an example of typical early exploratory behavior (a); an older girl carries a bamboo container filled with water (b); a toddler carries a bundle of fiber rope across the hamlet yard (c); a young girl explores a water-filled earth oven with a stick (d); a girl assists in the distribution of food for a feast (e); a young boy adds a stone to those being heated for cooking (f); girls play with and prepare food for cooking (g); two boys watch and participate in the removal of food from a wooden steam oven (h); an adolescent girl prepares bundles of vegetables for a feast (i); a girl helps her foster father put grated taro into a banana leaf for cooking (j).

FIGURE 123. LEARNING V. During a feast various approaches to experience practiced by the Fore young could be observed. Infants and toddlers usually remained in physical contact with mothers and caretakers, even while they were busy preparing the food, a vantage point from which they could closely observe the activities associated with feast making. Somewhat older children roamed about the feast area attending whatever interested them; and both solitary exploratory excursions as well as clusterings of children about common interests could be seen. Older children participated in the feast preparations. Here, a child closely watches food preparation by older children and adults (**a**); infants and toddlers take interest in the food preparation by their mothers and the older children (**b**); small children wander about the area observing things that interest them and picking up bits of food (**c**); children cluster at the site of a pile of food that has just been cooked (**d**).

FIGURE 124. INTEGRATING ACTIVITIES TOWARD COMMON ENDS. Although much of the activity of toddlers and young children tended to be hedonistic and exploratory, they did, even at this young age, begin to participate in the productive activity of others. Although they did this as play, rather than in recognition of the larger goals that may have been involved, it was, nonetheless, the beginning of a pattern that continued to emerge as they grew older and that led to the kind of social activity that characterized Fore life. In this sequence, an older boy dips water out of an earth oven with bamboo cylinders. Two toddlers become interested in participating by emptying the cylinders and returning them to the boy.

Tactile Communication and Social Integration

The considerable physical contact Fore infants and toddlers had with their caretakers allowed the development of relationships through tactile response. Even before they could talk, the Fore young were able to communicate needs, desires and feelings through physical contact to responsive mothers and other caretakers. This language of contact facilitated integration of the infant's needs and desires with his source of succor. The effectiveness of the manner in which Fore mothers dealt with breast biting *(see fig. 80),* for example, seemed to stem from the close attunement of mother to child, facilitated by this prelinguistic communicative contact. Since this type of communication was well suited to the most salient needs of the young child (i.e. nourishment, security, comfort and stimulation), and since it was within the capability of the pretalking child, its development proceeded easily.

Older children continued to make use of this language of touch and frequently engaged in tactile interplay when the desire for nourishment, security, comfort or stimulation was involved. For example, the tendency for young children to seek bodily contact with close associates when frightened was largely a security quest, as discussed above *(see figs. 92–97).* In face of less stressful uncertainty, such as that provided by exciting or unexpected events or novelty, there was a similar tendency to become physically "in touch" with an associate. In this case the act seemed to provide a vantage point from which one's immature cognitive and response apparatus was less likely to be overtaxed *(fig. 125).* Such contact seemed to provide both security and a guide to the appropriate response in unfamiliar circumstances. The early exploration of the materials, objects and situations of one's surroundings often proceeded in the vicinity of older associates *(see figs. 84–92).*

Recourse to physical contact not only offered security in the face of fear and the unknown; it also afforded sensual enjoyment, stimulation and comfort. Gratification through physical contact was refined in association with older caretakers during infancy and was later incorporated into the social behavior and play between young age-mates *(figs. 126, 127).* Through touch and tactile interplay, emotional states, affectionate impulses and desires were integrated into the social setting, in conjunction with an intimate sense of personal physical security.

Rich, meaningful social expression was evident in daily eating. From one's earliest days, food was provided through interaction with others, and as the Fore children grew older, their early experience of obtaining food in association with physical contact influenced their later feeding behavior. Thus, the association of nourishment and tactile interplay, which developed in early life, persisted in later childhood as a tendency to engage associates in physical contact when seeking food from them. This act reconfirmed their prior relationship, established closer rapport and conveyed interest in the food *(figs. 128, 129).*

Because tactile contact was nearly always a part of the infant's and toddler's normal experience; because his ability to control touch and physical relationship came before speech; and because touch and bodily contact lend themselves naturally to satisfying the basic needs of the young child, this early means of communication facilitated cooperative interaction between infants and their caretakers. Recognition and accommodation to the needs of one another could be based on tactile

FIGURE 125. TACTILE ASSOCIATION AND RESPONSE TO NOVELTY. The way in which Fore developed their behavioral repertoire and reacted to unanticipated, new or surprising occurrences around them was influenced by their access to security through bodily contact during their early lives. Thus, older children, as well as infants and toddlers, often responded to novelty and challenge while in bodily contact with others. For Fore infants and toddlers, this physical contact was a sanctuary of nurture and warmth, which gave them a base from which curiosity and interest could be safely maintained and to which they could retreat when their immature cognitive or response capabilities were overtaxed. The pattern remained as the children grew older; but unlike their younger colleagues, older children tended to turn more to their peers to provide the feeling of security coming from physical contact. In these photographs, children respond typically to the novelty of my presence and behavior in newly visited hamlets.

FIGURE 126. AFFECTIONATE PLAY AND TACTILE COMMU-
NICATION. Close physical proximity to and play with
individuals of interest and value to the child started
in infancy and led to the elaboration of stereotyped
interactive communicative responses. Much of the
affectionate playfulness seen among children involves
such communicative feedback based on tactile association. Here, a toddler grasps one of his older habitual
associates and is reassured in this act by the manner in
which his older friend curls his shoulders and grasps
his hand (a); a toddler relaxes his raised arms, the usual
signal to be lifted, as his friend clasps him, instead,

against his legs and abdomen in recognition of and
sympathy with this nonverbal request but not in full
acquiescence (b); a girl lightly touches an infant's back
with her finger tips, indicating proferred affectionate
attention (c); similarly, a toddler lightly touches another infant on the neck to indicate his affectionate but
not insistent interest (d); a toddler indicates his interest
in stimulating response from an infant by seductively
touching him on the chin (e); a girl touches a toddler
to reinforce the attention she is seeking from him (f);
a boy indicates desire for interplay with an older girl

206

by lightly holding her arm; but, because she is occupied with an infant making other demands on her, he also lightly taps her, an indication that he is deferring (g); a group of young children huddle together, touching one another so as to attract attention of their friends to their observations and interests, while they also grasp one another to reinforce their confidence in the face of novelty (h); a group of boys intertwine themselves in sensual play (i); a younger boy clasps his older associate, indicating his uncertainty with respect to my presence, and to increase his own sense of security (j); two girls maintain their solidarity and mutually reinforce their confidence and curiosity in the face of the novel stimulus of my presence (k).

FIGURE 127. TACTILE INTERPLAY. A good bit of the activity among Fore children included tactile interplay. In part, this seemed to stem from an association of tactile contact with good will, imprinted during early childhood. This resulted in a tendency to touch one's friends. Here, two young boys from the same hamlet strike different stances of tactile interplay as they stand with each other near my house.

207

FIGURE 128. TACTILE COMMUNICATION AND SHARING. Tactile communication was also associated with nourishment from one's earliest days. This association also carried over into later childhood, as tactile communication continued to play a part in food sharing. Above, a boy who has just finished eating the meat off one pig rib, renews his interest in the carving of more pork by tactile contact with one of the carvers. Below, young children strike different stances, indicating interest in the same piece of meat seen in the above series.

FIGURE 129. SHARING FOOD WITH THE YOUNG. Children expected their older close associates to share their food. By expression, gesture and tactile association, they received the food that interested them. The close association that developed among those who shared food was such that interest in food was most often communicated without need for spoken words. Indeed, many of the nonverbal ways of seeking food had developed even before the child was able to speak. Those within such communities of associates continually acted to assist each other in the satisfaction of wants and needs. The mutual understanding of one another in these small groups was such that appreciation of desires, interests and problems often preceded spoken communication and made explicit verbal construction unnecessary. Here, a boy indicates his interest in the pandanus nuts being opened by one of his hamlet-mates (a); a girl motions her desire for some food, which she cannot reach (b); a toddler reaches for a piece of reheated sweet potato being eaten by an older boy of his hamlet (c); an older female associate passes an ear of roast corn to a girl who was standing nearby (d); a young boy indicates his desire for a piece of food being eaten by an older hamlet-mate by his stance, his expression and a tap on the arm (e, f).

messages that soon became effective in securing assuagement, succor and stimulation.

The importance of tactile contact in social integration can be seen in situations in which sharing developed out of range of physical contact. When the circumstances under which sharing took place did not facilitate physical contact, such as in the delivering of food or materials from a distance, the act of sharing was more awkward and static. Even among age-mates and close friends, tentative proffering and avoidance of eye contact and passive facial expressions often characterized such incidents (*fig. 130*). It was almost as if it were difficult to utilize the other modes of communication in the absence of the tactile component at such times.

FIGURE 130. SHARING ACROSS SPACE. The sharing stance was quite different when the interaction was across intervening space. It was more tentative, sometimes diffident and usually extended only part of the way. Eyes were frequently averted. This kind of sharing may have marked a less close, or new, relationship between the sharers. However, it also reflected the de- creased assurance of even close associates when they were not in tactile proximity. Here, a girl partially extends a package of cooked vegetables to a friend (**a**); a boy presents a burning branch he has obtained to help his friend start a fire (**b**); a girl averts her eyes as she offers a bunch of cooked *piga* bean roots (**c**); a girl with eyes averted proffers a bundle of beans (**d**).

Resolution of Conflict

Fighting was rarely resorted to as a means to resolve conflict. The aggressive impulses of toddlers did not tend to cause fights, because they were ignored or distracted (see figs. 101–105). Older children seemed to have developed behavioral mechanisms that sidetracked squabbles and fights with their age-mates. Conflict was typically resolved by deference or cooperative activity in keeping with the Fore social pattern, based on support and succor among those who chose to be associated with one another. Only those children who were too young to have developed this cooperative sense typically demanded and obtained preferential consideration from their older hamlet-mates, as discussed above (see figs. 106–110).

At the ages when spontaneous aggressive acts began to cease, mechanisms that sidetracked the development of conflict began to take their place (figs. 131, 132).

Boys more than girls were apt to find themselves in situations in which the mechanisms forestalling conflict among close associates were not fully up to the task of resolving dispute. Conflict might develop because boys were more often in new situations and places and in contact with other boys whom they did not know intimately. The intimate cooperative sense developed by the Fore through close personal association in small groups did not easily extend to less familiar persons. Where boys who did not know one another well came together, contesting could occur (fig. 133). But, if in the course of contesting, one of the contestants showed even a trace of anger, the other usually deferred and laughed, in much the same way he would have to the demands and antics of a young child. This usually embarrassed the other, who frequently attempted to get out of this role by being magnanimous.

Socialization

The beginnings of socialization are complex, as in any culture, and most of the behavior so far discussed has a bearing on this socialization. Purposeful seeking of social activity, however, can be said to begin when children grow out of the toddler stage. At this time they began to demonstrate more

interest in other children of their own age and to pursue their company (fig. 134). Initially they did this in much the way that they made exploratory sorties from their mothers to investigate things attracting their attention in their nearby surroundings. Young children typically clustered about things of mutual interest (fig. 135).

At first, much of the play with age-mates was tactile; and part of that occurring among young age-mates could be characterized as sensually pseudo-aggressive (fig. 136). This early type of social encounter has been thought by a number of Western observers to be of aggressive or hostile intent; yet the Fore did not see it in this way. Although some of the expressions and acts involved in it appeared from the Western point of view to have aggressive components, the play was focused on exploratory physical play with sensual satisfaction by both parties. Such play was allowed to follow its natural course, and it rarely erupted into squabbles or fighting; the participants gave no evidence of intent to inflict displeasure. Oral biting games, frequently seen between older and younger children appeared to be related to this kind of pseudo-aggressive play.

The testing and feeling out of common interests, beyond those of mutual physical pleasure, began to develop as the toddlers became more mobile. Simple exploration of the environment and the individuals in it became integrated with increasingly complex social goals as the children became older. Much of the seemingly aimless moving about, one with another, which was characteristic of young Fore children, was probably instrumental in sorting out common interests and goals (fig. 137).

During this period of formative social integration, Fore children were often attracted to activities initiated by other children. The Fore freedom to pursue interest led to enlarged arenas for social contact in which preference could be expressed. This kind of social engagement probably also activated the interests of the young in the things around them. Like-minded individuals tended to be together more often, and, eventually, somewhat loosely defined groups of boys formed and reformed to explore, hunt, cook, eat and sleep together (fig. 138). They obtained and prepared their food cooperatively and built and shared shelter, a form of social integration directly related to the Fore proto-agricultural social organization.

This pattern of socialization, based on preference and cooperation, led directly into the informal

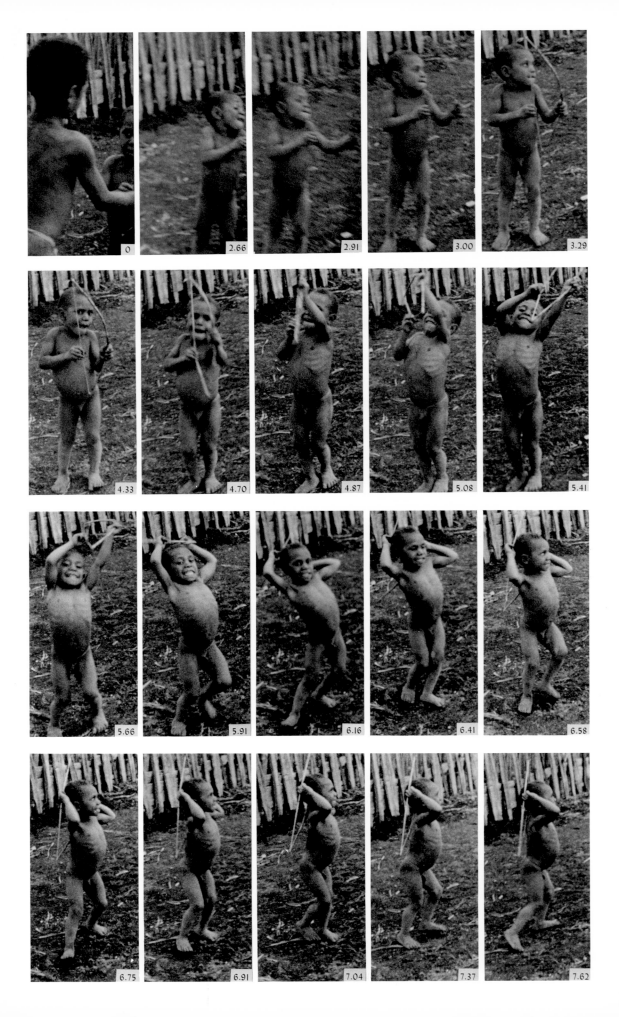

FIGURE 131. BEHAVIOR PATTERNS FORESTALLING CON-
FLICT I. Between the ages of about seven and eight
years, overt aggressive acts began to taper off and
behavioral mechanisms began to develop leading one
away from conflict as an outgrowth of anger or frustration. One of the kinds of mechanisms that appeared, as
this tendency to aggressiveness dropped off, was dancelike movement following provocation or frustration.
These dances were spontaneous and usually of short
duration; they seemed to take place in lieu of physical
aggression or retaliation. In this sequence, a young boy
responds with such a dance to the playful snatching
at his bow by a passing boy. Elapsed time from the
provoking incident is indicated in seconds in the lower
right corner of each frame.

FIGURE 132. BEHAVIOR PATTERNS FORESTALLING CON-
FLICT II. By the time Fore boys were about nine years
old, fighting among associates was unlikely to develop
out of a moment of anger. Another mechanism for side-
tracking anger, such as that which could develop during
rough play, is shown here. The boy on the bottom shows
a momentary trace of anger (b, c, d); he then goes limp
(e) for few a seconds, after which he resumes his activity
with the previous friendly elan. Elapsed time from the
first frame is in seconds as follows:

0.0	8.8	9.4
10.5	13.3	15.5
15.8	16.3	18.7
20.8	21.8	23.0

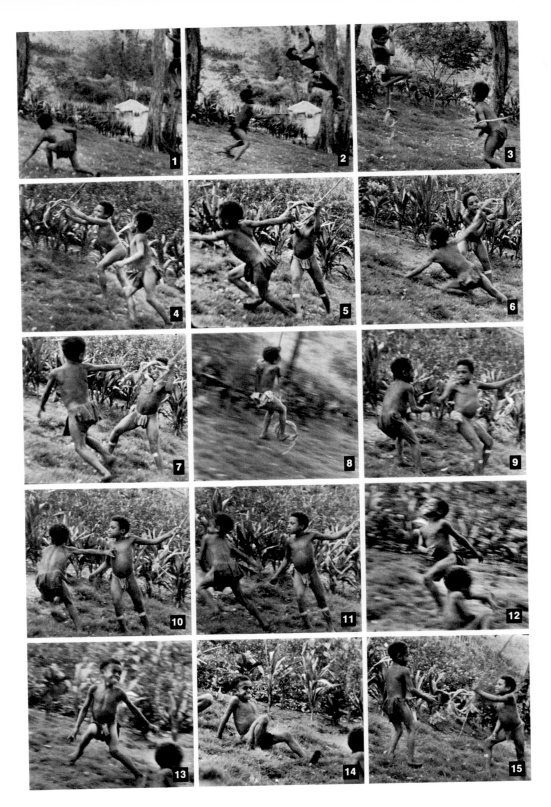

FIGURE 133. BEHAVIOR PATTERNS FORESTALLING CON-
FLICT III. Conflict, which could develop out of a mutual
but exclusive desire to use the same object or resources,
did not usually lead to physical aggression among young
Fore age-mates over about seven years of age. In this
sequence, two boys from different hamlets, but who
are somewhat casually associated, want to swing on the
same vine. A good-natured tilting develops, accompanied by laughter (1–3). The boy who had been
swinging keeps the vine for another swing, in spite of

the obvious desire of the other boy to take it (4–8). When he finished this swing, the contending boy approaches more insistently and provokes his adversary to an expression of anger (9–11). This amuses, rather than angers the contending boy, who disengages laugh-ing, just as he would over the irregular behavior of a small child (12–14). This embarrasses his adversary who takes a short swing and generously gives up the vine in a friendly way (15–17). Cooperative behavior and sharing of the vine develop (in the rest of the sequence).

FIGURE 134. SOCIALIZATION I. Young children were also attracted by the presence of age-mates; their exploratory activity soon turned to social encounter. Although their mutual interests were often associated with eating (see fig. 135), interest in joint exploratory play and physical contact also brought them together. As they grew older, they began to stimulate one another's interests and activities and to carry on joint cooperative activities.

FIGURE 135. SOCIALIZATION II. Youngsters tended to cluster around events of common interest and participate in similar ways. The commonality of interest and experience provided a basis for peer-group formation. Here, children gather around attractive food during a feast (**a, b**), eat the same things (**c, d**) and interact with each other in the gleaning of meat scraps from the inside of a pig skin (**e**).

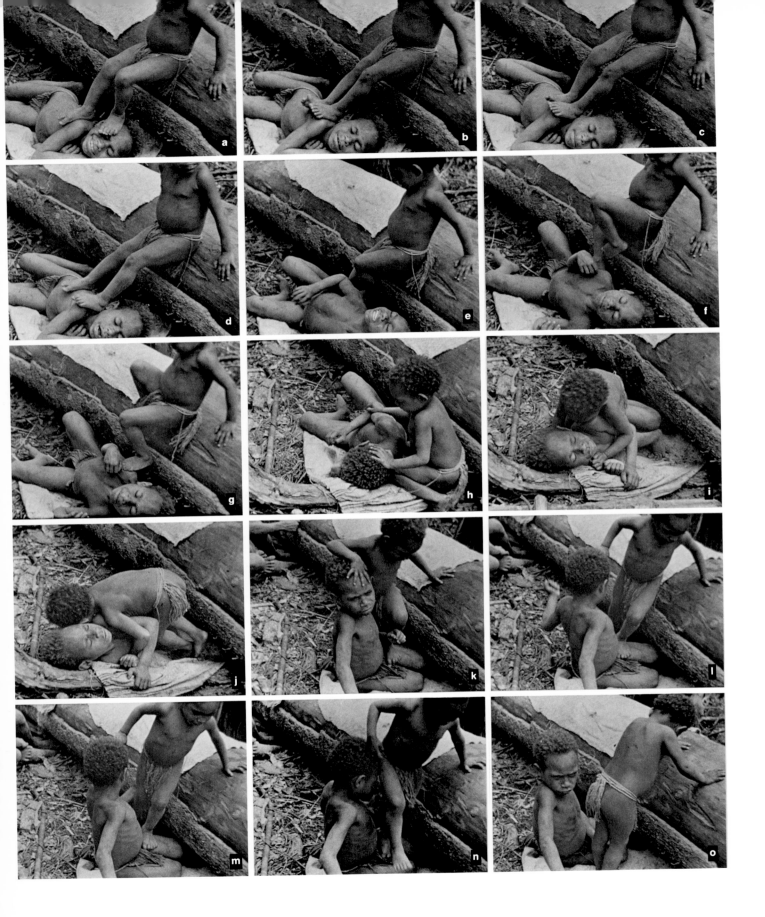

FIGURE 136. SOCIALIZATION III. Much of the early social contact with age-mates tended to center on exploratory physical contact. Some of this play included elements that Westerners might call hostile or aggressive, although the Fore did not see them as such. Adults gave little notice to such activities, neither overseeing them nor interceding in them. Here, two young children play near their mothers, who are making tapa (not seen in these pictures). The touching, caressing, hugging and hitting, much of which may be exploratory sensual play, is communicative and can, thus, be called social. It is voluntary and satisfying to each, otherwise the children would not remain with one another. Yet the interplay includes expressions reminiscent of anger (c, g, o), displeasure (f, j), and demand (e); and hitting is involved (l, m, n). The Fore do not consider these to be indicative of displeasure, aggressive intent or hos-

tility. That such play often continues for protracted periods and squabbles and fighting do not erupt supports this Fore assessment of such activity.

FIGURE 137. SOCIALIZATION IV. As Fore children grew older they began to spend more and more of their time with age-mates, and much of their play centered around common interests. The testing and feeling out of interests and responses, beyond those of mutual physical pleasure, began to develop fairly early. Mixtures of tactile communication, interpersonal enthusiasm and more complex social goals became more evident as the children became older. Much of the seemingly aimless moving about with one another, as in this sequence, was part of the process of sorting out common interests and goals.

FIGURE 138. BOYS' PEER GROUPS. In contrast to the girls, whose daily associations are predominantly within a group of women who live or garden together, boys tend to spend their time in the company of peers. As young boys, they rove and play together and develop their interests and objectives jointly. As they grow older, cooperative endeavors having to do with securing one's day-to-day livelihood become more common—a style of life that approaches that characteristic of adult Fore male society. Boys' interest groups and the mens' fraternal residential groups are similar in the way they work. In both, groups of close associates develop their interests and objectives together. Thus, the Fore boys enter the social and economic pattern governing the Fore way of life. Here, three boys jointly play with a vine (a); three other boys explore the lands near their hamlet with toy bows and arrows (b); a group of boys rest and talk in the *kunai* grassland near their hamlet (c); a group of boys who have collected food during the course of their roamings cook it and share it with other hamlet-mates (d).

nature of the adult social and residential groups. Polylocality and informal sociopolitical structure emerged. Residential groups were affinity groups; and within these groups personal property was transferred rather readily. Because of the difficulty in applying formal rules of affiliation, such as those of politics or kinship, the Fore social group was most appropriately defined as those who shared their lives and possessions with one another. Degree of association could be gauged by the degree of mutual activity and sharing. This basic structural principle of Fore society was but a more serious expression of the way groups of young Fore peers formed peer groups on the basis of personal predilection and affinity. The individualistic dovetailing of emotional, sensual and material interests led into cooperative association, which, in adult life was concerned with day-to-day livelihood and satisfaction.

Chapter 9 **Western Contact**

When the isolation of the Fore people came to an end through the advance of Western culture into their territory, their indigenous sociopolitical evolution was interrupted by a sudden flood of powerful new ideas and materials. Although it was the lifestyle and social organization of the Fore proto-agriculturalists that enabled them to respond quickly and innovatively to the arrival of Western man, in less than a decade, their egalitarian autonomy and this unique lifestyle had been drastically altered. Contact was easy. Early government officials did not have to oppose themselves to entrenched political elites, for there were none. Nor were the Fore restrained by rigid cultural interests from adopting the materials and ideas brought by the Western newcomers. They were accustomed to participating in whatever attracted them to the extent of their abilities and interests.

Furthermore, many of the new materials, tools and concepts brought by the Westerners were useful in the pursuit of traditional Fore goals. For example, the value of the steel axe or knife, cloth, medicine, court arbitration and public roads were immediately recognized. But the Fore also enthusiastically examined much more, and they experimented widely with the materials and ways of life introduced by the West. They were quick to grasp material advantage and extract whatever value they could find in any new opportunity. Innovation was not politically or socially discouraged. Just the opposite. From the child's earliest days, an experientially rich pattern of benign handling led easily to adaptive explorative behavior. This made it easier for the Fore to respond readily to Western culture in accordance with their own values and interests. And it made it easy for them to alter quickly the practices that had sustained their protoagricultural way of life.

Pax Australiana

The most obvious immediate effect of the arrival of Australian patrols in the Fore region was pacification. Fighting ceased almost spontaneously throughout the entire region. Most Fore groups did not wait to be told to cease fighting by the new administration but stopped on their own—almost as if they had been awaiting an excuse to give it up. A few, such as some of the Kamira people, maintained a warlike stance a bit longer than the others but without serious raiding. The Fore said among themselves that the *kiap* (government officer) was coming, so it was time to stop the fighting. They looked to his arrival as the beginning of a new era rather than as an invasion. Disputes that could not be settled by the Fore themselves were eagerly put into the hands of the patrol officers for arbitration, and an antifighting ethic quickly spread through the region. The aggressive posturing, which once accompanied assertions of rights and defense, faded away; talk of manliness in association with fighting prowess soon ceased.

Immense popularity was the lot of the early patrol officers, not only because of the peace, which had accompanied their arrival (and for which they got the credit), but also because of their introduction of new materials, tools and medicines. In the first years after the founding of Okapa Patrol Post, even the slightest innovative suggestion from the new authorities often brought rapid, sometimes excessive, effort to accommodate. When the newcomers were seen living in family houses, many Fore quickly gave up their separate men's and women's houses, and the men began to stop worrying about the supposed debilitating effect of familial contact with women. They gathered around any white man or woman who came among them and tried to attract missionaries and scientists to establish residence in their villages.

The receptive Fore reaction to Western presence seemed, at least in part, to be the result of the historical timing of the Australian arrival. Warfare had become a serious and disagreeable problem; yet indigenous political and social mechanisms for handling it had only begun to develop. The arrival of the Australian patrol officers permitted an immediate solution, and the Australian presence, by being the essential element in the peace (as well as the conduit bringing cloth, steel, salt and medicine), was considered millenarian.

This greatly facilitated the introduction of other key changes, such as public roads, government courts, trade and new concepts of social and economic organization. But the readiness with which new ideas and materials were adopted also depended on the high degree of individual freedom provided by the egalitarian Fore society. The new challenges and opportunities that came with Western presence were readily seized by the individual Fore, who was already accustomed to exploratory and innovative behavior.

Hamlet Convergence

Shortly after the founding of Okapa Patrol Post, patrol officers began to establish a system of thatched, native-built rest houses for overnight stops throughout the region as a means to facilitate census work and patrols, and to establish the government presence more effectively. Missionaries soon sponsored similar native-style buildings in many villages to be used for occasional church services. In keeping with their freedom to pursue preference, those Fore who wanted to be near the bearers of medicine and law (as well as the new steel tools, textiles, foods and knowledge) moved their houses to be near the new government rest houses or mission structures. In doing so, they developed much larger hamlets than they had had before, reversing somewhat their earlier tendency to segment and form new small hamlets (fig. 139).

The traditional residential pattern was that of nonpermanent hamlets, centrifugally dispersing outward from parent sites. There were loosely established group names relating to common origins or location; but as discussed in Chapter 6, there was not a sense of exclusively belonging to any permanent group. The Fore also dealt rather loosely (more loosely than many other Highland peoples) with formal kinship ties, and they formed new associations and relations readily when this was advantageous.

These practices led to a complex and fluid system of interhamlet allegiances, which could not easily be defined in terms of geographical or political units.

Faced with this situation, the early patrol officers assigned villages names somewhat arbitrarily to hamlet groupings as they established census units (see Chapter 2; map 6). They tried to base these groupings on what interhamlet affiliations they could discover while trying to maintain integral

FIGURE 139. CONVERGENCE OF HAMLETS AFTER WESTERN CONTACT. As the new Western government established public trails, roads, census sites, rest houses for government patrols and medical aid posts, the Fore began segmenting from their small, dispersed hamlets to settle near these centers of Western activity. Their segmentation was free, as it had been traditionally, but the effect was very different. Instead of centrifugally dispersing as small, segmenting groups into surrounding forest lands, there was a centripetal convergence on a central site. The government activities were often in the abandoned grasslands, causing the new settlements to be established in these previously abandoned lands in the centers of regions of population. As the Fore began leaving the edge of the forest to be near the edge of Western culture, they altered their protoagricultural movement and expanded their interests. The effect of Western presence, thus, was to convert the original outward movement of small protoagricultural bands to a consolidative, converging village-making movement where non-proto-agricultural interests could more readily be pursued. [a, In Paiti, between 1960 and 1963, many people moved their houses in from the surrounding land to be near the center of government activity in their region, represented by a census site, the terminus of a government trail, a rest house for government officials, and a government medical aid post. b, A similar development occurred later in Umasa at the site of a government rest house and trail in the center of their deforested central region]

geographical units. But the establishment of these named "villages" or census units began to obscure the indigenous sociopolitical complexity. All Fore individuals were ultimately assigned to one or another of these "villages"; they were required to be physically present at their "village" census site for the biannual census unless specifically excused by the patrol officer. Soon large, consolidated hamlets marked most of the census sites as Fore, wanting closer access to the material advantages provided by the new government, decided to live near these sites of contact. Government rest houses to accommodate the census and other patrols were also built at the sites of contact.

Even after the census affiliations had been formally imposed, many of the Fore continued to move to new hamlets and villages, taking up residence with new or old friends wherever they liked. This led in some hamlets to a situation in which the individual residents claimed several different villages (census units) as their own. But in spite of such complications, the village concept was generally accepted by the end of the first decade of administrative control, and most Fore had begun to associate themselves with their "village" when asked, and to think of it as a named region of collectively claimed forest and grassland where they could build their hamlets and make their gardens (see Chapter 2; map 7). It is now possible to elicit the village name of almost any area that is unambiguously in the region of a census site, although there is disagreement about areas distant from these sites.

The new practice of associating named geographical regions with enumerated people has led to occasional confusion, as when group segments have resettled in entirely new regions. For example, a sizeable group of Wanitabe villagers recently moved nearly halfway across the South Fore region to exploit new lands. Some called the new settled area "Wanitabe," because they were the Wanitabe people and were recorded in the Wanitabe census book. Others, however, who thought of Wanitabe as the *place* from which they had come, adopted the local place name, Onuri, to designate their new settlement. Still others felt that Onuri was not really a village name because there was no Onuri census book; when pressed for a village name to designate their settlement, some responded with the name of one of the two nearest officially recognized villages (Abomatasa and Kasokana). Although problems of this sort will undoubtedly continue to arise, the present trend is, nevertheless, toward less ambiguous, more discretely defined named territorial units to which individuals are attached or belong.

Roads

Before contact, Fore travel was restricted to that possible on the interhamlet and garden paths of friends and close associates.

Faced with a population unable to move beyond their own land or that of friends, the early patrol officers began to designate several intervillage trails as government "roads." With the participation of native labor, these were improved under government direction and declared free for all to use. This new kind of trail differed from the traditional type (figs. 140–141). Construction of a jeep road to bisect the Fore region was also started, and by 1960 it was possible to go by four-wheel-drive vehicle from Okapa to Purosa during dry weather.

Although free use of the public trails caught on somewhat slowly due to fear of sorcery, the new

FIGURE 140. GARDEN TRAIL. Most trails were made to go between gardens and hamlets. Within a population cluster such trails tended to form an interhamlet network. Virtually all travel was over such trails. Traditionally, there were no others. To go from one hamlet to another usually required using a combination of old and current garden trails. The existence of both depended on continued use. Here, a young girl leads me down such a trail to the next hamlet. [Yagareba, 1967]

FIGURE 141. GOVERNMENT TRAIL. As the Fore region was brought under government control, the early patrol officers designated and improved several interregional trails to facilitate administration and to make intervillage travel possible. Some of these followed older intervillage routes kept up by separated friends and associates; but many were also established on new, more direct rights of way. Here, part of a government team walks on the government trail between Ilesa and Kamira.

FIGURE 142. ROADS. The first roads in the Fore region were built with government encouragement and pressure and under the supervision of a patrol officer. Women, traditionally the gardeners, did most of the earth moving (a). However, by 1968, the value of roads as a means of getting coffee out to market had become evident, and Fore men assumed the responsibility for planning, engineering and constructing roads into their villages from the government road (b, c). The idea of public roads, open to all, gained acceptance quickly under the influence of the patrol officers, encouraging much more travel than had ever occurred before (d). [a, between Okasa and Sepuna, 1963; b, c, between Umasa and Takari, 1967; d, between Awande and Ke'efu, 1963]

jeep road was immediately accepted as a true public road (undoubtedly, because the government was credited with building it), and extensive travel over it to Okapa and beyond began almost immediately.

More than anything else, the completion of the jeep road opened up the Fore region, changing it almost overnight from an isolated region to one open to free travel, commerce and, more important, contact with the outside world. Hamlets moved down from their ridgetop sites in order to be nearer to the road, frequently consolidating with others as they did so. These larger roadside villages attracted desired visits by Western government officers, scientists, missionaries and traders.

The power of the road is hard to overestimate. It was a great artery where only restricted capillaries had existed before, and down this artery came a flood of new goods, new ideas, new peoples and above all, excitement. This new road, often impassable even with four-wheel-drive vehicles, was perhaps the single most dramatic stroke wrought by the new government. It was to the Fore an opening to a new world. As they began to use the road, they began to shed traditions they had evolved in the protective insularity of their mountain fastness. In their stead they adopted an emerging market culture similar to those forming throughout the Highlands around access to Western economy and under the aegis of Western government.

By 1966, men from previously hostile villages had begun to get together, without the backing or necessarily even the knowledge of the government, to plan roads across their lands in addition to those built under government sponsorship. Several were under construction by 1967 *(fig. 142)*. In another year vehicles of the government, missionaries, scientists, politicians and traders used them to penetrate more and more deeply to previously inaccessible villages. In 1968, the original government jeep track had become the trunk of a tree of roads, and by 1970, a rudimentary network was developing. Road-building techniques, including bridge building, were partially improvised but modeled on the construction method employed in the first government road. Some sections of the new roads were rebuilt after earlier tries proved unnegotiable. However, for the most part they were passable to four-wheel-drive vehicles.

"Walkabout," nonexistent as an institution before contact, quickly became an accepted way of life, and teenaged boys began to roam even hundreds of miles from their homeland in the quest for new experiences, trade goods, jobs and money. Like the classic practice of the Australian Aborigine, this "walkabout" took one away from his usual home and social group for periods of varying length. But unlike the Australian practice, it usually took the boys to jobs and schools rather than to a solitary life in one's traditional lands. Among the Fore it seems to have sprung from the traditional practice of allowing boys considerable freedom to pursue their own interests, including unrestricted visits and even temporary residence with their friends and kinsmen in other hamlets. With the abandoning of warfare and the development of public roads, the earlier limitations on roaming, imposed by the perils of trespass among unrelated or unknown peoples, disappeared. Simultaneously, the teenaged boys' role as warriors suddenly became superfluous, thus reducing the importance of their presence in the community.

The current "walkabout" practice may take the boys out of their villages for periods of several days or prolonged periods of several years. Some boys do not roam far, whereas others have found ways to go to distant cities. The roaming boys often seek places where they might be welcomed as visitors, workers or students for a while. Mission stations and schools, plantation work camps and the servants' quarters of the European population became way-stations in the lives of the modernizing Fore boys. Recently, small, enduring Fore residence groups with fluctuating membership have developed in commercial and administrative centers such as Goroka, Lae and Port Moresby.

New Tools and Gardening Practices

The increasing Fore population over the past century had created a demand for more gardens, both to feed the increased numbers of people and to support increased pig raising. The stone axe and the fire-hardened digging stick were originally quite adequate to prepare what new gardens were needed. Soil in the forest was considered the best for gardens, and there had been no need to look elsewhere as long as there was plenty of forest. By the time of contact however, boundaries in several areas had become more strictly defined, limiting the continued migration into new forest land (fig. 143). In a few, older settled regions, where much of the forest had been removed, previous garden sites were recultivated. There was no problem where secondary forest growth had developed, but it was not easy to clear the thick, matted sod of the grasslands with the traditional tools.

With the arrival of the government came the steel axe and spade. The superiority of these implements was immediately grasped by the Fore. Even the women, who were much slower to adopt other introduced materials, began using the new spades as soon as they could get them—long before they took up cloth for clothing or tins or pots for cooking. Application of these more efficient new tools caused a spurt in the pig population and a more rapid invasion of the remaining forest.

Soon the women wielders of the spade discovered that it not only markedly facilitated normal gardening, but that it could also be employed to cut away grass and sod. They started extending exist-

ing gardens back into the grassland. In deforested regions, this return to the grasslands occurred more quickly (fig. 144). The spade also facilitated the development of the new, large hamlets, since it enabled the Fore to create large tracts of consolidated garden.

Although the Fore generally continued to believe that soil in reclaimed lands was inferior to that of the forest, the women had discovered that some areas of grassland supported some crops better than others and that for a few crops the grassland was at least as good as forest land. Some women also claimed that some crops grew better in the drier locales of these open sites during the rainy season. Many others also preferred the openness of the grassland sites and the easier access to gardens across grassland trails. But these new trends have only become important since the introduction of the spade; and it is on this tool that much of the credit must fall for the return of the Fore to some of their abandoned sites of earlier agricultural activity.

FIGURE 143. REGION OF LAND PRESSURE. In some regions, separate Fore populations began expanding into the same regions, removing the previous virgin forest lands that had once separated them. When there was insufficient forest land left to support contiguous protoagricultural migratory movement, alternatives had to be sought. Traditionally, this problem was solved by segmentation to distant new lands. However, increasingly full settlement of available lands limited this alternative in some regions. Thus, attempts were also made to move garden sites into the last remaining clusters of trees in old lands and to regarden lands that were not too thickly matted with sod. [Amora, 1967]

FIGURE 144. GRASSLAND SETTLEMENT. The residents of Kinenti hamlet (Yagareba) are among the early representatives of the movement back into grasslands. Before the introduction of the steel spade, gardens in this area had come up to the edges of streams and gulleys. Now garden activity is turning back into the previously abandoned grasslands.

The Coffee Revolution

In the early 1950s, before the Fore region had been brought under administrative control and before Okapa Patrol Post was established, coffee planters in the Kainantu area, across several language groups to the north, had begun to welcome the so-called uncontrolled natives from the northern North Fore villages as laborers. They were thought to be more congenial workers than other Highland people.

Impressed by the care and attention lavished on their coffee by European planters and by the money they saw paid to local Kainantu native coffee growers, these Fore workers returned home with coffee beans to plant in their own villages. It was not until 1957 that coffee was introduced to the South Fore region. Demonstration coffee plantings were started at Okapa Patrol Post, and natives working at the station sometimes received coffee beans to take to their villages in return for services. Government officers later encouraged further interest by establishing demonstration coffee plantings in several villages and by distributing coffee beans to Fore asking for them. Many of the South Fore were eager to get these seeds, because they had learned that coffee growing brought money, which could be traded for such highly prized items as steel axes and spades, cloth and knives.

Coffee grew well on the Fore hillsides, and by the early 1960s, when the first sizeable crop matured, natives who previously had felt lucky to earn a few dollars found themselves able to earn a few hundred dollars. Just as this discovery was made, groups of young men, many now knowledgeable in coffee growing, began returning from the first of the newly instituted two-year stints as laborers in Europeanized parts of New Guinea.[51] Many of these "returnees" had worked on coffee plantations. These young men, together with those who had been locally instructed, created a sizeable group able to grow coffee. A rush to plant coffee ensued *(fig. 145)*. Contributing to the general eagerness to grow coffee was the elimination of the need for men to spend their time as guardians of their women and lands and in the negotiation of ceremony and alliance. Many eagerly seized upon coffee production to fill this gap. When these gardens became productive in the late 1960s the Fore income from coffee had increased to nearly a quarter of a million dollars. The coffee revolution was established.

At first, the coffee was carried on the backs of its growers (sometimes for several days) over steep, rough mountain trails to a place where it could be sold to a buyer with a jeep. However, as more and more coffee was produced, the villagers began to turn their efforts to developing jeep roads in association with neighboring villagers and cutting roads through the mountains and bush in an effort to make it possible for coffee buyers to come to

FIGURE 145.   COFFEE GARDENS. Coffee as a cash crop was adopted with enthusiasm by the Fore people. In 1963, young coffee plantings, protected by sun shades, could be seen in nearly all villages (**a**). By 1967, mature coffee plants were bearing well (**b, c**), and the harvest began to bring more and more money to the Fore villagers. [**a,** Wagiri hamlet, Kamira, 1963; **b, c,** Yagareba, 1968]

their villages with Land Rovers and trucks. The newly built roads and the new monetary wealth of the people, in turn, stimulated further economic development and the opening of new trade stores throughout the region.

The first two trade stores were opened at Okapa Patrol Post by 1961 to serve the government staff, but as soon as the Fore began to obtain money, they too were welcomed as customers. Items the Fore found particularly desirable were: cloth, clothes, matches, tobacco, salt, rice, nails, kerosene, cooking oil, tinned meat, sugar and powdered milk. By 1963, other small stores had been opened primarily for the Fore—two on the road to Kainantu in the North Fore region and one irregularly opened mission store in the South Fore region at Purosa. By 1966, a few thatched huts had been built by local Fore entrepreneurs and were lightly stocked with trade goods for sale. In the year that followed, several such stores were built. By 1968, virtually all Fore were within a two- or three-hour walk from a trade store. In 1968 also, more permanent trade stores belonging to European trading companies began to appear along the new roads. Since these were much better stocked and sold their goods at lower prices, they began to take the trade away from the modest native stores, many of which were discontinued by the end of 1968.

FIGURE 146. PLANTINGS OF CASUARINA TREES. Among the earliest of the South Fore to adopt the Casuarina as a means to regenerate the land were the residents of Amora and Kume. By 1968, several groves of Casuarina punctuated previously uniform grassland. Some of these were planted as shade for coffee plantings, but others were simply planted from cuttings in the newly abandoned gardens. [Hamlets seen: Sevoi (Kume), lower right; Yasumit (Amora), upper center; Yasagavinti (Amora), upper right]

The Casuarina Tree and Land Tenure

Although no Casuarina trees grew in the South Fore region a generation ago, within the last 10 years, rapidly growing stands have begun to appear in most villages *(fig. 146)*. Many of the trees were brought in to provide shade for the new coffee gardens. The Fore soon noted that this fast-growing tree grew well in abandoned gardens and quickly provided shade that retarded growth of the *kunai* grass. It also grew well in established grasslands. Land planted in Casuarina trees, it was believed, also became fertile sooner than land left fallow to grass and was easier to recultivate. Furthermore, it provided a source of firewood, otherwise hard to obtain in grassland regions, thus facilitating habitation there.

In some areas, small groves of Casuarina began to appear in abandoned gardens. Later these trees were cut to reestablish the garden *(fig. 147)*. Since tree planting, like garden planting, allowed one to control the ground, these groves (along with the coffee plantings) instituted a more permanent type of land tenure. With their earlier crops, the Fore could only temporarily preempt land. Casuarina trees were an enduring crop, which the Fore viewed in the same way they viewed other crops, applying the traditional concept of land rights to them.

But application of the traditional practice governing land right in this case worked to undermine the traditional pattern of land tenure. For the first time, continued land tenure became feasible. Casuarina trees were planted in abandoned gardens to be cut down when the land was again regardenable, and when this garden was again given up, new Casuarina trees were planted. The same owner remained.

There is no evidence the Fore were aware that in adopting the Casuarina tree they were in fact altering their traditional practice of temporary land tenure to one allowing long-term or even permanent tenure. This situation is a clear demonstration of how the introduction of a new element into a cultural system may have unanticipated implications for that system—even when the new element is treated according to traditional practice.

FIGURE 147. NEW GARDEN CUT FROM A CASUARINA GROVE. Recent plantings of sweet potato dot the ground beneath the dead trunks of Casuarina trees in this new garden. Note the similar girth of the trunks, indicating equivalent ages. Uncut Casuarina remain beyond the garden on two sides.

Chapter 10 Socialization and Cultural Change

The nondirective Fore approach to child handling and rearing supported their protoagricultural existence by molding an unrepressed, explorative personality able to respond readily to new opportunity and challenge. Their dispersive interests encompassed novelty; but there was little interest in change for the sake of change. *Innovation-ready* but not innovation-questing, the Fore differed significantly from the more compulsive kind of innovative individuals seen in the West.

The Fore style of innovativeness facilitated adaptive pioneering penetration of the latent economic opportunities provided by virgin lands; and it fostered the flexible social segmentation and alliance practices so useful in this penetration. In the larger sense the Fore lifestyle abetted response to new opportunity while simultaneously bestowing contentment with the established protoagricultural existence.

The child-handling and rearing practices detailed in Chapter 8 provided the means by which this innovation-ready, protoagricultural character was passed on to succeeding generations and by which the Fore way of life was established as a way-station in cultural evolution.

As an expression of a more general New Guinea Highlands protoagricultural existence, this approach to enculturation may have persisted for a long time. To what degree it was similar to those of other protoagricultural people cannot yet be known, although in New Guinea, at least, there were clear parallels.[52] Elsewhere, in climates where close body contact and physical interaction were obstructed by heavy clothing, alternative patterns may have developed.

The innovation-ready Fore personality, molded by their approach to child rearing and socialization, was undoubtedly an important factor in the dramatic cultural change that followed exposure to the material largess of the West. Already attuned to innovative economic adaptation, it was easy for them to adopt quickly the new tools, goods and practices that began to flood in.

Ironically, perhaps, the adaptive protoagricultural character, which made it so easy to respond to these new opportunities, also provided a pattern of receptivity striking at the very practices spawning this character. Hidden in the persisting Fore protoagricultural way of life was an Achilles heel: In the face of lavish and sustained new economic opportunity and example, they were vulnerable to fundamental change.

The style of innovation, experimentation and exploration practiced by the Fore focused economic inquiry on surrounding opportunities. Expressed neither compulsively nor anxiously, the associated innovative behavior was relaxed. It was not based on efforts to be different or better. Novelty only became interesting and exciting when experienced as play among peers. It was approached in the company of like-minded friends *(see figs. 84, 85, 86, 87, 106, 107, 114, 125, 126)*, and when interest in something novel did not spark some degree of consensus appreciation, it was not likely to persist. In this respect, the approach to novelty paralleled the approach to protoagricultural exploitation. Both were basically cooperative and consensual; neither was competitive.

These approaches emerged as a culturally specific form of behavior during childhood and youth. Infants and toddlers experienced novelty and exploratory interest in the enveloping richness of the sociosensual opportunities provided by the bodies of caretakers *(see figs. 72, 76, 84, 85, 94, 107, 114, 120, 125, 126, 127)*. During childhood the focus shifted to the things and activities provided by the community, which the developing child could discover. This was done in the company of age-mates who reciprocally provided an exploratory security, through sociosensual contact and mutual interest, as they moved into the broadened community arena away from their older caretakers. Thus, exploration and novelty continued to be expressed in a personal gestalt of physical proximity and contact originally established in infancy.

As adulthood was approached, novelty tended to be valued according to its socioeconomic potential —how it might bring the good things in life. It was oriented about food, valued objects, materials and the related reciprocal exchanges of assistance or affection among associates.

Usually a novel practice had a short life, flowering and dying in the rich social life of the small Fore communities, to be replaced with new interests as other aspects of the surrounding environment were approached. However, when a new activity or approach attracted the interest and imagination of several individuals because it embodied a potential reward not previously noticed, it could become anchored in the community as an accepted practice. Sometimes such practices spread to neighboring communities to become part of the general regional culture—as during the "cargo-cult-like" movements, which rapidly altered the Fore way of life after Western contact.

The lack of frustration in Fore infancy and childhood may have had a fundamental effect upon their approach to novelty: During infancy and toddlerhood, the child's basic physical and emotional requirements were quickly and readily fulfilled. Frustration was minimal. The child was not required to elaborate abstract mental constructions of time, space and human relation in order to feel secure in the world about him. The richly responsive world of tactile communication and human interaction lessened the need for this less personal type of cognitive adaptation. As a result, the Fore child did not face the subordination of childlike desires experienced by children reared in cultures where households are organized by rule, schedule and behavioral ideals. Unlike such children, Fore infants had no need to elaborate concepts of order and regularity in order to relate to sources of sustenance and comfort. They did not have to internalize abstract concepts of social order based on arbitrary behavioral norms or schedules. No deep, emotional commitment to security-associated, abstract behavioral concepts developed. Neither

sense of well-being nor peace of mind were very dependent on altering or manipulating people or surroundings to fit an abstract program.

It may also be important that the Fore young were rarely frustrated in their efforts to obtain security, nourishment, warmth and stimulation. This condition more than anything may distinguish their psychological development from that more common in Western culture. The Fore did not have to face the contradiction inherent in having their basic emotional commitments traumatically installed. Not captured by this type of Jekyll-Hyde existentially paradoxical behavioral coin, the Fore did not have to commit themselves either to punctilious and demanding allegience to concepts of order, or to nihilistic, rage-engendered rejection of such commitment. Nor did they have to suffer the trauma and confusion caused by shifting from one side of this coin to the other.

With a basic behavioral program patterned by less traumatic, early handling, Fore social dynamics proceeded less rigidly, less traumatically and with a more stable internal sense of personal identity—one not so dependent on name, place, position or status.

With little to provoke angry withdrawal or "lashing out," destructive impulses directed at family, loved ones or way of life did not become ingrained in the Fore behavioral repertoire. Molded by an everpresent means to assuage discontent, there was little to give rise to these kinds of antisocial behavior patterns within their communities. Such common problems in the West as "generation gap," sibling rivalry, social domineering, adolescent rebellion and similar expressions of alienation did not disrupt the small Fore communities. Consistent with this pattern, the approach to innovation and change was adjustive and responsive, not aggressive, competitive, traumatic or destructive. It was based on good feeling among close associates, not on existential anxiety, anger, jealousy, compulsion or traumatically imbedded commitments to abstract principles.

A flaw in the underlying protoagricultural psychosocial development was that it did not extend so easily to strangers. Exacerbation, anger, violence and conflict could arise rather readily among aliens, as when moving into the same regions. But, even though the two poles, ingroup and outgroup, were psychologically far apart to the Fore, different degrees of rapport could arise to unite these rather adaptable people variously along the scale between.

It is not yet possible to say exactly how the Fore adaptability emerged. Undoubtedly it originated during prespeech infancy, when tactile communication provided a virtually uninterrupted, very personal interactive communication with caretakers. This "language" meant that the Fore infants rarely had to wait helplessly to have their needs fulfilled. Needs for sustenance, comfort, security and stimulation could be readily and responsively gratified, according to messages of touch, expression and movement. Much of the frustration experienced in other cultures was sidetracked by the Fore child-handling practices, and a pattern of relating to associates and the world around in a gratifying, sociosensual way was established.

In the absence of commitment to security-associated abstract concepts, challenges to existing belief or practice were not threatening. This left the Fore freer to think and behave in new ways. In it lay the basis for their cognitive flexibility, an important trait that facilitated both protoagricultural exploitation as well as cultural change.

How names were used reflected this cognitive flexibility. Names of persons, places and groups were not very binding. An individual's name was less a formally established identity than simply what he was called; and, particularly for children, this could change over time and from place to place.

As discussed in Chapter 9, the lack of commitment to formal names had made census identification difficult. Soon, however, the efforts of the new government began to stabilize names; the Fore rather willingly adapted to the patrol officer's insistence on the same names each year in the formal census and in connection with other governmental activities. Before this, both personal and place names were like nicknames, in that they could change depending on rapport, mood, habit, association and situation.

The closest thing to an enduring formal name was assigned during initiation. But even these names were not necessarily permanent nor were they necessarily used by one's associates. Name flexibility was particularly marked in children. Not uncommonly were they renamed on the basis of some event or deed with which they were asso-ciated. For example, a young boy running in a somewhat unusual way might jokingly, or affectionately, be called "grasshopper." Similarly a boy might be called "aid post" or "kiap" because of his interest, involvement in, or association with these aspects of the new government presence. Often these were transient, but they could stick. Some such spur-of-the-moment names have achieved permanence when patrol officers innocently recorded them as "official" names in census books.

Similarly, place names were not formally established before the arrival of the patrol officers. Places were often renamed after something interesting that had happened there. The place names with the greatest permanence were derived from outstanding natural features or well-established groups living there.

Recognition that all people did not necessarily use the same names for places or individuals also affected usage. For example, local usage was usually adopted by individual visitors, but migrating groups often used their own names. Different people sometimes used different names for the same person, and an individual would usually respond to the name he knew himself to be known by. Various names were similarly assigned to place. Since names were used primarily for communication rather than to establish preeminence, usage followed this need. Names could even fade away to be replaced by others, according to usefulness and consensus.

The ease with which the Fore were able to modify or abandon names is another indication of their relatively low commitment to abstract concept.

Similarly, they were only weakly committed to social and moral codes. The emotional focus of the Fore seemed to be a pleasurable cooperative association with friends, in the quest of material things generally appreciated. Interest in defending precepts or ideals did not fit this pattern. This seemed to make it easier to modify practice and belief, and it may have been a major factor in the diversity of belief and practice noted among the Fore. It also made it easier for the Fore to join (or absorb) individuals from other, quite different groups. Undoubtedly it facilitated mobility and polylocality.

Cognitive flexibility also facilitated formation of informal clusters of individuals with similar views and interests. In the absense of formal obstacles to spontaneous personal affiliation, the Fore could readily reassociate themselves with other individuals who had similar interests, objectives and values. I call this kind of group formation *cognitive clustering,* because it involves the association, at least temporarily, of people with similar views.

Obviously, cognitive clustering will occur more frequently among cognitively flexible people. And the social formations and reformations resulting will lead rather quickly to diversification of practice, custom, belief and language. Cognitive clustering provides a ready way to take advantage of new possibilities, and it may explain the rather remarkable cultural, linguistic and behavioral diversity seen across New Guinea.[53]

The potential for change demonstrated so dramatically by the protoagricultural Fore stems, at least in part, from their cognitive flexibility. In turn, cognitive flexibility fostered cognitive clustering, which, then, fostered divergent adaptation. Sociopolitically expressed as informal, flexibly constituted affinity groups, cognitive clustering provided an appropriate psychological basis for affiliative kinship, sociopolitical looseness, egalitarian social structure, mobility, unrestricted social segmentation and polylocality.

Whether the fashion in which cognitive clustering occurred among the Fore was only a temporary phase in the sociopolitical evolution or an ancient trait may not be possible to determine. However, since it fit so well with the protoagricultural situation, it seems reasonable to assume that it emerged from similar economic and ecological foundations.

The rather dramatic culture change of the Fore after Western contact also seemed to emerge naturally from the protoagricultural situation. But it appears as if the power of this change may have been so dramatic as to threaten seriously the conditions that made the change occur so easily. Adoption of clothing, commerce and principles of land tenure; schools, churches, courts and law; money, radios, roads and jobs all add up to something distinctly different from the protoagricultural way of life.

It could be argued that the entire Fore socialization process, as well as the evolution of their nondirective, egalitarian social structure, depended on practices necessitated by climate—obviously an oversimple explanation, but one containing a germ of truth. Close physical contact may have been necessary in the temperate mountains of the Fore homeland; for the Fore lacked materials from which to make warm clothing. Tactile communication may have naturally emerged from this condition; cognitive flexibility from tactile communication, then loose sociopolitical structure and then the protoagricultural ability to adapt to new challenge and opportunity.

It may be significant that now, for the first time in Fore history, an alternative to sustained physical contact between infants and mothers is possible. How they will use this alternative and how much difference it will make in the molding of future Fore character is as yet impossible to evaluate. Already women are beginning to wear blouses and sleep in blankets. Is it significant that some of these women have complained that their babies cry too much? Since the wearing of blouses was not suffciently widespread at the time of my field studies, I cannot draw any precise conclusions.

Another change brought by Western contact, which may have important future implications, is the abandonment of separate men's and women's living quarters in favor of nuclear family dwellings. In traditional Fore hamlets, the separation of men and women effectively made the hamlet the indivisible basic social unit. Close interpersonal and economic ties extended through other houses as strongly as they did in one's house of residence. The nuclear family changes this and puts all those individuals with the closest ties in one house. Not only does the nuclear household thus fragmentize somewhat the social unity of the hamlet, but it also begins to restrict that earlier freedom of movement enjoyed by children. In the traditional hamlet it was never very clear where they should be or to whom they might be responsible.

The introduction of encoded rules of behavior by the Australian patrol officers may be another important force in the demise of the protoagricultural character of the Fore. There is now concern with such rules, after the Australian example. Fore boys have begun to take interest in games with formal rules, such as marbles and kickball, and they improvise other games, such as "kiap" (patrol officer), "police" and "doctor boy," during which they play at rule application and the giving and taking of orders.

Some changes in some of the more basic patterns of child interaction were also detectable by 1968: In the modernized hamlets, annoyance expressed

FIGURE 148. AGGRESSIVE BEHAVIOR IN MODERNIZED HAMLETS I. By 1968, aggressive behavior by older children toward their younger hamlet-mates was detectable in the modernized hamlets. Particularly when games governed by rules were played, older children could be seen pushing their younger associates about and rejecting their company in order to play the game better. Here, a younger boy gets in the way of an older one as they play marbles (c). At first, the older boy throws a pebble at his younger hamlet-mate (d); then he pushes him out of the way (e) and finally threatens him (f).

by older children with younger children could occasionally be seen, particularly during play, an apparent consequence of playing at "rules." This was a distinct departure from play behavior in the small traditional hamlets. Sometimes younger children were even pushed about because they interfered with the proper playing of a game. Youngsters also began to take aggressive, rather unyielding stances with one another *(figs. 148, 149).*

It is still too early to evaluate the implications of the new developments and practices. However, it is obvious that the approach to child rearing and socialization, which hitherto sustained the Fore way of life, was rather vulnerable to the materials and practices introduced by Western culture. Probably the combination of clothing, nuclear family social organization and authoritarian sociopolitical structure will prove strong enough to end the approaches to child rearing and socialization that made it so easy to adopt them.

FIGURE 149. AGGRESSIVE BEHAVIOR IN MODERNIZED HAMLETS II. Aggressive behavior, aimed at controlling the behavior of others, could be noted in modernized Fore hamlets by 1968. In part, this seemed to stem from an attempt by Fore boys to model their behavior on that of the Western government officials and missionaries who had settled in their region; and, in part, it may represent their interest in experimenting with rule-governed behavior because it represented a new challenge. Here, older boys adopt stances of aggressive demand in their relationship to young boys (a, b, c).

In the modernized hamlets, older children could also occasionally be seen retaliating when they were the subject of aggressive acts of young children. To what degree this indicates the development of a new pattern of response cannot yet be determined. At left, an older boy retaliates when attacked by a younger hamlet-mate, instead of being amused or affectionate as was the usual practice (d-o).

Notes

1. The archaeological findings of White (1967) suggest cultural continuity in the Eastern Highlands from the earliest evidence of human occupation.

2. Watson (1965a, 1967b) discusses the introduction of agriculture and of the sweet potato into the Highlands.

3. This classification is based on a lexicostatistical survey of the New Guinea Highlands by S. A. Wurm (1962, 1964).

4. Although Scott (1963) formally demonstrated three dialects of Fore, his sample of the Ilesa area may not have been complete enough to determine whether it, too, might have qualified as a separate dialect. Many Fore refer to the Ilesa way of speech as distinguishably different from that of the other major regions.

5. The first complete census of the Fore was completed by patrol officers from Okapa Patrol Post in 1958. The population figure given here is from the *Annual Census Report* (1958) of the Okapa Subdistrict, Territory of Papua and New Guinea.

6. These population densities are based on the population figure reported in the *Annual Census Report* (1958), divided by the approximate area of land occupied by people speaking these dialects.

7. Berndt (1962) and Glasse (1967) have also described cannibalism in this Highland region.

8. Glasse (1967, p. 753) states: "Although precise dates cannot be established, it appears that cannibalism spread into the kuru region from the north: the Keiagana-Kanite adopted the custom a few generations ago; the North Fore, about the turn of the century; and the South Fore, 40 to 50 years ago, a decade or so before the first appearance of kuru there." In my own studies of kuru epidemiology in the South Fore, I frequently heard first-hand stories about the early practice of cannibalism in the various villages. Persons over about 50 years of age frequently remembered when cannibalism was first practiced in their villages. In the western South Fore, cannibalism was even more recent.

9. Gajdusek 1963a, p. 152.

10. Bennett, Rhodes and Robson 1958; Bennett and Robson 1958.

11. Gajdusek, Gibbs, Alpers 1967; Gajdusek, Gibbs, Ascher and David 1968.

12. Glasse 1963; Matthews, Glasse and Lindenbaum 1968.

13. Zigas and Gajdusek 1957.

14. Alpers 1965; Alpers and Gajdusek 1965.

15. Gajdusek, Zigas and Baker 1961; Gajdusek and Zigas 1959.

16. Annual Census Report 1963, Okapa Subdistrict, Territory of Papua and New Guinea.

17. Glasse, Shirley 1964, p. 36. She also reported that in the village of Wanitabe, where she lived, 50 percent of the men were without wives.

18. I restrict the term sorcery to that practiced by the malicious human sorcerers. The Fore also believed sickness and death to be caused sometimes by natural spirits, ghosts of recently dead relatives, violation of food taboos or excessive association with women.

19. Reid and Gajdusek (1969) reported a nutritional evaluation of traditional Fore diet in the North Fore village of Moke. Oomen et al. (1961) and Keleny (1962) describe the dietary role of sweet potato elsewhere.

20. Twenty tons is probably rare. However, Glasse (1962) recorded yields as high as 21 tons in the South Fore. Ten tons per acre in a good garden is probably a more common yield. My figures were based on the number of standard *bilums* of sweet potato yielded by a very good garden over a three-month period. Since this did not include the driest part of the year, my figure may be a little high for that garden.

21. Shirley Glasse (1963b) listed over 300 ethnobotanical items used by the Fore.

22. Watson (1965a) also discusses the evidence for a shift from hunting and gathering in a nearby part of the Eastern Highlands. Lindenbaum (1971b) mentions the degree to which Fore oral tradition involves hunting and gathering. Diamond (1966) notes that the Fore system of zoological classification indicates they may have depended more heavily on wild animals and plants only a few generations ago.

23. A detailed discussion of this ecological transformation is contained in the next chapter. Robbins (1963a) also discusses the anthropogenic origin of the New Guinea Highlands grasslands; and Bowers (1968) deals with the problem of the ascending grasslands for the Kaugel valley to the west.

24. For comparative accounts of other Highlands peoples see: Berndt (1955, 1962, 1964), Brookfield and Brown (1963), Brown (1960, 1963, 1964), Brown and Brookfield (1959), Bulmer (1960), De Lepervanche (1967–68), Du Toit (1962, 1964), Fischer (1968), Gardner and Heider (1969), Heider (1970), Kelly (1968), Langness (1964), Meggitt (1958, 1964, 1965, 1967), Pospisil (1958, 1960, 1963), Rappaport (1967ab), Read (1951, 1952ab, 1954ab, 1959, 1965), Reay (1959ab, 1967), Ryan (1955, 1959, 1961), Vayda (1961), Vayda, Leeds and Smith (1961), Watson (1967ab).

25. The evidence dealing with the introduction of the sweet potato into the Pacific regions has been presented by Yen (1960, 1963), Conklin (1963), and Nishiyama (1963). O'Brien (1972) summarizes the evidence for the introduction of the sweet potato into the Highlands via the Markham valley. Watson (1967b) discusses the introduction of the sweet potato into the Tairora region of the Eastern Highlands.

26. This is consistent with Brookfield's (1964, p. 21) hypothesis that "taro is an older crop than the sweet potato in the Highlands." Watson (1967b, p. 89) also reports that "some highlands peoples do believe the sweet potato to have been introduced and superseded taro as a principal crop."

27. In the Fore, yields per unit of land were much greater with sweet potato than with any of the other crops. Occasionally they approached 20 tons per acre from especially good gardens, although a more common "good" yield would be around 10 tons per acre per annum. Glasse (1962, p. 4) discusses yields of five to 21 tons per acre. The implications of such yields have been discussed by Watson (1965ab, 1967b), Robbins (1963a) and Bulmer and Bulmer (1964).

28. Man-made grasslands elsewhere in the Highlands have also been discussed by Robbins (1963b) and Bowers (1968).

29. Watson (1965a) feels the effect of sweet potato introduction on population was so dramatic that it can be spoken of as a population explosion. Brookfield and White (1968) suggest other factors may limit this, and that population increase is not quite so dramatic. It is clear, however, that, where sweet potato opens up new lands to agricultural exploitation, it also allows a population density hitherto not possible. Thus, population densities in these regions may become much greater than before. But where sweet potato is introduced into lands already ecologically despoiled by earlier crops, it may depopulate a region by making migration to higher altitude virgin lands elsewhere more advantageous.

30. Watson (1965a, p. 300) also believes this to be the region from which the Agarabi and Tairora (to the north of the Fore) obtained sweet potato: "All the numerous pre-contact varieties, including those which they considered the oldest, traditionally reached the area from the people immediately to the west (Kamano) or, in a few instances, from still farther west."

Read (1952a) provides an excellent account of the much more elaborate and formal *idza nama* festivals (pig-exchange feasts) of the Gahuku, where the event is much more important to the total culture than among the Fore. This is also true of the Chimbu, who slaughter hundreds of pigs for a single exchange feast affirming their clan affiliations (Brookfield and Brown, 1963). Berndt (1962) describes the smaller, less elaborate pig feasts of the Usurufa, Kamano, Yate and North Fore. Read (1954a) believes the pig-exchange feasts serve to express and confirm political ties. He also states (1952a, p. 17): "The integrative importance of the *idza nama* can hardly be overestimated . . . it seems pre-eminently to acknowledge political alliances and obligation. Traditional ties between groups are renewed . . . As many as a thousand people may be gathered." Berndt (1962, p. 64) makes the following statement for the lesser exchange feasts in the Usurufa, Kamano, Yate and North Fore: "The visitors to

whom the pig meat is given are those belonging to what I call here the sphere of political influence. Peace between some of the units within this range has been established, for the time being at least."

31. This was done using Dr. L. A. Cavalli-Sforza's genetic network computer program. Based on the results of the ecological-genetic analysis presented here, Dr. Wiesenfeld is continuing further genetic examination of the blood-genetic data with special reference to my suggestion of the Kamano as a major origin site.

32. Robbins (1963b, p. 50) discusses the importance of the Markham valley agricultural routes to the Highlands: "It is concluded that these migrants (Markham valley peoples), in common with New Guinea native peoples, generally, were forest-clearers and gardeners and that they would have passed through areas of dense lowland rainforest to reach the interior. For this group there is no lack of vegetational evidence. . . . Nowhere else along the postulated routes of entry into the Highlands is there this extent of modified and disclimax vegetation, such as would be created in the course of a large-scale migration. Only thus can the now largely abandoned upper Markham grasslands be readily explained."

33. Robbins (1963b, p. 52) shows that stabilized, short grasslands, including Imperata, may not appear for several centuries after initial Miscanthus grasslands have replaced gardens: "Miscanthus regrowth successions may persist over several centuries, however, before the final short-grass stage is attained. Gradual changes leading to the establishment of the short-grass disclimax involve floristic shifts in the associated woody shrubs of the Miscanthus sword-grass communities."

34. Watson (1965a) found that both Agarabi and Tairora people cited the Kamano region as that from which sweet potato was introduced into their regions. Furthermore, sweet potato had, at the time of contact, just replaced taro as the staple in the southern part of Region 2 *(map 8)*, among the Awa and the southernmost Tairora and was still replacing taro among the Anga.

35. The Anga and Agarabi occupy a single branch in map 10 while the Gimi-Labogai occupy another. This does not mean that the Anga and Gimi-Labogai are not genetically similar—even more similar to each other than to other groups in their own branches. Genetic networks reflect overall relations among all groups. Because of this they may not emphasize specific close relationships between two groups when this relationship does not extend beyond these two groups, as where hybridization between two groups in different branches has not extended to the other groups to which the two groups are separately related. (This could occur because their contact has been recent or because geographic or political barriers prevent more extended liaison). Such hybridization would not always be strong enough to affect the more dominent overall genetic relationships that placed the two groups in separate branches.

36. An example is the Nosuguri population cluster. Most of its people migrated to its present site to become more closely allied with each other in a previously unexploited region adjacent to the Kamira population cluster. However they continued to maintain their own hamlets, rather than merge with Kamira hamlets. Some of the neighboring people

began referring to their region (and its people) as Nosuguri, not Kamira, the region in which they had settled, or Ketabi, the region from which they had migrated. Others did refer to these new hamlets as Kamira, and others called them Ketabi. Some even called them Purosa. The social and political affiliations of the Nosuguri people were at least as strong with Ketabi people as they were with Kamira people; in fact more interhamlet feasts were held between Nosuguri and Ketabi hamlets than with Kamira hamlets in 1963–64. Another example is the Gimi village of Eteve, which was originally a large segmenting group from Ketabi. These people took their name with them (Ketabi and Eteve are the same name with the typical phonemic shifts between Fore and Gimi changing the "k" to a glottal stop and the "b" to "v.") These people are now linguistically and culturally indistinguishable from their Gimi neighbors. Another Fore group, Paiti, settled in the same part of the Gimi lands and kept its Fore language and culture, sustained contact with Ifufurapa communities, but adopted a local place name.

At the time of Western contact, the people who were living in what is now called Agakamatasa did not use this word to identify themselves. Rather the population then making up the Agakamatasa settlement was still using the names of the population clusters from which it had emigrated: Wanitabe, Mugaiamuti and Awarosa. The name, Agakamatasa, was originally Agakamati, a smaller place-name in that region. Partly as a result of government activities centered there, this name came to be applied to the entire population cluster so as to define it better for government purposes. None of the people there now use their old origin site names to refer to themselves.

37. Gajdusek and Zigas (1961, p. 87) discovered that ". . . on first entry of civilized man into the region, the population was in a state of flux with recent shifts and migrations." Berndt (1962, p. 27) states: "One of the (lineage's) most important attributes is its fluidity, expressed through changing personnel." Lindenbaum and Glasse (1969, p. 166) believed: "Individual and group mobility was great, partly as a result of dispersal following defeat in war." Glasse (1970, p. 211) states that before contact . . . hamlet members traveled widely and frequently within the Fore territory and occasionally beyond."

38. Some of these have been noted by other observers: C. Berndt (1953, p. 116) notes: "Thus Asafina, one of the Fore districts, driven from its home in the south, came eventually into the Usurufa territory where it joined forces with the district of Moife . . . and settled down on their land to build houses and cultivate gardens." Gajdusek (1963b, p. 183), while studying kuru, documented two other migrations: "The Agakamatasa group split from the Mugaiamuti group of Purosa . . . to escape the ravages of kuru. They crossed the densely forested summit above the Purosa valley to Awarosa on the slopes above the Lamari river south of Ilesa . . . They were still plagued by kuru at Awarosa and, thus, returned to Mugaiamuti. Later they left for Agakamatasa . . . Likewise the Kasarai people moved south down to sago country at Abonai on the west side of the Yani River, driven from their homelands by the Misapi Gimi" (where they lived for a generation or so). Gajdusek (1967) suggests a Fore origin for the Genatei people: "The Tainoraba peo-

ple . . . state definitely that these people [the Genatei] had migrated here from somewhere in the South Fore after a quarrel in which their group had split, some remaining with the Fore, others coming here."

39. The people of Urai, Umasa, Agakamatasa, Awarosa and Orie did not move far to establish new hamlets.

40. Glasse (1962, p. 10) reports: "Though defeat in warfare was formerly the main reason for parish dispersal, individuals shift residence temporarily or permanently, for many reasons. If in a personal fight a man injures or kills a member of his own parish, usually he leaves voluntarily and remains away until feelings simmer down . . . A man may also leave his parish-territory for a long visit to his matrilateral kin . . . A small percentage of Fore men reside bilocally as a normal practice and maintain gardens on two parish-territories. A few men live several periods of a year or more away from their natal territory; some never return. Thus, Wanitabe clansmen (born at Wanitabe) now live in at least nine other parish-territories: Mentilesa, Purosa-Ketabi and Takai, Agakamatasa, Pusarasa, Amora, Kamira, Yasubi, and Okasa."

41. Lindenbaum and Glasse (1969, pp. 168-69) agree with this in their discussion of Fore age-mate bonds: "Reciprocal support is the cornerstone of the relationship. A man will call for the help of his *nagaiya* in any difficult or dangerous situation . . . Age mates provide sanctuary for each other when a clan is dispersed by war, and they furnish food and lodging at all times."

42. See Scott (1963) for dialect differences and Chapter 5 for genetic differences.

43. In a study of marriage in the South Fore, Glasse (1970, p. 37) made a similar observation: "In New Guinea, those who behave towards one another in a positive, reciprocal manner regard each other as kin . . . Once a man demonstrates his loyalty to a group by appropriate acts and participation in corporate affairs he belongs to the group in a full sense. The other members care little whether he is an agnate, a cognate, or even an unrelated man." Berndt, (1955, p. 184) who believed that North Fore society was patrilineally organized, admitted that "cooperation and common interests (may) entirely modify one's allegiance to one's local clan."

44. That females were more restricted possibly was because they were an indispensible element in marriage exchanges (an important means of establishing and maintaining political and economic liaison between groups) and the principal producers of food. Their failure to be as mobile as males may also be related to their living in smaller houses with more stable memberships than did the men and boys. This may have given them a stronger sense of belonging to particular adults, while at the same time limiting their opportunities for broader close association. It would be a mistake to see the women as pawns in the sociopolitical maneuverings of the men or as food-production resources. Strong bonds of affection and mutual regard existed between those who called each other brother and sister, and it was this mutual regard that was often cited when a girl was protected or returned to her village by her brothers. S. Glasse (1963, p. 3) has also commented on the close relationship between brothers and sisters: "One of the most important kinship ties for a Fore woman is the tie with her

brothers. From early childhood girls show concern for them. A young girl often tells her parents that she wishes to give the produce of her first garden to her brothers. Her parents agree that she should do this and tell her she may expect fine gifts in return. After marriage, too, the girl continues to send food to her brothers and they give her possums or tinned meat, beads, clothing or money. A woman's brothers are an insurance of her protection if she is ill-treated by her husband. The brothers of a Purosa girl . . . said that in the past they took greater care of their sisters than their parents." Even as boys, Fore show concern for the welfare of their sisters, who reciprocate by finding ways to give good food to their brothers, and after her marriage they continue to look out for her welfare.

45. Sometimes polylocality was easier for children than for adults. Children did not have to worry about the need to maintain established socioeconomic relationships—a matter of some concern to adults. Children were not expected to be economically adept or productive. Furthermore, they were welcomed in places where, had they been adults, they would not have been because they were freer of possibly competitive socioeconomic ties. Child mobility was also facilitated by the inclination of most Fore young adults to enjoy the attention of a child attracted to them and looking to them for support and guidance. On the other hand, children were less able migrators than adults because they were small and not as experienced and they lacked the confidence and knowledge needed to negotiate unfamiliar territory.

46. Gajdusek (1963b, p. 78) speaks of Kukukuku (Anga) youngsters who had joined (adopted) him when he had visited their village during a medical survey. They were adopted later by a Fore boys' group. I have witnessed similar occurrences; and boys from remote villages have stuck with me on my travels across the Highlands eventually to become adopted by boys or adults in other villages where they had never been before. In one case, a boy of about nine years followed my expedition further and further away from his home, trying to maintain his welcome by being useful. He became attached to one of the carriers, and when the expedition was ended, he took up residence with this young man and began to call him "father" (devakamba). This boy, who was not Fore, quickly became involved with the peer bands in his new village and began to call some of his new age-mates "brother" (desamu) and others "very close age-mate kinsman" (nagaiya). Lindenbaum and Glasse (1969) explored the nagaiya relationship in some detail; however, they attribute it more specifically to coinitiation or cobirth.

47. Berndt (1955, p. 167) speaking of the Kamano, Usurufa, Yate and North Fore as a unit states: ". . . land may be said to be owned by the patrilineage, the eldest physically able member holding it in trust. . . . The land then belonging to the patrilineage, can be apportioned between the younger members as circumstances demand. . . . Virtually all inheritance of goods takes place through the male patri-line." And (1962, p. 34): "Social relations within the patri-lineage are based upon common agnatic descent."

48. Berndt (1962, p. 24) speaking of just the North Fore states: "Here lineages of the same name occupying different villages within one district consider themselves interrelated whether or not they can work this out genealogically. This relationship cuts across village membership, where the emphasis is on coresidence."

49. Berndt's wife, C. Berndt (1953), speaking more specifically of the Kamano and Usurufa, speaks of their degree of patriliny: "Land is normally owned by and inherited through the patrilineage, shared among its living members."

50. It is this patrilineal bias in the population clusters that I believe led Glasse (1962) to speak of the "patrilineal clan" as the basis of political organization among the South Fore. He qualified this later (Lindenbaum and Glasse 1969, p. 166): "As in other parts of the Highlands unilineal descent is of limited importance and it might be more appropriate to speak of cumulative patrifiliation." In 1970 Glasse (1970, p. 20) departed even further from the patrilineal concept: ". . . to use unilineal terminology suggests a greater concern with formal principles than the people manifest in their speech and behavior. Fore genealogies are short, seldom exceeding five generations; their clans bear local, not ancestral names; people rarely invoke unilineal descent to justify or to sanction social acts; they do not distinguish agnates from non-agnates in the local groups, either in terminology or by different access to clan resources." Glasse and Lindenbaum (1969) take a similar view on the looseness of patriliny among the Fore.

51. Soon after government administration was established, the natives were encouraged to sign government-supervised, two-year labor contracts taking them to jobs on plantations and as laborers for European entrepreneurs. Many Fore boys and young men eagerly seized this opportunity to make money and to go to Europeanized parts of New Guinea. Their eagerness for this approach to new experience and material largess dropped off rather quickly when the first groups returned to their villages not much richer than when they left and with stories of hard, supervised and scheduled work.

52. During a preliminary survey of the Gimi, Keiagana, Auyana, Simbari, Labogai, Chimbu, Usurufa, Kamano and Gahuku, I found child-rearing and socialization practices similar to those of the Fore. Heider (1969) observed that the child-rearing experiences of the Dani were not very different.

53. Even within a given Fore village, there were differences in belief and practice. For example, there was not village-wide agreement on the practice of cannibalism. Some villagers were avid cannibals, and others shunned it. In adjacent villages, where some residents practiced alternative residence among one another, the eating of pythons was viewed differently. Some men thought it would enhance fighting prowess; others thought it debilitating. Similarly, a few Fore groups in the southwest encouraged juvenile sexual activity in the belief that it was helpful in attaining proper adult development, while other Fore discouraged it because they believed it to be injurious and weakening. Juvenile homosexuality was approved in a few eastern fringe hamlets; it was laughed at in other places.

Appendix 1   The Research Film Theory and Method

Introduction

If the techniques of motion picture recording had been available to Herodotus, Xenophon or the chroniclers traveling with Cortez, Magellan or Captain Cook, what sort of cinema record would we today most value from these great voyages? The concept of the research film as a way of preserving the maximum information possible about changing and disappearing ways of life has been shaped by this question.

Very few scholars would today dispute the value of motion pictures such as suggested by the above anachronistic conjecture. If such records existed, they would now be used for endless scientific and historical inquiry and for ends undreamed of by their filmers or the thinkers of the time. Yet, serious scholars would not be totally satisfied with only edited productions dictated by the philosophical and scientific tastes of the time, or with only that footage selected by a filmmaker, according to his idea of what best supported his beliefs or his concept of aesthetic excellence.

Byers (1966) said that "cameras don't take pictures . . . people take pictures." This statement is useful because it cleverly stresses the subjective aspect of photography. But it is only half accurate. While it is true that cameras do not take pictures, it is not true that people take pictures. People only select the pictures to be taken. Quite literally it is the film that *takes* the picture. Its light-sensitive emulsion takes light energy emanating from a scene to produce objective chemical changes that capture a permanent record of the pattern of light received. Because of this, the basic condition in any approach to research filming is the mutual dependence of human selection of what to film and the ability of film to preserve an objective chemical facsimile of the pattern of light it re-ceives. In this equation the camera is only a facilitating device. Its sole purpose is to form under human guidance an image on the film and to control the amount of light admitted in order to produce a readable chemical image of the scene selected.

Although film emulsions record objective visual data, the use of cameras is, nevertheless, dependent on human direction. Thus, whatever is photographed in the field depends on the objectives, desires and personality of the filmer. This intrudes a necessary and important subjective element into the collection of the research filmed data. Although in some special settings, such selectivity may be partially alleviated by use of a randomly directed and triggered camera, nonetheless, in any field investigation and filming program, human selection must play a decisive role. A peculiar myth that has developed in recent years is that anthropological films cannot be scientific because their content is always governed by selective interests. This rather reckless notion ignores the degree to which selectivity and special interest underly *all* scientific inquiry. In research filming, as in science generally, avoidance is not even desirable. It is method that is crucial. In order for visual records of changing ways of life to be a valid scholarly resource, they need to be shaped by scientific methodological considerations that govern the investigation of nonrecurring phenomena. Interpretability and verifiability must be stressed. Credibility is key. This requires that selective factors be indicated in the research films so that future scholars using them can take into account the distortions and emphases that may characterize the filmed record. These selective factors may be indicated in titles, on a narrated soundtrack and in accompanying journals and typescripts.

We cannot always anticipate the questions we and future scholars will find important or meaningful. For this reason, it is important that the full motion picture record be preserved—not just those sequences selected for an edited production. The problem to be faced, when trying to maximize the potential scholarly usefulness of film, is not one of what sequences to keep, but, rather, how to make all the exposed footage and the basic data contained in it usable and recoverable by research workers for study and film presentation.

Research films are therefore not a summation of information, a demonstration of a conclusion or the imposition of an already structured idea or system of knowledge. Rather they serve as a source of material for viewers with research interests in events of the past. In contrast to the production of usual motion pictures, the work of preparing research films is principally that of the extensive identification of subject matter in its original time sequence and the correlation of the filmed data with other associated material. All episodes are identified in time, place and subject, and the filmer's objectives and predilections are indicated. Such research films can be returned to again and again as the source of data for diverse further research stimulated by advances in the methods and findings of the human sciences.

The Research Film Method thus is a means to increase the research potential—present and future —of any film, whether taken for specialized research, demonstration or educational purposes. It is particularly designed to meet the pressing need to preserve unanalyzed data from nonrecurring events such as those of a changing culture. Annotated film records reveal a range of human behavior in its cultural and environmental settings and allow a variety of studies of human behavior, potential and organization that otherwise would be impossible to make. Not only do such phenomenological records capture subtleties and complexities of social interaction and movement unobtainable in any other way, but they also record unappreciated and unanticipated data, thus providing the possibility of sustained reevaluation of early deductions. Research films may therefore serve in lieu of real events no longer accessible to direct research; they contain more information than just that sought or comprehended by the filmer *(see Chapter 8; Theoretical Considerations)*. They are also interpretable in light of the selective factors governing their content, and they provide a basis for substantiation and verifiability of data emerging from unrepeatable events.

Research film footage meant to serve as a scientific or humanistic resource may be distinguished from other kinds of anthropological film primarily by the methods and objectives governing its production. Meant to provide a credible source of information for continued analysis and rework, record footage is different in format and use from films constructed to reveal an anthropologist's understanding of a culture or from films in which a language of visual flow is developed to communicate anthropological insight in new and more powerful ways.

Theoretical Approaches

We may think of four distinct kinds of information that play a role in increasing the scientific usefulness of visual records of passing phenomena: 1) undifferentiated information; 2) structured information; 3) personal insights; and 4) time and space constants.

UNDIFFERENTIATED INFORMATION

Undifferentiated information has not yet been consciously perceived, structured or organized by the human mind. Such information exists everywhere, but for cultural, technical or biological reasons we are not tuned into all of it. At times in the course of history, as well as during crucial stages in our individual lives, becoming aware of such information allows changes in understanding and capability, sometimes leading to new schools of thought, technological breakthrough and broadened possibilities for man's expression of himself. When such information is contained in research records, it becomes a richer source for later discoveries. Because film records a facsimile of visual phenomena by means of objective changes in light-sensitive chemicals, it records considerable unseen and undifferentiated data simultaneously with collection of selected data. Strategies may be devised to increase the content of this kind of information in visual records.

Structured Information

Structured information is that mediated by the human mind. It takes its form from our habitual way of looking at the things around us, according to the concepts, ideas and values bestowed upon us by our training, as limited by the forms of mind and capabilities provided by our evolutionary background. It permits us to handle the continuous phenomena about us symbolically by organizing them into discrete categories and patterns manipulable by rules of language and logic. Such structured information permits us an intellectual grip on experience and gives us the ability to plan our own movements relative to it. It provides the basis for our discussions, conjectures and studies, and is the "known" to which we relate discovery to learn its significance. A research record must be oriented around structured knowledge in order to be grasped intellectually.

The publicly accessible, organized knowledge of a scientific discipline is such a structure. Because they come from an extensive, interlocked body of validated data, scientifically established facts and their measured relationships furnish a basis to which other phenomena can be related and so take on meaning. However, we cannot be sure that the scientific insights we have today will be totally adequate for the research objectives of tomorrow. Thus editing or polishing visual records meant for research (as opposed to reports of research results) is to be avoided. Such structuring sacrifices much of the important undifferentiated information and thus that which remains to be discovered and understood.

Personal Insights

Personal insights and predilections fall somewhere between undifferentiated and structured information and contain elements of both. The selective interests and perceptive eye of individual workers impelled by inclinations, impressions and partially formulated ideas are a powerful force in the discovery of data and the interpretation of it. Research records influenced by such forces reflect the early stages in the formulation of ideas and data from sense impression and make possible analysis of them as no other medium yet has. With such records, an approach to the problem of verifiabil-

ity and substantiation of data coming from unrepeatable field studies becomes possible. Therefore, one must shun attempts to rework, restructure or polish research records to fit subsequently derived ideas or generally accepted aesthetic forms. Such creative manipulation is important for many purposes, but visual records are better without it.

Time and Space Constants

Very fundamental among those structural tools that permit us to analyze and organize phenomena for their precise communication and use are our assumptions of time and spatial order. From the discovery of consistent ways to measure observed phenomena in relation to a postulated, uniform flow of time and a defined geometry of space, much of our contemporary science has been built. And it is primarily on these constants that the precise communication of a scientific construct depends and upon which its validation rests. In many kinds of studies, physical and temporal separation are the critical functions, as when concepts of development, differentiation, diffusion and communication are involved. Because of this, extensive and accurate documentation of time and place is needed in research documents. Records in which the true time sequence of the original phenomena has been disrupted, or in which the places shown are not geographically identifiable, are poorer in their research potential than those that scrupulously preserve such information.

Sampling Strategies

With an eye to the above theoretical considerations and drawing from insights gained during a decade of collecting visual data from disappearing cultures, three basic strategies have emerged.

Although we may, with film, make windows, however small, through which we can review past events, the value of these windows depends on how they are made. How, where and when should these camera windows be placed in order to obtain a potentially more productive or representative sample?

A great wealth of visual information emanates from all natural events. To attempt a "complete" record of even a small event would be a fruitless pursuit of an unachievable fantasy. Many more than thousands of "channels" would be needed to show "all" micro and macro views of everything from all angles and perspectives. We can only *sample*.

In my own research filming efforts, I have found that we increase the potential scientific value of visual records of passing phenomena by adopting a basic tripartite sampling strategy based on *Opportunistic Sampling, Programmed Sampling* and *Digressive Search*. These strategies permit us to 1) seize the opportunity we "see," 2) take advantage of the collective knowledge of our culture, and 3) look into the unknown. They take advantage of the unique ability of film emulsions to preserve a chemical facsimile of unrecognized and unappreciated visual information, and they parallel three basic elements of scientific inquiry: 1) the significance-recognizing capability of the human mind; 2) an accepted, rationalized body of knowledge; and 3) the desire to learn.

Opportunistic Sampling

Seize opportunities. When something interesting happens, pick up the camera and shoot. Opportunistic filming, a freewheeling yet indispensable approach to visual documentation of naturally occurring phenomena, takes advantage of events as they develop in unfamiliar settings.

Some degree of opportunistic filming is useful in filming any natural event. The world in its dynamic diversity continually churns out transformations. We can never fully anticipate what is going to happen or when or how it will occur. What is "normal" here and now may not be so later or elsewhere. Expectations, insofar as they are constructed from past experience and patterns of awareness, are not completely reliable as guides of what will come. Opportunistic filming documents unanticipated and poorly understood phenomena as they occur. It relies on that most basic tool of discovery and the source of all our knowledge, the individual human mind. It uses to advantage the selective interests and perceptive eye of individual workers by tapping intuition, impression and partially formulated ideas.

When a photographer is filming opportunistically, he flows with the events of the day and cues into them at some personal level, suddenly noticing that "something" is about to happen and following such events intuitively, without a worked-out plan. He takes it as it comes. Thus, the visual data sample achieved reflects the personality of the filmer: It takes its form and content from his interests, inclinations and style. But by linking the camera to the pattern-recognizing capability of the human mind, the visual sample reflects prearticulated stages of discovery. Such footage may not always be directly relevant to a predetermined scientific study, but it can be a powerful resource in the quest for knowledge.

Because observers with or without cameras always affect what is observed, opportunistic film records made during early contact help to reveal the nature of the influence. As a setting reacts to the presence of fieldworkers, subtle transformations and adaptive restructuring of relationships, attitudes and responses begin to take place. The kinds of information fieldworkers get often depend upon the nature of the relationships that they develop with selected persons and things within the community. An early record, continued through the familiarization period, makes it easier to see the nature of the change and thus to gauge the effect of one's own presence on the situation being documented.

In spite of its advantages, opportunistic sampling remains an unformulated sampling procedure. It allows us to cope with an unfamiliar situation profitably but according to a personal style that is not always, and never completely, obvious. Its major strength as well as its weakness is that selection of the sample is controlled by the interests and personality of the photographer. One of its most important advantages is that it allows the cameraman to flow with and in fact be controlled by the events as an integral part of the scene.

Programmed Sampling

Programmed sampling is filming according to a predetermined plan—deciding in advance what, where and when to film. It is therefore based on a cognitive framework and a concept of significance. Pictures are taken according to a preconceived structure: There are pigeonholes to fill.

A program can be very simple (e.g., taking pictures of a single category of activity, such as nursing behavior or agricultural practice) or it can be a complex attempt to sample broadly.

Like opportunistic sampling, the programmed approach also relies on human interests and ideas, but instead of unstated personal impressions and inclinations, a formulated statement governs the filming. This makes programmed visual samples easier to interpret and more scientific. They extend beyond the narrower, personal preoccupations of an individual to take advantage of the accumulated, systematized and articulated knowledge that unites him with colleagues and a cultural heritage.

Programmed sampling depends on structured information rather than intuitions and inclinations to guide the filmer. This structured information takes its form from our articulated way of viewing things according to the concepts, ideas and values bestowed upon us by our training and background. It provides us with a means of dealing symbolically with the undifferentiated phenomena about us by relating them to discrete categories manipulable through rules of language and logic. Structured information gives us an intellectual grip on experience and enables us to plan our own movements relative to it. It provides an anchor for discussion, conjecture and study, and is the "known" to which we relate discovery in order to learn its significance.

A postulated uniform flow of time and a defined geometry of space are indispensable structural concepts in the scientific analysis and description of phenomena. They are fundamental in the construction and validation of scientific knowledge. In studies dealing with development, differentiation, diffusion or communication, physical and temporal separation are the critical functions. Thus, time and space parameters must be part of any research filming program.

Programming the sampling procedure according to any stated conceptual model is also useful. Not only do such models bring order into our minds and help us to "see" into the muddle of the real world, but they also enable us to place the footage shot in a more clearly defined context both for ourselves and for others.

Thus, programmed sampling helps to break the egocentricity of opportunistic sampling by imposing a comprehensible structure over the often hard-to-grasp vagaries of human inclination. It does this by drawing from the public knowledge of a culture. However, programmed samples represent ethnocentric distillations of human interests, desires and inclinations. But because of the more public nature of ethnocentric bias, especially in cultures with written histories, the skewing effect can be taken into consideration more readily than in opportunistic samples.

DIGRESSIVE SEARCH

Neither programmed nor opportunistic sampling solves the problem of how to branch out beyond our personal predilections or the structural concepts of our culture. Programmed sampling is limited to preconceived ideas about what is important to document. In essence, it prejudges importance and therefore misses categories of events not considered. Opportunistic sampling avoids this problem by deliberately taking advantage of unanticipated events, but because it is subject to the personal inclinations and vision of the photographer, it, too, prejudices and skews the sample, but in a less decipherable way.

A digressive search helps to solve these difficulties by deliberately intruding into the "blank areas," i.e. those places and events outside our range of recognition or appreciation. This tactic allows us, somewhat blindly at first, to expand our vision as we visually sample and document events alien to our structured formats and habitual shooting instincts. By digressing inquisitively, we may penetrate areas and situations peripheral to our attention, beyond our range of awareness or comprehension, and interstitial to our points of view and predilections.

This kind of sampling requires that we turn our attention away from the obvious to the novel—even to what may seem pointless, aberrant or meaningless. We have to be purposefully digressive, in both space and subject matter, turning our gaze from the familiar and "important" to events that appear incoherent and insignificant. A randomness must be intruded into the way we direct attention; I have also called the digressive search semirandomized (1973). We must sample in places we know nothing of or in areas lying between the kinds of locales and events to which

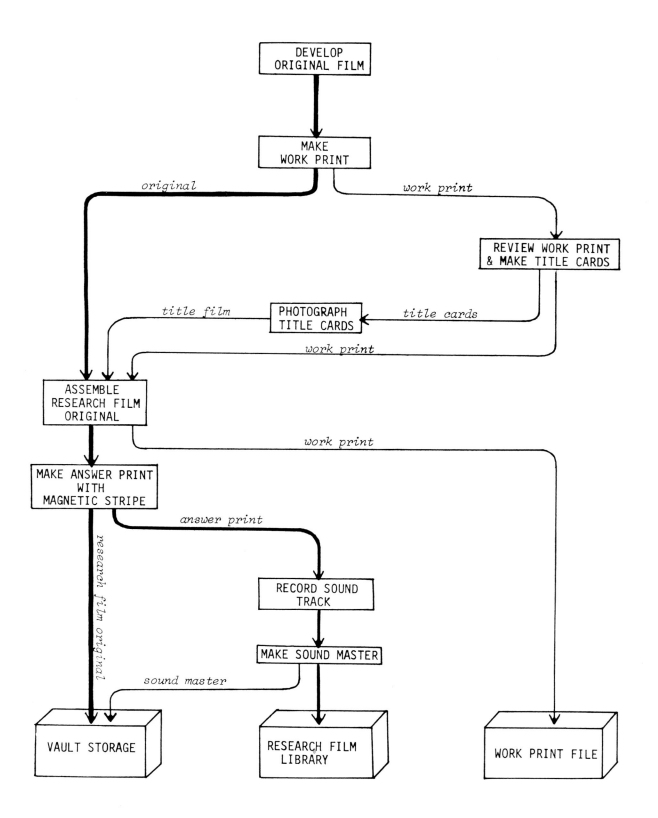

FIGURE 150. BASIC STEPS IN THE PRODUCTION OF RESEARCH CINEMA FILMS.

our sampling program or interests are anchored.

Digressive tactics such as these can broaden a visual data sample beyond the originally defined scope of a programmed sample and the undefined scope of habitual and unstated shooting predilections. To extend our observations and visual data sampling into fringe areas of understanding and attention, and thus beyond presumption and habit, is deliberately to add unanticipated, interstitial visual information to the research film sample. It is in this aspect that the greatest potential of research filming as a tool for discovery may lie.

*   *   *

The theoretical format underlying research filming as developed during this study relies on three basic general strategies: (1) seizing the opportunity we "see"; (2) taking advantage of the collective knowledge of our culture; and (3) looking into the unknown. These strategies take advantage of the unique ability of film emulsions to record unrecognized and unappreciated visual information objectively. They parallel three basic elements of scientific inquiry: (1) the significant-recognizing capability of the human mind; (2) an accepted, rationalized body of knowledge; and (3) the desire to learn.

Each of the three basic strategies has its own merits. Opportunistic sampling can be quite easy, particularly in unfamiliar or novel situations. Opportunistic sampling also permits a flexibility in approach, which allows greatest advantage to be taken of personal impressions and insights.

On the other hand, programmed sampling enables us to take advantage of the parameters and structural concepts that have already been developed and proved significant (at least in our own culture). Such programs, drawing from sources broader than just ourselves, help us to sample more comprehensively and lead us to types of events that would otherwise escape attention. They also give us a starting point in an unfamiliar situation and the explanation of what we are doing among the people we may be filming. The articulated existence of such filming programs makes the visual samples obtained more widely intelligible and interpretable. Furthermore, when a program asks for things that cannot be found, attention is directed to an absence that in itself may be significant.

Both programmed and opportunistic sampling rely on forms of mind and habit reflecting the past: They depend either on the state of publicly accepted knowledge as developed through history, or on the sensory abilities, interests and habits provided by human evolutionary background, as programmed by his life experiences.

We may begin to move away from these limitations by adopting a deliberately digressive (or semirandomized) search and, with camera in hand, by recording what we may neither appreciate nor "see." Such an approach allows us to increase the content of unrecognized information in a visual record by moving, even if blindly, beyond the constraints of either personal intuition or sophisticated program, to document ahead of understanding and awareness. A digressive search makes it possible deliberately to impregnate the visual sample with information yet to be discovered.

Each of the three strategies has advantages and disadvantages. Each skews the sample in a different way. But in concert, they begin to balance one another so as to increase the informative potential of the visual records.

Annotation

As stated above, precise documentation of time and place are usually required for developing scientific constructs. Indeed, much of the disenchantment with film as a scientific resource can be traced to the failure of adequately preserving the time and place information of the event filmed. Such failure makes it impossible confidently to interrelate parts of the films or to correlate what is seen with other data, such as specimens, written records, still photographs, tapes, weather reports, ethnographic notes, political activity and government reports.

The traditional methods of movie making do not make it easy to preserve the necessary time and place information rigorously with film. As a result, many research efforts have been impaired. Irreparable mixups have occurred when films were processed, stored or edited. Because of this, it is wise to put permanent time and place identifications into the original filmed record.

No film record independent of the subjective interests of the filmer is possible. One of the important limitations affecting programs aimed at the collection of data on changing and vanishing ways of life and culture is that completely objective records are unachievable. To film at all is to film selectively. However, this is not as much of a drawback as it might seem at first glance. It is important to recognize that in film inquiry, as in all types of inquiry, the selective interests and perceptive eye of the inquirer are among the most valuable forces at work in the discovery of data and in its interpretation. To that degree that selective interests of the filmer can be made known in research films, the data contained in the films becomes more accessible and usable to other scholars.

Many of these subjective influences operating on the selection of material filmed can be documented so as to make it possible for intelligent users to make valuable deductions with reference to them. Major selective factors, such as the purpose for which the filming project was undertaken, can be stated in titles, as can the perhaps more subtle influence of the sponsoring institution. The names of the filmer (and his coworkers) who influenced the use of the camera can also be included in titles. Circumstances not apparent from viewing the film, but that had an affect on the behavior of the filmed subject (or the cameraperson's activity) can be mentioned and discussed in a narrated synched soundtrack. The more subtle psychological factors that influence the filmer become increasingly evident as more of his work becomes known. And a most valuable source of such data can come from a personal journal kept daily during the fieldwork in which observations, ideas, plans, interests and frustrations are discussed. Detailed camera logs can also be useful in revealing many of the forces that influence the behavior of both the camerapersons and the subject.

The Method of Assembling Research Films

The research film assembly method is a means to increase the research potential—present and future—of film taken for any purpose, including specialized research, demonstration or education.

It has been designed to meet the pressing need to preserve unanalyzed data from nonrecurring events, such as those of changing culture, and to do so within the limits of today's financial exigencies. The research films produced by this method preserve more information than just that sought or comprehended by the filmer; they are meant to be interpretable in light of the selective factors governing their content; and they provide an approach to the important problem of substantiation and verifiability in studies based on unrepeatable events.

This method evolved during the course of the study of the Fore, as follows:

1) Each roll of film was identified as to time, place and subject, as it was taken out of the camera. In addition, a watch was photographed at least once in each camera roll to facilitate chronological assembly of the films and to permit correction in cases of mixup by the film laboratory.

2) Before being sent to the processor, the exposed rolls of film were lined up in chronological order and assembled in batches of 800 to 1,200 feet per batch on the basis of the evident natural groupings imposed by time or subject matter.

3) Each roll in each batch was serially numbered to correspond to the order in which it was filmed. The processor was instructed to assemble and process them in this order and return the developed film on a single core, accompanied by a work print.

4) The work print was examined to make sure the correct order was maintained during processing; errors were corrected by moving the out-of-place rolls in both the work print and original film to their correct chronological positions by referring to the picture of the dating watch in them.

5) The work print was reviewed for final verification of correctness of order. Titles were composed to be placed in the film at each major change in time, place or subject. Introductory titles gave the general name of the people or peoples filmed, the name of the region in which the filming took place, the inclusive dates of filming covered by the reel, and a brief statement of the purpose of filming. Sheets of paper on which these titles were written were numbered, and a corresponding number was placed on a piece of tape put on the work print where the title was to be inserted.

6) Technically useless footage, where no image remained, was cut out of the work print. Technically poor but informative material was retained.

7) Title cards were composed and photographed for each of the numbered titles.

8) After development of the title film, the numbered work print was used as the guide to splice the titles into each reel of original film, as indicated by the numbered tabs on the work print.

9) A timed print with a magnetic recording strip was made from the assembled original. This print was used for the analysis.

10) Matching series of reference edge numbers were sequentially printed along the edges of the print and original, so that a sequence in one could be found in the other by referring to these numbers.

11) The research print was reviewed for insurance of correct assemblage and for familiarization with its contents preparatory to narrating background information onto the magnetic soundtrack.

12) With the use of a projector with magnetic recording and erase heads, additional information relating to the events filmed and to circumstances of filming was narrated from memory, aided by notes, onto the magnetic soundtrack. Mistakes were corrected and revisions made by reversing the projector and re-recording the section in question in the same manner in which one would use a tape recorder. Usually this was done extemporaneously on the first run of the film through the projector, although sometimes the print was studied carefully first.

13) The sound on the magnetic stripe was copied onto 16mm magnetic film to serve as a sound master. The research film was not used for study until after this sound master was made, in order to protect against loss by accidental erasure, physical damage to the stripe or breaks in the film.

14) The projection print was deposited in the research film library along with associated copies of field notes, journals, charts, maps, logs, appended typescripts, still pictures and tape recordings.

15) The research film original and its sound master have been stored in the film vault at less than 40°F and between 35% and 38% relative humidity.

16) Abstracts and indexed descriptions of the contents of the films were prepared.

Appendix 2   Abstracts of the Initial Body of Research Films

The following research films, on which the study of Fore child behavior was based, are now preserved as a permanent scholarly resource in the National Research Film Collection of the Smithsonian Institution. Inquiries related to their use may be made to the Coordinator, Research Film Studies, National Anthropological Film Center, Smithsonian Institution, Washington, D.C. 20560. Use of the films is usually restricted to individuals engaged in scholarly studies requiring them.

63-12A *SOUTH FORE Kuru Survey I; Villages of Agakamatasa, Miarasa, Ketabi, Waisa and Wanitabe, Eastern Highlands, East New Guinea; September 16–20, 1963.*
16 mm Kodak Commercial Ektachrome, 24 frs./sec., narrated and synchronous field sound, 936 ft., 26 min.

Most of the film is devoted to neurological examinations by Dr. Jon Hancock, medical officer stationed at the Okapa Patrol Post, of two kuru victims. One of these (Kabuinampa) is filmed with synchronous sound and includes a medical history with translation between Neo-Melanesian Pidgin and Fore by a native medical assistant.

In Agakamatasa village, there are several children who had gathered at the Medical Aid Post, two visiting Simbari Kukukuku's, and an Awa mother with her toddler. The toddler plays close to his seated mother and occasionally makes short sorties to objects in the immediate vicinity. Many of the preadolescent children of Agakamatasa coquettishly avoid the camera, while seeming to invite further camera attention. There are panoramas of the Agakamatasa Aid Post, the grounds surrounding Akilankamuti hamlet of Wanitabe, and of Anati hamlet of Waisa village.

63-12B *NORTH FORE AUYANA; Congenital Tremor Survey, Eastern Highlands, East New Guinea; September 22–23, 1963.*
16 mm Kodak Commercial Ektachrome, 24 frs./sec., narrated and synchronous field sound, 1,158 ft., 32 min.

Medical examinations of the tremor victims are conducted by Dr. Jon Hancock. The examination of Arufu is filmed with synchronous field sound, as is part of that of Koko. Instructions are given by Dr. Hancock in Neo-Melanesian Pidgin and translated into and from Auyana by a native medical assistant.

A somewhat dissimilar clinical picture is characteristic of each: Koko displayed a marked tremor around the mouth and tongue; Arufu had a side-to-side tremor of the head and marked dysarthria; and Aokapara had a severe extrapyramidal tremor involving arms and legs, weakness and an apparently paralytic strabismus.

Sequences taken in Okasa, en route to the Auyana, show the inspection of the medical aid station by Dr. Hancock, the camp site at the government rest house at Okasa and the several people from the village who had gathered. An affectionate young girl sits between the legs of her seated father as other preadolescent girls playfully dash away out of camera view in a coquettish manner, seemingly designed to attract further attention. In Arora, very young children run when frightened by the camera, as older children and adults stand about watching. Koko is seen together with her daughter, granddaughter and great-grandson.

63-12C *SOUTH FORE Kuru Survey II; Villages of Okapa, Miarasa, Kaga and Yasubi, Eastern Highlands, East New Guinea; September 25–27, 1963.*
16 mm Kodak Commercial Ektachrome, 24 frs./sec., narrated sound, 577 ft., 16 min.

Major attention is given to several kuru victims. However, occasional sequences show some of the country, hamlets and people encountered. A small child plays haphazardly with a knife; several sequences show the site of a new hamlet under construction and the fitting and attaching of prefabricated *pitpit* wall sections to the house framework. Among the group following the patrol, there is a variety of skin tone in the children; a small boy walks with a typical Fore posture, with arms about shoulders; a young girl tends a younger sibling; and several children are seen in the hamlet adjacent to the Miarasa haus kiap as a light rain begins to fall. From Okapa, a panorama shows some of the grounds, including a few European-style houses, distant hills and valleys of Awande and Tarabo villages and the summit of Mt. Michael.

63-12D *SOUTH FORE Kuru Survey III; Villages of Wanitabe, Kamira, Ketabi, Amora, Kume and Yagareba, Eastern Highlands, East New Guinea; October 2–10, 1963.*
16 mm Kodak Commercial Ektachrome, 24 frs./sec., narrated sound, 1,215 ft., 34 min.

Although major attention is given to persons with kuru, the camera was diverted occasionally to show geographical settings, child behavior and hamlet surroundings in the places visited. Included are panoramas of several hamlets and their surroundings. Mothers nurse, fondle, delouse and play with their infants; a father shields his daughter's eyes from the camera; and children are carried and lifted and are seen crying and being comforted. They climb fences and use small practice bows to shoot stems of *kunai* grass. House construction is under way in some hamlets.

63-12E *SOUTH FORE Kuru Survey IV; Villages of Wanitabe, Kamira and Yagareba, Eastern Highlands, East New Guinea; October 11–16, 1963.*
16 mm Kodak Commercial Ektachrome, 24 frs./sec., narrated sound, 1,543 ft., 43 min.

The proportion of the total reel devoted to kuru victims is small, the bulk centering on other activities going on in the hamlets of the kuru region. Several sequences show the plaiting of the flattened *pitpit* grass stalks into prefabricated walls for new houses under construction. Bundles of *pitpit* stalks are brought in from nearby fields, flattened by beating and slit with a bamboo knife. Repeated sequences over the course of a day cover the manufacture of a stone axe haft and the binding onto it of a stone axe head. These include the location of an appropriate branch in the top of a tree, the cutting of the tree top, its trimming, the fashioning of the branch into a traditional haft, and its binding onto the stone axe head. In the course of documenting the wall construction section and axe manufacture, the camera, with zoom lens, repeatedly focuses on children in the hamlet yards as they move about and play. A boy of about three years of age is seen as he repeatedly and idly hacks and whittles a sliver of bamboo, first with a knife and then with a machete. Children gather about a fire to warm themselves and cook ears of corn. Affection and indulgence for the very young children by the older is evident. Incipient modesty is seen as a young boy with obvious satisfaction tests the covering characteristics of a new *laplap* (wrap-around lower garment introduced by Westerners). Young children are tumbled and lifted; one tries to balance on a *pitpit* bundle; they walk, run and nurse, and are seen in attitudes of preoccupation, play and aggression. One toddler repeatedly hits a seated man with a *pitpit* stalk, and a girl of about eight years of age delivers cooked food to a relative and waits for him to receive it. A man considered by his villagers to be *longlong*, the Pidgin expression for dementia or a behavior peculiarity, prances, runs about and pretends to shoot arrows.

63-12F *SOUTH FORE Music; Wanitabe village, Eastern Highlands, East New Guinea; October 22 and 26, 1963.*
16 mm Kodak Commercial Ektachrome, 24 frs./sec., synchronously recorded field sound, 635 ft., 15 min.

Filmed entirely on the land of Wanitabe village with synchronously recorded sound, this film is of Fore flute playing and *singsing*. The first part is in the rainforest at a place of spirits of the Wanitabians, where a demonstration of the playing of the Fore sacred flutes by several Wanitabe men takes place. This is followed by a Wanitabe man who was discovered singing a song as he fashioned an axe haft near his hamlet.

63-12G *SOUTH FORE Kuru Survey V; Villages of Yagareba, Yasubi, Amora, Wanitabe, Ketabi and Waisa, Eastern Highlands, East New Guinea; October 27–31, 1963.*
16 mm Kodak Commercial Ektachrome, 24 frs./sec., narrated sound, 1,600 ft., 44.5 min.

In addition to the attention given to kuru victims, there are also sequences of an achrondroplastic dwarf, women working in a garden and several episodes of activity among children of Keiamungagori hamlet. A brother and sister sit close and occasionally hug. Their dispute over a discarded cigarette box is resolved after a gesture of displeasure, as both play casually with it. Nearby, a young boy of about six years squirms about and swings a stick while in the lap of his mother. She, somewhat annoyed, puts him down on the ground. Her son responds by hitting and poking her with a stick before running off grinning in a stylized, dancelike movement to join his father. An infant is carried by his sister to his mother to nurse.

63-12H *KANITE NORTH FORE, KAMANO; Congenital Tremor Survey; Eastern Highlands, East New Guinea; November 1, 1963.*
16 mm Kodak Tri-X, 24 frs./sec., synchronous field sound, 1,160 ft., 32 min.

This is the film record of a medical survey to locate, examine and film persons in the Kanite, Kamano and North Fore linguistic groups who have previously been reported to have an unusual tremor syndrome called *Kogaisantamba* by the Auyana and *tavaravain avie* or *kogaisa en avie* by the Fore. The persons seen here had come to various points along the Okapa to Kainantu Land Rover road and are examined by Dr. Jon Hancock. His examination and interview are recorded with synchronous sound-translation between Neo-Melanesian Pidgin and the native languages.

63-12I *SOUTH FORE Wedding Feast; Kagumuti hamlet, Wanitabe village; Eastern Highlands, East New Guinea; November 2, 1963.*
16 mm Kodak Commercial Ektachrome, 24 frs./sec., two soundtracks (narration and synchronous field sound), 1,210 ft., 33 min.

Filmed entirely during the course of the day of a South Fore wedding feast, about 80% of the film is with synchronously recorded field sound. This wedding feast marked the transition of Abeiya, a girl who had been living in Kagumuti hamlet, to a married woman. Gifts of food, net bags and the full skirts of the married women were presented and fastened upon her in a short ceremony at the end of the feast. Filming was done at various intervals during the day with the attention given to pig butchering and food preparation in the social atmosphere in which they occur. The children as they play with the parts of the raw pig's carcass, assist in the preparation of the food, play idly with each other and are cared for by older siblings or relatives.

63-12J *SOUTH FORE Kuru Survey VI; Villages of Ketabi and Amora; Eastern Highlands, East New Guinea; November 3 and 22, 1963.*
16 mm Kodak Tri-X and Commercial Ektachrome, 24 frs./sec., synchronous field and narrated sound, 546 ft., 15 min.

This film is restricted to the medical examinations of kuru victims. Kabuinampa is examined by Dr. Jon Hancock with his questions and instructions recorded synchronously with the filming. Dialogue is in Neo-Melanesian Pidgin and South Fore, with translations by a native medical assistant. Kabuinampa was unable to stand or walk without support, maintain a posture of outstretched hands, or adequately perform the heel shin test. Her speech was slurred, but she was able to reply intelligently to questions asked. On direct questioning, she complained of pain in the knees but nowhere else. There was slight titubation of head and trunk and marked intention tremor. Extraocular movements were normal, and there was no strabismus. Deep tendon reflexes were normal; plantar responses flexor; and sensation in the feet apparently normal. During the examination, she showed an almost constant dull smile.

Dr. Paul Brown examined Tigi and Isu briefly. Tigi's reflexes appeared essentially normal, as did the finger to finger test. Isu showed a typical kuru tremor of the legs, which was accentuated by an unsupported posture. He demonstrated brisk deep tendon reflexes and a marked left internal strabismus with an ability, nevertheless, to deviate the left eye laterally.

63-12K *SOUTH FORE Initiation Feast; Poiagori hamlet of Waisa village, Eastern Highlands, East New Guinea; November 26, 1963.*
16 mm Kodak Commercial Ektachrome, 24 frs./sec., narrated sound, 780 ft., 21.5 min.

The sequences in this reel were taken on the day of the initiation feast for a boy of Waisa village. While the boy remained in seclusion in the initiation house, preparation of the feast is documented. After the opening of the cooking pit, the initiate, with escort, comes out of the house long enough to be dressed in new clothing and receive the sizeable gifts of food.

During the feast preparation, the camera focuses repeatedly on the activities of the children in the feast area and on the adults preparing the food. Young children climb, fall, nurse, run, eat, throw sticks, play with knives and stones, explore their surroundings and react to accidental annoyances. They are lifted and carried and are the subjects of affectionate and tolerant actions by older children and adults.

While women prepare food, men prepare the cooking pit. One woman weaves a net bag as she sits waiting. Among the assembled people is Tatobi, a man with an un-kuru-like tremor, who claimed to have been previously diagnosed as having kuru.

63-12L *SOUTH FORE Kuru Survey VII; Villages of Ketabi and Wanitabe, Eastern Highlands, East New Guinea; November 28, 1963.*
16 mm Kodak Tri-X, 24 frs./sec., narrated sound, 412 ft., 11.5 min.

The first half of the film is devoted to a neurological examination of Kabuinampa of Ketabi by Dr. Paul Brown. She is in the terminal stage of kuru and shows very little spontaneous movement. A number of large decubitis ulcers are present, and there is an apparent edema of the feet. Tendon reflexes are still present normally in the arms, extraocular movements appear normal, and there is no strabismus. Kabuinampa has a fixed grimace but is able to cooperate intelligently in the examination and to follow a finger with her eyes. There is a short panorama of Wesnari hamlet.

The second half of the film is devoted to showing the evasive, seductive and coquettish avoidance behavior of young South Fore girls at Wanitabe village. They had been en route from gardens to their hamlets, and emboldened by the presence of several young boys visiting the research house, they also stopped. Their behavior is characterized by flashing eyes and giggling retreats whenever attention is paid to them. The commotion caused by this attracted more girls from nearby Akilankamuti hamlet, who run up to join in the same game of alternating advancing and retreating. Some of the girls carry infants on their backs. Akilankamuti hamlet is seen briefly in panorama.

63-12M *SOUTH FORE Marriage Payment Feast; Yemagori hamlet of Ketabi village, Eastern Highlands, East New Guinea; December 1, 1963.*
16 mm Kodak Commercial Ektachrome and High Speed Ektachrome, 24 frs./sec., narrated sound, 556 ft., 15 min.

Although the wedding had been completed months earlier, a bride payment feast was celebrated, as payment had not been fully made. Several pigs were cooked and other valuable items such as tapa, newspaper, sugar cane and vegetables were brought for distribution to the appropriate relatives of the bride. Piles of tapa are rolled up in preparation for presentation, dead pigs lie about and are butchered, and the gifts are bundled up in parcels. One woman holds a newborn baby and another carries her two infants, one under each arm. Children inflate the discarded bladders of the pigs like balloons; and as men butcher and women prepare vegetables, children sit about or play in the hamlet yard. Some infants show the typical fear reaction to being approached by strangers. Stones are heated before placing them in the cooking pit; pig skins are seared; and meat and vegetables are placed on top of steaming rocks in the pits and covered with leaves and dirt. Water is poured into the sealed pits through bamboo tubes extending down to the hot stones in the bottom. Men remove the food when it has been cooked, and the feast participants sit about eating before carrying the excess off to their homes. Food preparation includes peeling sweet potato; trimming and peeling *pitpit*; bundling sweet potato, *pitpit* and other vegetables; and placing the bundles of food in the cooking pit.

63-13A *SOUTH FORE Children I; Villages of Waisa and Wanitabe, Eastern Highlands, East New Guinea; December 6 and 8, 1963.*
16 mm Kodak Commercial Ektachrome, 24 frs./sec., narrated sound, 994 ft., 28 min.

This is the first reel of a series dealing with the study of child behavior in the South Fore. Although the concentration of this study was the South Fore children in Waisa village, where much data in other forms were also collected, this first reel deals primarily with the children's activities in nearby Wanitabe village. There are many sequences of children, predominantly between three and 10 years of age, playing in a very large rain puddle. There are also fright reactions to strangers by toddlers who seek solace in close contact with older children or attempt to hide in thick *pitpit* and *kunai* grass. Nakedness modesty is demonstrated by a young boy, whose many age-mates still wear nothing; and the typical coquettish shyness of the Fore girls is seen in an adolescent girl bartering food.

During the course of the filming, the camera was diverted several times to record the thatching of the roofs of two of the new houses under construction in Akilankamuti hamlet of Wanitabe. The *kunai* grass is tied into bundles and then inserted and bent into and around the closely spaced supports of the roof. Women bring additional grass from nearby *kunai* fields, and a young girl delivers small bundles of the grass from the ground to her father on the roof via a rickety ladder with a broken rung.

The latter part of the film deals with the beginning of the child study at Waisa village. Among the curious children visiting the research house, there is a protracted oral play between two brothers, the older of whom is repeatedly and playfully bitten by the younger in a peculiar puppylike frolicking, seemingly generated by shyness in the younger. During the course of this play a younger sister sleeps in her older brother's lap. Nearby a posttoddler demonstrates the typical fright of the young Fore children to strangers.

63-13B *SOUTH FORE Children II; Kamira and Waisa villages; Eastern Highlands, East New Guinea; December 9–13, 1963.*
16 mm Kodak Commercial Ektachrome and Tri-X, 24 frs./sec., narrated sound, 821 ft., 23 min.

This film opens with a long sequence of a neurological examination of Oreke, a nine-year-old boy with kuru, showing patellar knee jerk, ankle jerk, right biceps reflex, muscle tone and eye follow. Throughout the examination the severe ataxia (trunkal and of extremities) and kuru tremor of limbs, trunk and head are apparent. Strabismus is present.

The rest of the film concentrates on children in various hamlets of Waisa village. Several are seen climbing small trees. An older child defers to a smaller youngster, relinquishing a film wrapper on the insistent demands of the younger. A small girl also tries to climb in the trees but is discouraged as a smaller boy hits her head several times. She withdraws to swing back and forth from the tree trunk and moves away in a somewhat stylized, dancelike movement. In another hamlet, a feast is in preparation and many sequences show preparation of the food. Mothers are with children and there is eating and nursing. In yet another hamlet a woman spins the fibers from tree bark into a string, which will later be woven into a net bag. Another woman nurses her child, who crouches to his mother and holds her breast in his mouth without sucking, as the camera approaches.

63-13C *SOUTH FORE Hamlets; Village of Waisa, Eastern Highlands, East New Guinea; December 14, 1963.*
16 mm Kodak Commercial Ektachrome, 24 frs./sec., narrated sound, 1,048 ft., 29 min.

The bulk of this film is the result of an attempt to visit and photograph many of the hamlets of Waisa village and to make panoramas of other villages on distant hillsides, ridges and valleys that are visible from the Waisa grounds. Waisa hamlets are seen in closeup, and the more distant inhabited sites are seen by telephotography during panorama. Along the trails are garden sites situated in the bush between hamlets. A few people are seen moving along these trails: One boy drinks from a small stream, and another munches on raw *kumu* discovered growing wild along the trail. A woman

and girl carry *kunai* grass for house thatching to their hamlet, and two girls work in a remote garden. In the hamlets are a few people. One man weaves a basket, and in another hamlet a young boy runs away from the camera. Another small boy attempts to cross a difficult stile and is helped by older boys.

During a respite at Yagoenti ground, several boys play. One clowns by taking large mouthfuls of grass and jumping and twisting about in a pseudodemented fashion, very much like the few oddly behaved people called *longlong* in the region; there is play, mimicking traditional dances with the binding back of the lips; some boys climb and swing on a vine suspended over the Mugagarampa gorge; others spontaneously start to wrestle, with almost all the boys joining in briefly; and a small boy playfully and repeatedly menaces an older boy with a stick and throws stones at another.

63-13D *SOUTH FORE Children III; Village of Waisa, Eastern Highlands, East New Guinea; December 15, 1963.*
16 mm Kodak Commercial Ektachrome, 24 frs./sec., narrated sound, 1,130 ft., 31 min.

Most of this film is devoted to the activities of children at the typical Fore feasts where the food is cooked en masse in a pit in the ground for a large number of people. One feast takes place in the largest hamlet of Waisa; and, as is customary in the larger feasts, the men and women sit in separate areas during the preparation, cooking and eating of the food. Most of the photographic attention is on the children, who play among the adults and in nearby weeds, deliver food to and receive food from adults, help in the preparation of the food to be cooked, play in the dirt, run, crawl, walk, eat and nurse. Older children are tolerant and amused when hit by toddlers, although they sometimes playfully snatch the object with which they are being hit and even occasionally lightly and somewhat mockingly wrestle with the toddler. One toddler, learning to walk, uses a stick for balance as he practices taking a few steps upright by himself. Another child in pursuit of a rooster is followed by a toddler, who repeatedly trips and falls. One toddler pulling the hair of another has his hand gently, almost casually removed by his mother.

Another much smaller, family-sized feast is seen in preparation in one of the very small hamlets. Girls peel sweet potato, and a man breaks the tops from *pitpit* stalks, while stones are being heated on a fire preparatory to being pushed into the cooking pit.

During the visits to other hamlets in the Waisa region, gardens, rain shelters, trails and hamlets are seen. Young boys en route along the trails stick flower petals to their faces, eat raw *kumu (agatno)*, and drink water from rivulets and springs. In Anati hamlet an old house, no longer used, is burned, and work on other new houses is in progress. Women clear ground for foundations of new houses in front of others nearing completion.

63-13E *SOUTH FORE Children IV; Waisa village, Eastern Highlands, East New Guinea; December 16, 1963.*
16 mm Kodak Commercial Ektachrome, 24 frs./sec., narrated sound, 1,155 ft., 32 min.

A 360° panorama from the Palontavinti hilltop in Waisa

village reveals five hamlets of Waisa village and 12 hamlets of surrounding South Fore villages. There are telephoto zoom views of each inhabited site.

Near Mimori, as two boys bathe in a stream, one boy manages to shame the other into lending his soap, a prized item among the Fore. This Fore technique is frequently used to gain the use of the property of another without directly requesting it.

The bulk of the film was taken in Mugagori hamlet where a feast was in progress. Its preparation includes views of women preparing vegetables and men pushing stones, preheated on the nearby fire, into the cooking pit; placing bundles of food into the pit; and sealing the pit with banana leaves. Some of the women cook *kumu,* an edible leaf, in bamboo cooking cylinders on separate small fires. One boy helps his mother start such a fire by helping her bring burning branches from another fire. Among the people attending the feast, one boy hugs his infant cousin, a man watches over an infant as he plays with a plate, a small girl carries her infant brother, another girl sucks her fingers and plays with her lip, a mother prechews sugar cane for her infant son and an adolescent girl chases chickens. A toddler defecates in the hamlet yard while his mother and a girl clean up previous discharges, and his mother finally takes him off to clean him up. Another toddler plays with an axe head and later hits an age-mate with a stick, causing nearby children to laugh as they take the stick from him, show it to the aggrieved and throw it away. Girls return from bathing in a nearby stream, a young girl repeatedly hits her mother with a stick, infants nurse and older children and adults eat *kumu, pitpit* and sweet potato. As the feast ends, people pack the uneaten food into net bags and carry it off.

63-13F *SOUTH FORE Children V; Waisa village; Eastern Highlands, East New Guinea; December 17–19, 1963.*
16 mm Kodak Commercial Ektachrome, 24 frs./sec., narrated sound, 1,026 ft., 28 min.

A visit to the most remote hamlet of Waisa village includes several panoramas showing the setting, plan and gardens nearby. Two 360° panoramas are from within each of the two parts of this divided hamlet and show all the buildings, which include both the old, round-style Fore house, as well as the newer square style. A few of the inhabitants of the hamlet are present, and one mother is seen holding her infant daughter and chewing off the harder outside parts of a piece of sugar cane so that her daughter will be able to manage the softer, more succulent inner portions. While waiting, the girl idly strikes at baby pigs loitering nearby.

Several boys of various ages demonstrate their techniques and abilities in climbing a vine suspended from a tree, taking turns swinging. A typical indulgence by older Fore children for younger is seen as older boys delay their turns swinging to help a very young boy who wanted to swing on the vine. Competition for turns on the vine swing develops between two boys, who repeatedly contest for the vine. This is resolved easily, after a momentary trace of anger by one, without fighting or overt hostility. One boy of about 10 years of age loses his loin cloth while swinging. Self-consciously and hurriedly he recovers it from a smaller boy, who had retrieved it and was running off. Among views

of the several boys gathered at the vine swing there are episodes including swinging, climbing, falling, eating, wrestling, running and crying.

63-13G *SOUTH FORE Children VI; Waisa Village, Eastern Highlands, East New Guinea; December 21–26, 1963.*
16 mm Kodak Commercial Ektachrome, 24 frs./sec., narrated sound, 1,009 ft., 28 min.

An *embokaba* beetle, considered a tasty treat by many Fore, is captured by some boys in a tree and later cooked and eaten. A panorama from Bamus hamlet shows the geographical setting of some of the hamlets of Kalu, Mentilasa and Intamatasa villages across the valley. The play of children in the hamlet yard of Bamus ranges from idle toying with bows and arrows to chasing and wrestling among the boys. One boy performs an unusual, seemingly stylized set of motions almost like a dance in response to an older boy's grabbing momentarily at his bow. Later, near Anati hamlet, a young boy refuses food offered by his father until given the piece he wants. Another boy climbs a tree, and others sit around idly eating. One of the young men of Waisa plays with two small boys by rolling and crawling in the grass with them. Boys are seen swinging on a vine at Yagoenti while other boys and some girls watch and run and crawl about. The help extended by older boys to younger is seen as they help a small boy not quite able to mount the vine by himself.

During a Christmas visit to the Awande mission, kuru orphans are seen playing in their new Christmas clothing. This is followed by panoramic sequences showing the hospital and buildings of the mission. A few costumed natives pass through en route to the annual *singing* about to begin in Okapa.

63-13H *FORE, GIMI, KEIAGANA, KANITE Singsing; Large annual celebration at the Okapa Patrol Post, Eastern Highlands, East New Guinea; December 26 and 27, 1963.*
16 mm Kodak Commercial Ektachrome, 24 frs./sec., silent, 579 ft., 16 min.

An early patrol officer at the Okapa Patrol Post induced the people of his subdistrict to gather at Okapa annually between Christmas and the New Year for a large feast and *singsing.* This has become traditional.

In this film, groups of Gimi or Keiagana in elaborate costume sing and dance along the road to Okapa, and Fore, Gimi, Keiagana and Kanite celebrate at Okapa, where many pigs and piles of sweet potato have been accumulated and are prepared and cooked in pits for the gathered throngs. Hundreds of performers in village groups sing, dance and play their instruments on the celebration field. A wide variety of costumes include elaborate shell and feather headdresses—large ornamental structures extending several feet above the head—faces and bodies smeared with mud and various paints, and other unusual body coverings. Many of the men are armed.

63-13I *SOUTH FORE Children VII; Wagiri hamlet of Kamira village; Eastern Highlands, East New Guinea, December 31, 1963–January 2, 1964.*
16 mm Kodak Commercial Ektachrome, 24 frs./sec., narrated sound, 1,052 ft., 29 min.

This film concentrates on the play and casual activities of children in a small, old-style hamlet. There is also a long series of sequences dealing with the manufacture and demonstration of a bird snare learned by one of the Fore boys during a recent sojourn among the Kukukuku. Three ill people are seen.

Activities going on in and around the hamlet include corn planting with a digging stick, fence building, cooking sweet potato in coals, cooking *kumu* leaves in bamboo cylinders, washing food, bathing in a nearby stream and eating. Sequences of children's activities include running, walking, crawling, fence climbing, wrestling and autoerotic play. Some Fore boys demonstrate the technique by which they shoot small arrows of *kunai* grass by flicking them from their thumbs and fingers. Children are seen in attitudes of playful menacing, shame, anger and affection. One small girl has a tantrum, which elicits the normal tolerant adult response. Short games occasionally develop among the children in the hamlet yard and include snuggling, crawling and following, pushing against a fence, chasing, physical contact and balance upsetting. Objects lying about, such as old cooking cylinders, sticks and onion stalks, become occasional toys. The casual Fore attitude toward the very ill and infirm is seen as a boy dying of kuru is ignored, except when he is the subject of medical attention, while normal hamlet activity and play go on about him.

64-1A *KEIAGANA, GIMI, LABOGAI, SOUTH FORE; Exploratory patrol through and beyond the peripheral kuru region, Eastern Highlands, East New Guinea; January 4– February 1, 1964. (Part 1, January 4–8)*
16 mm Kodak Commercial Ektachrome, 24 and 64 frs./sec., narrated sound, 1,213 ft., 34 min.

This filmed record of a kuru epidemiological patrol consists of four reels and deals with the people and places of the western edge of the kuru region and into the nonkuru region further to the west.

A neurological examination of Kopuyaga by Dr. Gajdusek reveals trunkal, extremity and head tremor not associated with the marked locomotor ataxia; slightly hyperactive deep tendon jerks; and nonsustained ankle clonus.

In each of the places where the patrol stopped, there are sequences of the inhabited sites and their people. In a family at Ke'efu, a wide range of skin tone is noticeable. A young girl who is considered behaviorly abnormal plays in an odd fashion with others. Food purchase for the patrol is seen, and among the people in some of the hamlets are a woman carrying firewood on her head, children carrying infants, women working in gardens, small children carrying loaded bags of food, men smoking, a toddler making short, exploratory excursions from his seated mother and returning to nurse, and a man with a mid-epigastric hernia.

Many views show inhabited sites seen along the trails, and in Henegaru a 360° panorama from the hilltop hamlet of Taturu reveals 15 inhabited sites in the surrounding valleys.

64-1B *KEIAGANA, GIMI, LABOGAI, SOUTH FORE 1964; Exploratory patrol through and beyond the peripheral kuru region; Eastern Highlands, East New Guinea; January 4–February 1, 1964. (Part 2, January 8–14)*

16 mm Kodak Commercial Ektachrome, 24 frs./sec., narrated sound, 1,142 ft., 32 min.

Part 2 of this patrol film was taken as the patrol passed through the Gimi villages of Negibi, Uvai, Amusa and Misapi; the South Fore village of Pai'iti; and at the Iyavipi and Omiuyarai camp sites in the uninhabited rainforest between Pai'iti and Heroana. In Uvai live a number of mentally defective people, including one boy who could neither hear nor talk. Among the many spectators at our camp site were fearful younger children, some crying and being comforted by their mothers. There is casual eating by some toddlers and older children as they mill about the camp; a few *mai* initiates with their long braided hair are in this group. Early morning views and panoramas show one of the hamlets as the residents start stirring about.

As the patrol moves through the Gimi country, typical vine suspension bridges cross swollen rivers. One of these is under construction. In Misapi a man considered peculiar (*longlong* by the villagers here) plays with snakes. At Pai'iti, women, some of whom carry and nurse infants in typical fashion, bring food for trade. In the uninhabited rainforest between Pai'iti and Heroana, two patrol camps are built.

64-1C *KEIAGANA, GIMI, LABOGAI, SOUTH FORE 1964; Exploratory patrol through and beyond the peripheral kuru region; Eastern Highlands; East New Guinea; January 4–February 1, 1964. (Part 3, January 15–23)*
16 mm Kodak Commercial Ektachrome, 24 frs./sec., narrated and synchronous field sound, 1,028 ft., 28.5 min.

This reel deals with the passage of the epidemiological patrol from Heroana, Labogai, to Takarai, South Fore. In Heroana, there is an old leper from a distant Yar village who, with his two wives and two sons, claimed to be the only survivor of the massacre of their village of Lolo. It was, he said, his first contact with white man. Gajdusek's interview with him via interpreters, speaking Neo-Melanesian and Yar-Pawaia, is with synchronously recorded sound.

As the Heroanans gather for an orientation regarding the shortly to-be-held first New Guinea-wide election, several young children of about three to five years of age play in and around small trees nearby. Climbing, aggression, oral behavior, running, idle play, resting and sensual play are recorded.

The crossing of a vine suspension bridge en route to Uwagubi precedes sequences of curious children standing around in Uwagubi. Fearful children run to their mothers, food is prepared for cooking, and a boy of about six years of age carries a sibling.

As the patrol passes through Mani village, a feast is in preparation with much of the food being cooked in large, hollow, upright log sections. The setting of Mani and its surroundings are seen in panorama. A nearby garden is cultivated by two women. In Agotu an initiation for several boys is going on in nearby I'amam'aberai hamlet. Part of the dancing and singing is filmed with synchronous sound. Here, too, food is cooked in upright, hollow log sections by means of hot stones. The initiated boys are seen emerging from the men's house, where they had been secluded for several days. Cooking logs are opened and the food is distributed and eaten. There is a panorama of the Agotu valley from the trail on the way to Gimi. Mani village is seen briefly, and another suspension bridge is crossed en route to Takarai. There is a new hamlet under construction, not yet inhabited, in Takarai, consisting of the newer style, round houses.

64-1D *KEIAGANA, GIMI, LABOGAI, SOUTH FORE*
1964; Exploratory patrol through and beyond the peripheral kuru region, Eastern Highlands, East New Guinea; January 4–February 1, 1964. (Part 4, January 24–February 1)
16 mm Kodak Commercial Ektachrome, 24 frs./sec., narrated sound, 1,028 ft., 29 min.

In Umasa, panoramas and telephotography show the inhabited sites and gardens and a new, large, as yet, uninhabited hamlet, with the new round-style houses nearing completion. Ivaki kuru victims are examined in front of their houses and near their hamlets; cargo carriers lounge and walk about the camp site and affectionately greet friends who have come to visit them; a toddler crying of fright is pacified by nursing; and a snake is brought for photography. Upon leaving the highlands of New Guinea via Lae there are air views of the Markham River valley, the forest and *kunai* grass-covered mountains to the south, and the Wau air strip.

References

ALPERS, M. P.

1965 Epidemiological changes in kuru, 1957 to 1963. In: *Slow, Latent, and Temperate Virus Infections.* NINDB monograph no 2. Edited by D. C. Gajdusek, C. J. Gibbs, Jr. and M. P. Alpers. Washington, D.C.: U.S. Government Printing Office, pp. 65-82.

ALPERS, M. P., and D. C. GAJDUSEK

1965 Changing patterns of kuru: Epidemiological changes in the period of increasing contact of the Fore people with Western civilization. *American Journal of Tropical Medicine and Hygiene* 14:852-879.

Annual Census Report

1958 Okapa, Eastern Highlands, Territory of Papua and New Guinea: Okapa Subdistrict, Department of District Affairs.

1963 Okapa Eastern Highlands, Territory of Papua and New Guinea: Okapa Subdistrict, Department of District Affairs.

BATESON, G., and MARGARET MEAD

1942 *Balinese Character: A Photographic Analysis.* New York Academy of Sciences, Special Publications, Vol. 2.

BENNETT, J. H., F. A. RHODES, and H. N. ROBSON

1958 Observations on kuru. I. A possible genetic basis. *Australian Annals of Medicine* 7:4 (Nov), 269-275.

BENNETT, J. H., and H. N. ROBSON

1958 A possible genetic basis for kuru. Abstract in: Proceedings of the Tenth International Congress of Genetics, Montreal, Canada, Aug. 20–21, Vol. 2. Toronto: University of Toronto Press, p. 22.

BERNDT, C. H.

1953 Sociocultural change in the Eastern Central Highlands of New Guinea. *Southwestern Journal of Anthropology* 9:112-138.

BERNDT, R. M.

1955 Interdependence and conflict in the Eastern Central Highlands of New Guinea. *Man* 55:105-107.

1962 *Excess and Restraint: Social Control Among a New Guinea Mountain People.* Chicago: University of Chicago Press.

1964 Warfare in the New Guinea Highlands. *American Anthropologist* 66(4, pt. 2):183-203.

BIRDWHISTELL, R. L.

1952 *Introduction to Kinesics.* Louisville: University of Louisville Press.

1970 *Kinesics and Context.* New York: Ballantine.

BOWERS, N.

1968 *The Ascending Grasslands: An Anthropological Study of Ecological Succession in a High Mountain Valley of New Guinea.* Unpublished Ph.D. thesis, Columbia University, New York, N.Y.

BROOKFIELD, H. C.

1964 The ecology of Highlands settlement: Some suggestions. *American Anthropologist* 66(4, pt. 2):20-38.

BROOKFIELD, H. C., and PAULA BROWN

1963 *Struggle for Land: Agriculture and Group Territories among the Chimbu of the New Guinea Highlands.* Melbourne: Oxford University Press.

BROOKFIELD, H. C., and J. P. WHITE

1968 Revolution or evolution in the prehistory of New Guinea Highlands. *Ethnology* 7:1(January), 43-52.

BROWN, P.

1960 Chimbu tribes: Political organization in the Eastern Highlands of New Guinea. *Southwestern Journal of Anthropology* 16:22-35.

1963 From anarchy to satrapy. *American Anthropologist* 65:1-15.

1964 Enemies and affines. *Ethnology* 3:335-356.

BROWN, P., and H. C. BROOKFIELD

1959 Chimbu land and society. *Oceania* 30:1-75.

BULMER, R. N. H.

1960 Political aspects of the *moka* ceremonial exchange system among the Kyaka people. *Oceania* 30: 1-13.

BULMER, S., and R. BULMER

1964 The prehistory of the Australian New Guinea Highlands. *American Anthropologist* 66(4, pt. 2):39-76.

CAVALLI-SFORZA, L. A., and W. F. BODMER

1971 *The Genetics of Human Population*. San Francisco: W. H. Freeman.

CHANOCK, F. O., and E. R. SORENSON

1973 Research films and the communications revolution. Proceedings and abstracts of the 9th International Congress of the Anthropological and Ethnological Sciences, Chicago, Sept. 1–8. (Also in: *Principles of Visual Anthropology*, edited by P. Hockings, The Hague: Mouton, 1975).

CONKLIN, H. C.

1963 The Oceanian-African hypotheses and the sweet potato. In: *Plants and the Migration of Pacific Peoples*. Edited by J. Barrau. Honolulu: Bernice P. Bishop Museum.

CROW, J. F., and M. KIMURA

1970 *An Introduction to Population Genetics Theory*. New York: Harper and Row.

DARWIN, C.

1872 *The Expression of Emotion in Man and Animals*. London: John Murray.

DASHIELL, J. F.

1927 A new method of measuring reactions to facial expressions of emotion. *Psychological Bulletin* 24:174-175.

DE LEPERVANCHE, M.

1967–68 Descent, residence, and leadership in the New Guinea Highlands. *Oceania* 38:2, 134-158, 38:3, 163-189.

DIAMOND, J.

1966 Zoological classification system of a primitive people. *Science* 151:1102-1104.

DU TOIT, B. M.

1962 Structural looseness in New Guinea. *Journal of the Polynesian Society* 71:397-399.

1964 Filiation and affiliation among the Gadsup. *Oceania* 35:85-95.

EKMAN, P., and W. V. FRIESEN

1969a Origin, usage, and coding: The basis for five categories of nonverbal behavior. In: *Lenguaje y Communication Social*. Edited by E. Vernon, et al. Buenos Aires: Nueva Vision.

1969b The repertoire of nonverbal behavior. *Semiotica* 1:49-98.

EKMAN, P., E. R. SORENSON, and W. V. FRIESEN

1969 Pancultural elements in the facial expression of emotion. *Science* 164:86-88.

FISCHER, H.

1968 *Negwa: Eine Papua-Gruppe im Wandel*. Munich: Klaus Renner Verlag.

FRIEDLAENDER, J. S.

1974 A comparison of population distances and population structure analysis. In: *Genetic Distance*. Edited by J. F. Crow. New York: Plenum Press.

GAJDUSEK, D. C.

1962 Personal communication

1963a Kuru. *Transactions of the Royal Society of Tropical Medicine and Hygiene* 57(3):151-169.

1963b *Kuru Epidemiological Patrols from the New Guinea Highlands to Papua*. August 21–November 10, 1957. Monograph, limited edition. (August). Bethesda, Maryland: National Institute of Neurological Diseases and Blindness, National Institutes of Health, 204 pp.

1963c *New Guinea Journal*. June 10–August 15, 1959. Monograph, limited edition. (October). Bethesda, Maryland: Institute of Neurological Diseases and Blindness, National Institutes of Health, 165 pp.

1967 Personal communication.

1970 Personal communication.

GAJDUSEK, D. C., C. J. GIBBS, JR., and M. ALPERS

1967 Transmission and passage of experimental "kuru" to chimpanzees. *Science* 155(3759), 212-214.

GAJDUSEK, D. C., C. J. GIBBS, JR., D. M. ASHER, and E. DAVID

1968 Transmission of experimental kuru to the spider monkey (*Ateles geoffreyi*). *Science* 162(3854), 693-694.

GAJDUSEK, D. C., and V. ZIGAS

1959 Kuru, clinical, pathological and epidemiological study of an acute progressive degenerative disease of the central nervous system among natives of the Eastern Highlands of New Guinea. *American Journal of Medicine* 26(3), 442-469.

1961 Studies on kuru. I. The ethnologic setting of kuru. *American Journal of Tropical Medicine and Hygiene* 10(1), 80-91.

GAJDUSEK, D. C., V. ZIGAS, and J. BAKER

1961 Studies on kuru. III. Patterns of kuru incidence: demographic and geographic epidemiological analysis. *American Journal of Tropical Medicine and Hygiene* 10(4), 599-627.

GARDNER, R., and K. G. HEIDER

1969 *Gardens of War: Life and Death in the New Guinea Stone Age.* New York: Random House.

GLASSE, R. M.

1962 *South Fore Society: A Preliminary Report.* Mimeographed. Department of Public Health, Territory of Papua and New Guinea. Reissued Bethesda, Maryland: National Institutes of Health.

1963 *Cannibalism in the Kuru Region.* Mimeographed. Department of Public Health, Territory of Papua and New Guinea, 14 pp. Reissued Bethesda, Maryland: National Institutes of Health, 14 pp.

1967 Cannibalism in the kuru region of New Guinea. *Transactions of the New York Academy of Sciences* (Series 2), 29:748-754.

1970 Marriage in the South Fore. In: *Pigs, Pearlshells and Women: Marriage in the New Guinea Highlands.* Edited by M. J. Meggitt and R. M. Glasse. New Jersey: Prentice Hall.

GLASSE, R. M., and SHIRLEY LINDENBAUM

1969 South Fore politics. *Anthropological Forum* 2:3, 308-326.

GLASSE, SHIRLEY

1963a *A Note on Fore Medicine and Sorcery,* with an ethnobotanical list. Mimeographed. Department of Public Health, Territory of Papua New Guinea.

1963b *The Social Life of Women in the South Fore.* Mimeographed. Department of Public Health, Territory of Papua and New Guinea. Reissued Bethesda, Maryland: National Institutes of Health.

1964 The social effects of kuru. *Papua and New Guinea Medical Journal* 7(1), 36-47.

HALL, EDWARD T.

1959 *The Silent Language.* New York: Doubleday.

HARPENDING, H., and T. JENKINS

1973 Genetic distances among Southern African populations. In: *Methods in Anthropological Genetics.* Edited by M. H. Crawford and P. L. Workman. Albuquerque: University of New Mexico Press.

HEIDER, K.

1969 Personal communication

1970 *The Dugum Dani.* Chicago: Aldine Press.

IZARD, C. E.

1971 *Face of Emotion.* New York: Appleton-Century-Crofts.

KELENY, G. P.

1962 The origin and introduction of the basic food crops of the New Guinea people. *Papua and New Guinea Agricultural Journal* 15:7-13.

KELLY, R. C.

1968 Demographic pressure and descent group structure in the New Guinea Highlands. *Oceania* 39:36-63.

KIDD, K. K., and L. SGARAMELLA-ZONTA

1971 Phylogenetic analysis: Concepts and methods. *American Journal of Human Genetics* 23:235-52.

LANGNESS, L. L.

1964 Some problems in the conceptualization of Highlands social structures. *American Anthropologist* 66(4, pt. 2):162-182.

LINDENBAUM, SHIRLEY

1971a Sorcery and structure in Fore society. *Oceania* 41(4), 277-287.

1971b *The South Fore: 1961–1963.* Unpublished M.A. thesis, University of Sydney, Sydney, Australia.

LINDENBAUM, SHIRLEY, and R. GLASSE

1969 Fore age mates. *Oceania* 39(3):165-173.

LOMAX, ALAN, and NORMAN BERKOWITZ

1972 Evolutionary taxonomy of culture. *Science* 177: 228-239.

MATHEWS, J. D., R. GLASSE, and SHIRLEY LINDENBAUM

1968 Kuru and cannibalism. *Lancet* 2:449-452.

MEAD, MARGARET, and F. C. MACGREGOR

1951 *Growth and Culture: A Photographic Study of Balinese Childhood.* New York: Putnam.

MEGGITT, M. J.

1958 The Enga of the New Guinea Highlands. *Oceania* 28:253-330.

1964 Male-female relationships in the Highlands of Australian New Guinea. *American Anthropologist* 66(4, pt. 2):204-224.

1965 *The Lineage System of the Mae-Enga of New Guinea.* Edinburg: Oliver and Boyd.

1967 The pattern of leadership among the Mae-Enga of New Guinea. *Anthropological Forum* 2:20-35.

NISHIYAMA, I.

1963 The origin of the sweet potato. In: *Plants and the Migrations of Pacific Peoples.* Edited by J. Barrau. Honolulu: Bernice P. Bishop Museum.

O'BRIEN, P. J.

1972 The sweet potato: Its origin and dispersal. *Journal of the American Anthropological Association* 74:342-365.

OOMEN, H. A. P. C., W. SPOON, J. E. HEESTERMAN, J. RUINARD, R. LUYKEN, and P. SLUMP

1961 The sweet potato as the staff of life of the Highland Papuan. *Tropical and Geographical Medicine* (Amsterdam) 13:55-66.

POSPISIL, L.

1958a *Kapauku Papuans and their Law.* New Haven: Yale University Press. Yale University Publications in Anthropology (54).

1958b Social change and primitive law. *American Anthropologist* 60:832-837.

1960 The Kapauku Papuans and their kinship organization. *Oceania* 30:188-206.

1963 *The Kapauku Papuans of West New Guinea.* New York: Holt, Rinehart and Winston.

RAPPAPORT, R. A.

1967a *Pigs for the Ancestors: Ritual in the Ecology of a New Guinea People.* New Haven: Yale University Press.

1967b Ritual regulation of environmental relations among a New Guinea people. *Ethnology* 6:17-30.

READ, K. E.

1951 The Gahuku-Gama of the Central Highlands. *South Pacific* 5:154-164.

1952a Nama cult of the Central Highlands, New Guinea. *Oceania* 23:1-25.

1952b Land in the Central Highlands. *South Pacific* 6:440-449.

1954a Cultures of the Central Highlands, New Guinea. *Southwestern Journal of Anthropology* 10:1-43.

1954b Marriage among the Gahuku-Gama of the Eastern Central Highlands, New Guinea. *South Pacific* 7:864-870.

1959 Leadership and consensus in a New Guinea society. *American Anthropologist* 61:425-436.

1965 *The High Valley.* New York: Charles Scribner's Sons.

REAY, MARIE

1959a *The Kuma: Freedom and Conformity in the New Guinea Highlands.* Melbourne: Melbourne University Press for Australian National University.

1959b Individual ownership and transfer of land among the Kumu. *Man* 59:78-82.

1967 Structural covariants of land shortage among patrilinear peoples. *Anthropological Forum* 2:4-19.

REID, LUCY, and D. C. GAJDUSEK

1969 Nutrition in the kuru region. II. A nutritional evaluation of traditional Fore diet in Moke village in 1957. *Acta Tropica* 26:331-345.

ROBBINS, R. G.

1963a Anthropogenic grasslands of New Guinea. In: *UNESCO Symposium on Humid Tropics Vegetation.* (Goroka 1960). Canberra: Canberra Government Printer.

1963b Correlations of plant patterns and population migration into Australian New Guinea Highlands. In: *Plants and the Migration of Pacific Peoples.* Edited by J. Barrau. Honolulu: Bernice P. Bishop Museum.

RYAN, D. J.

1955 Clan organization in the Mendi valley. *Oceania* 26:79-90.

1959 Clan formation in the Mendi valley. *Oceania* 29:257-289.

1961 Gift exchange in the Mendi valley. Unpublished Ph.D. thesis, Sydney University, Sydney, Australia.

SCOTT, G. K.

1963 The dialects of Fore. *Oceania* 33:280-286.

SIMMONS, R. T., J. J. GRAYDON, V. ZIGAS, J. BAKER, and D. C. GAJDUSEK

1961 Studies on kuru V: A blood-group genetic survey

of the kuru region and other parts of Papua New Guinea. *Journal of Tropical Medicine and Hygiene* 10:639-664.

SIMMONS, R. T., J. J. GRAYDON, D. C. GAJDUSEK, M. P. ALPERS, and R. W. HORNABROOK

1972 Genetic studies in relation to kuru. II. Blood group genetic patterns in kuru patients and populations of the Eastern Highlands of New Guinea. *American Journal of Human Genetics* 24:39-71.

SORENSON, E. R.

1967a A research film program in the study of changing man: Research filmed material as a foundation for continued study of non-recurring human events. *Current Anthropology* 8(5), 443-469.

1967b The concept of the research film. Proceedings of the Annual Meetings of the Society for Applied Anthropology, Washington, D.C., May 5, 1967.

1968a The retrieval of data from changing culture: A strategy for developing research documents for continued study. *Anthropological Quarterly* 41(3), 177-186.

1968b *Growing Up As a Fore.* Scientific report film presented at the postgraduate course in pediatrics, Harvard University Medical School. (Original in the National Research Film Collection, Smithsonian Institution).

1971a *The Evolving Fore: A Study of Socialization and Cultural Change in the New Guinea Highlands.* Unpublished Ph.D. dissertation, Stanford University.

1971b Toward a national anthropological research film center: A progress report. *PIEF Newsletter* of the American Anthropological Association 3:1.

1972 Socio-ecological change among the Fore of New Guinea. *Current Anthropology* 13:349-83.

1973a Research filming and the study of culturally specific patterns of behavior. *PIEF Newsletter* of the American Anthropological Association 4:3-4.

1973b Visual records, human knowledge, and the future. Proceedings and abstracts of the 9th International Congress of the Anthropological and Ethnological Sciences, Chicago, September 1-8, 1973. (Also in: *Principles of Visual Anthropology.* Edited by P. Hockings, The Hague: Mouton, 1975).

1973c Ecological disturbance and population distribution among the Fore of New Guinea: A proto-agricultural phenomena. Proceedings and abstracts of the 9th International Congress of the Anthropological and Ethnological Sciences, Chicago, September 1-8, 1973. (Also in: *Anthropology of the Pacific World.* Edited by W. Sibley, The Hague: Mouton, in press).

1973d Culture and the expression of emotion. Proceedings and abstracts of the 9th International Con-

gress of the Anthropological and Ethnological Sciences, Chicago, September 1-8. (Also in: *Psychological Anthropology.* Edited by T. Williams, The Hague: Mouton, 1975).

1974 Anthropological film: A scientific and humanistic resource. *Science* 186:1079-85.

1975 To further phenomenological inquiry: The National Anthropological Film Center. *Current Anthropology* 16(2):267-269.

SORENSON, E. R., and D. C. GAJDUSEK

1963 Investigation of nonrecurring phenomena: The research cinema film. *Nature* 200:112-114.

1966 The Study of Child Behavior and Development in Primitive Cultures. Supplement to *Pediatrics* 37(1), Part II.

1969 Nutrition in the kuru region. I. Gardening, food handling, and diet of the Fore people. *Acta Tropica* 26:281-330.

SORENSON, E. R., and ALLISON JABLONKO

1973 Research filming of naturally occurring phenomena: Basic strategies. Proceedings of the 9th International Congress of the Anthropological and Ethnological Sciences, Chicago, September 1-8, 1973. (Also in: *Principles of Visual Anthropology.* Edited by P. Hockings, The Hague: Mouton, 1975).

SORENSON, E. R., and P. E. KENMORE

1974 Proto-agricultural movement in the Eastern Highlands of New Guinea. *Current Anthropology* 15(1): 67-74.

TOMKINS, S. S.

1962 *Affect, Imagery, Consciousness,* Vol. One: *The Positive Affects.* New York: Springer.

1963 *Affect, Imagery, Consciousness,* Vol. Two: *The Negative Affects.* New York: Springer.

TOMKINS, S. S. and R. McCARTER

1964 What and where are the primary affects? Some evidence for a theory. *Perceptual and Motor Skills* 18: 119-158.

VAYDA, A. P.

1961 Expansion and warfare among swidden agriculturalists. *American Anthropologist* 63:346-358.

VAYDA, A. P., A. LEEDS, and D. B. SMITH

1961 The place of pigs in Melanesian subsistence. In: Proceedings of the Annual Meeting of the American Ethnological Society. Edited by V. E. Garfield. Seattle: University of Washington, 69-77.

Watson, J. B.

1965a From hunting to horticulture in the New Guinea Highlands. *Ethnology* 4:295-309.

1965b The significance of recent ecological change in the Central Highlands of New Guinea. *Journal of the Polynesian Society* 74:438-450.

1967a Tairora: The politics of despotism in a small society. *Anthropological Forum* 2:53-104.

1967b Horticulture traditions of the Eastern New Guinea Highlands. *Oceania* 38:81-98.

White, J. P.

1967 *Taim Bilong Bipo.* Unpublished Ph.D. dissertation, Australian National University, Canberra, Australia.

Wurm, S. A.

1962 The languages of the Eastern, Western, and Southern Highlands, Territory of Papua and New Guinea. In: *A Linguistic Survey of the South-Western Pacific.* 2nd edition. Edited by A. Capell. South Pacific Commission, Noumea, Technical Paper No. 136, 105-128.

1964 Australian New Guinea Highlands language and the distribution of their typological features. *American Anthropologist* 66(4, pt. 2):77-97.

Yen, D. C.

1960 The sweet potato in the Pacific: The propagation of the plant in relation to its distribution. *Journal of the Polynesian Society* 69:368-375.

1963 Sweet potato variation and its relation to human migration in the Pacific. In: *Plants and the Migration of Pacific Peoples.* Edited by J. Barrau. Honolulu: Bernice P. Bishop Museum, 93-118.

Zigas, V., and D. C. Gajdusek

1957 Kuru: Clinical study of a new syndrome resembling paralysis agitans in natives of the Eastern Highlands of Australian New Guinea. *Medical Journal of Australia,* 2:21 (November 23), 745-754.

Index

C

Cabbage, 50
Cameras, use of, 147
Cannibalism, 32, 243; decline of, 36; familial, 194
Caressing, 162
"Cargo-cult," 14, 16
"Cargo-cult-like" movements, 236
Carrots, 50
Carrying the young child, 153
Cassowary, 57, 59
Casuarina tree: and land tenure, 233; plantings of, 231
Census, 27, 222, 224, 237; units, 28, 222, 224
Central Range, 17
Change: ecological, 82, 97; pattern of, 93; sociopolitical, 91
Character: innovation-ready, 235; protoagricultural, 235
Chemical changes, objective, 247
Chiefs, 16
Child: aggression, 181, 182, 184; care, voluntary, 155; carrying of the young, 153; desires, deference to, 155, 185-189; discontent, 160; exercise of preference in seeking security, 175; frustration, 16; handling of young, 151; holding the young, 153; mobility, 246; polylocality, 246; retaliation, 160; supervision, 165
Child handling, 151; nondirective, 235; sociosensual, 237
Childhood, 16
Child rearing, Dani, 246
Chimbu, 244
Clearings, satellitelike, 85
Clothing, adoption of, 238
Cloth, bark, 68
Coffee, 48, 50; gardens, 230; marketing, 230; revolution, 230
Cognitive: clustering, 238; confusion, 15; flexibility, 237-238
Comforting, access to, 177
Communication: interactive, 237; interpersonal, 140; interrogative, 15, 140; prelinguistic, 204; tactile, 150, 204, 206, 208-210, 219, 237-238; unspoken, 209
Community: character of, 134; harmony, 135
Condiments, 59
Conflict, 40, 97, 132, 211; behavior patterns forestalling, 213-214; resolution of, 211
Congestion, territorial, 132
Constants, time and space, 249
Contact: affectionate, 162; sociosensual, 236; Western, 13, 27, 221, 236
Cooking, 62, 73; collective, 63; preparing leaf vegetables for, 65
Cooperative activity, 135; association, 134, 220; behavior, emergence of, 151; endeavors, 220
Corn, 48-50, 63-64
Cornerstone of sociopolitical unity, 134

Crayfish, 59
Crying, attention to, 177
Cucumber, 50
Cultural barriers to inquiry, 146
Cultural enclaves, neolithic, 17
Cultural evolution, way-station, 235
Culture change, 14-16, 221-222, 224, 227-228, 230-231, 233, 238; and socialization, 235; vulnerability to, 235
Cuscus, 57-59, 63, 67, 73
Customs, divergence of, 246

D

Dani, child rearing, 246
Data, visual, 16
Debts: death, 68; intercommunity, 68; settlement of, 93
Defecation, 177-178
Defense, grassland burning, 82
Deforestation, 14, 81-82; taro-caused, 109, 120
Deforested regions, Fore homeland, 108
Delocalization, 132
Demographic: discontinuities, 116; dispersion, 130; flux, 245; organization, 127-130
Demography effect of sweet potato on, 244; male/female ratio, 243; patrilineal character of, 135
Desires of the young, deference to the, 185-189
Development: economic, 14; political, 92; psychological, 236
Dialect chain, 19, 21; group, 127, 130
Dialects, 21
Dialect: Atigina, 27; Ibusa, 27; Ilesa, 28; Pamousa 28; Purosa, 28
Dietary staple, 54
Digressive search, 251
Discourse: interrogative style of, 140; question-and-answer, 15
Dispersal, 130, 132, 134; dramatic, 132; kindred, 132
Dispersion: centrifugal, 19; demographic, 130, 132; residential, 128, 132
Dispute, settlement of, 93
Dissonances, communicative, 16
Distress, 177
Distribution, population, 130
Disturbance, ecological, 82, 97
Divergence of subpopulations, 103
Divergent settlement, 16
Diversity: behavioral, 238; linguistic, 17, 21
Division of food, 73
Documentation, phenomenological, 16
Dogs, wild, 57
Domestication, semi: animals, 57
Dunantina River, 106
Dunkwi, 35
Dwellings, family, nuclear, 238

burning of, 82, 85, 87-88, 90; configuration of, 106; expansion of, 99, 106; formation of, 79, 82; manmade, 244; stability of, 82; taller, 90; uninhabited, 97, 125

Grass: *kunai,* 82, 88; pitpit, 82; for salt making, 60

Greens, 62

Groups, affinity, 135, 220

Growing up, 135-136, 145

Growing Up as a Fore, 150

Grubs, 63

H

Habitation patterns, 28

Hamlet, 81, 126-128, 238; consolidated, 130, 224; convergence, 222; formation of, 52, 222, 224; modernized, 16, 238, 241

Handling the young child, 151

Hens, 57

Herbs, 59; medicinal, 59; wild, 59

Higitaru, 95

Historical reconstruction, 93

Holding the young child, 153

Honeycomb, 59

Horticultural expansion, pioneer, 123

Horticulture, 13, 17; slash-and-burn, 43, 91

Houses: boy's, 16; men's, 19, 26; women's, 19, 26

Hugging, 163

Human development, way-stations of, 145

Hunting and gathering, 13, 57-58, 77, 106

Hybridization, 106

I

Idza Nama, 244

Ibusa, 21-22, 99; dialect, 27

Ibusa-Moke, 22

Ifufurapa, 245

Ilesa, 21-22, 33, 45, 82, 109, 224; dialect, 27

Implements, stone, 17

Indona, 19, 21

Infancy, lack of frustration, 236

Infants and toddlers, affectionate care, 163

Infants: attention focused on, 162; balance, 157; care and handling of, 151, 154-155, 162-163; carrying of, 151; grasp, 157; physical contact provided to, 150; resting, 153; sleeping, 153

Informal adoption, 133-134

Information: interstitial, 146; structured, 249; undifferentiated, 146, 248; visual, 147

Inheritance, 134

Initiation, 59, 68

Innovation, tolerance of, 91

Innovativeness, 235

Inquiry, 165; and affection, 164; cultural barriers to, 146; and exploratory behavior, 165

Insects, edible, 58

Insights, personal, 249

Integration, social, 204, 211

Interaction, tactile, 150-151

Interdigitation: demographic, 114, 119; protogracultural, 119

Interhamlet affinity groups, 127, 130; development of, 132

Interplay, tactile, 204, 207

Intimacy, 15, 135

Isolation, 15, 17; visual, 137

Ivaki, 22, 90

Ivingoi, 40, 114

J

Jeep road, 30

K

Kagu, 22

Kagumuti, 31

Kainantu, 18, 230

Kalu, 22

Kalugori, 31

Kamano, 99, 244; region, 101; proto-, 104

Kamata, 30, 40, 82

Kamira, 30, 40, 224, 245 ,

Kangaroo, tree-climbing, 57, 59

Kanigitasa, 40

Kanite, 99

Kasokana, 69-70, 224

Kasoru, 22

Kavantari, 30

Kawaina, 19, 21

Kaza River, 22, 98, 109

Keiagana, 21, 99

Ke'efu, 226

Ketabi, 22, 64, 245

Keyanosa, 22

Kiap, 221. See also Patrol Officer

Kindreds, localization of, 132

Kinenti, 69, 229

Kinship: adoptive, 133; affiliative, 133-134, 238, 246; informal, 245; and land pressure, 135; looseness of, 133-134, unconcern for lineal, 133

Kissing, 162

Knives, child access to, 167-168

Koventari, 82

Kratke Range, 17-18, 106
Kukukuku, 21
Kume, 95, 231
Kumu, 43, 48-49, 64, 69, 71
Kunai, 82; grass, 88
Kuru, 36-39, 132, 243; effect on sorcery, 39-40; epidemiological studies of, 14; social effect of, 36, 38

L

Labor contracts, 246
Lamari gorge, 17
Lamari River, 15, 17-18, 35, 98, 106
Lamari valley, 22, 100, 109, 112, 120
Lamari-Puburamba confluence, 112
Land: competition for, 92; congestion of the, 92; pressure, 40, 92, 130, 132, 229; rights, 32; tenure, 126, 132, 233; tenure and Casuarina tree, 233; tenure, permanent type of, 233
Language, 17; frontiers, 19
Larva, edible, 58-59
Learning, 198-200, 202; of gardening, 200; kinesthetic, 199, 202; by mimicry, 177; as pursuit of preference, 199; socioeconomic 203; socioeconomic skills, 198
Lemon, 50
Lettuce, 50
Liaison, interregional, 132
Linguistic: barriers, 16; diversity, 17; group, 130; setting, 17; stock, East New Guinea Highlands, 21
Lizards, edible, 59
Lunati, 31

M

Mage, 22, 99
Maize, 50, 73
Mango, 59
Manioc, 50
Mapping, 15, 28
Mareta, 64
Markham range, 18
Markham River, 106
Markham valley, 104
Marriage, 59, 68, 135; exchanges, 245; study of, 245
Meals, daily, 63
Medicine men, 16
Migrations, 119, 130, 245; contiguous, 97; discontiguous, 95, 97, 114, 116; dispersive, 244; protoagricultural, 104
Missionaries, 15, 222
Mobility, 130, 132, 134-135, 237-238; child, 246
Modernized hamlets, 16, 241

Moke, 22
Morandugai, 35
Motherhood, determining of, 133
Mourning, 32
Movement into the Fore region, 106
Movement: protoagricultural, 119, sweet potato, 105, 119; taro, 105, 119
Mt. Tamiloa, 45, 120
Mt. Wanivinti, 87
Mugaiamuti, 22, 245
Mugugori, 64
Mumu, 70
Mushrooms, 58-59, 63, 67

N

Nagaiya, 245
Names, loose character of, 237
Naming of regions, 125-126
Neolithic cultural enclaves, 17
Net bags, 50
Networks: interregional, 132; personal, 126; socioeconomic, 126
Niginosi, 31
Nonrecurring phenomena, 247
North Fore, 244
Nosuguri, 244-245
Nourishment, free access to, 159
Nursing, 151, 159
Nuts, wild, 58-59

O

Objective chemical changes, 247
Observation, selective, 150
Ofafina, 99
Okapa, 22, 99, 109, 224
Okapa Patrol Post, 221-222, 230
Okasa, 19, 21, 226
Onion, 50
Onuri, 224
Opoiyanti, 22
Opportunistic sampling, 250
Oral affection, 162
Oralty, 194
Organization: residential, 16; social, 40, 133-134, 135-136; sociopolitical, 16, 127
Orie, 114, 245
Oriondamuti, 45, 52
Oven, earth, 63

P

Pacification, 221
Paiti, 85, 114, 222, 245
Paiyanili, 81
Palm, 63; wild *limbum,* 67; wild, black, 59
Pamousa, 21; dialect, 28
Pandanus, 53, 68; nut, 50, 53; red, 50, 53, 64
Paparoti, 31
Patriarchs, 16
Patrifiliation, 134; cumulative, 246
Patriliny, 134; and land pressure, 134; proto-, 134-135
Patrol Officer, 15, 28, 221-222, 226, 238
Patrol Post, 14, 36, 41
Patrol Post, Okapa, 221-222, 230
Pawpaw, 50
Pax Australiana, 221
Peanut, 50
Peas, 50
Peer-groups: boy's, 220; formation of, 211, 217, 220
Personal insights, usefulness of, 249
Personal rapport and land use, 126
Personality: explorative, 109; innovation-ready, 235; innovative, 109; protoagricultural, 109
Phenomena, nonrecurring, 16, 247
Physical capabilities, developing, 170
Physical contact: close, 238; uninterrupted, 151
Pig feasts, 63, 68, 71; diffusion of, 92; formal, 63; inter-group, 92; political importance, 244 and population density, 92 as rapprochement, 93
Piga, 71
Pig-exchange feast, 92-93, 95, 244
Pigs, 54, 56, 73; butchered, 68; care of, 54, 56; delousing of, 55; domestic, 54; economic unit, 77; exchange feasts, 54; husbandry, 54-55; husbandry, changing patterns of, 56; political use of, 77; population, 54; scavenging, 56-57; socioeconomic importance of, 77; wild, 57, 59; wild, decline of, 77, 92
Pineapple, 50
Pioneer: peoples, 17; region, 97
Pioneering penetration, adaptive, 235
Pitpit, 43, 48, 62, 64, 71, 82
Place names, 125-126, 222; flexibility of, 246; formation of, 237
Play: affectionate, 162, 206; biting, 191, 194-195; experimental, 200; exploratory, 195, 198, 200, 216; exploratory sensual, 219; garden, 200; physical, 192; pseudoaggressive, 211; rules, 241; sensual, 192; as socioeconomic learning, 195, 200
Plovinti, 31
Political consolidation, 39, 93
Polylocality, 132-134, 220, 237-238; child expression of, 246
Ponamenti, 30
Population clusters, 28, 125, 127-130; names of, 127; patrilineal bias in, 135, 246

Population density, 21, 27; and pig feasts, 92
Population distribution, 27, 104; classification of, 127; factors in, 95, 97
Population: aboriginal, absorption of, 119; aboriginal, evidence of, 195; Anga-like, 116; congestion, 130; dispersion of, 92; dynamics, 105; expanding, 99; explosion of, 244; prehorticultural, 103; regions of, 106, 123, 125, 127, 130; spread of, 97
Pork, 62
Potato, 50
Preference: child, 171; exercise of, 165
Prehorticultural populations, 103
Principal-components analysis, 102-103
Programmed sampling, 250
Propinquity in social organization, 133
Protoagricultural: exploitation, 106; mixing, 109; routes, 119; spread, 98, 100-101; spread, confined, 100
Protoagricultural movement, 79, 91, 95, 97, 103-104, 106, 109; discontiguous, 109; sweet potato-based, 104; taro-based, 97, 103
Protoagricultural personality, traits of, 136, 150, 235
Protoagriculture: defined, 13; Eastern Highlands, 97
Protohorticulture, 50, 54
Protopatriliny, 134-135
Psychological development, 236
Puburamba River, 17, 22
Puburamba River valley, 109
Puburamba valley, 109, 112
Pumpkin, 50
Purosa, 224, 245; dialect, 28; origin site, 85
Purosa-Takai, 22, 25
Purosa valley, 25, 98, 109
Python, 57

Q

Question-and-answer discourse, 15

R

Ramu River, 18, 106
Rapport: social, 135
Rats, 57, 59; edible, 59
Recultivation, 43, 79
Reed, salt, 61
Refuge, 132
Regeneration, forest, 90
Regions, naming of, 125-126
Regions of population, 106, 125, 127, 130
Regions of settlement, ecologically defined, 106
Relationship: adoptive, 133; affiliative, 133
Research film, 16; analysis of, 150; basic steps in the production of, 252; concept of, 247; method of as-

sembling, 254; sampling strategies, 249; theoretical approaches, 248; theory and method, 247
Resettlement: centrifugal, 98; dispersive, 132
Residence: afamilial, 133; alternative, 132; male/female, 26; sex-segregated, 63
Residence privileges, 134
Residential: dispersion, 128; flexibility, 132; pattern (traditional), 222
Revolution, coffee, 230
Roads, 224, 226-227; building techniques, 226-227; impact of, 227; public, 226
Rodents, 59, 63
Rule application, 238

S

Saburosa, 53
Salt, 59-62; commercial, 59, 62; native-made, 59
Salt makers, Anga, 60
Salt making, 61; decline of, 62
Sampling strategies, 249
Sampling: opportunistic, 250; programmed, 250; randomized, 147
Search, digressive, 251
Security: child's quest for, 175-176; through body contact, 171
Segmentation, 16, 91, 130; discontiguous, 130; flexible social, 235; group, 130; protoagricultural, 97; unrestricted, 132, 238
Self-sufficiency, 17
Semidomesticated animals, 57
Sepuna, 226
Setting, linguistic, 17
Settlement: divergent, 16; grassland, 229; horticultural, 81; noncontiguous, 99; patterns of, 22, 126
Sevoi, 231
Sharing, 208, 210; of food, 59, 208-209; of food in relation to social structure, 75-76
Shrimp, fresh water, 59
Sibling association, 134
Sibling rivalry, lack of, 162
Simbari Anga, 35
Slash-and-burn horticulture, 43
Snakes, 57, 59
Snares, 59-60; cuscus, 60; rodent, 60
Social code, looseness of, 237
Social cohesion, 135-136; fluid, 136
Social contact with age-mates, 219
Social horizons, narrowed, 92
Social integration, 204, 211
Social order, abstract concepts of, 236
Social organization, 40, 133; cooperative, 136; dependence on rapport, 143; effect of anger on, 143; effect of land pressure on, 136; personal basis of, 126, 135; propinquity in, 133

Social segmentation, unrestricted, 238
Social structure: egalitarian, 238; in relation to casual eating, 62-63
Socialization, 211, 216-217, 219, 238; and culture change, 235; patterns of, 211
Socioecological change, 79
Socioeconomic activity, focusing of, 134
Sociopolitical: change, 91; cornerstone of unity, 134; development of groupings, 92; diffuseness, 125; identity, 126; informal structure, 220; looseness, 238; obscuring of complexity, 224; organization, 16, 127; protoagricultural organization, 123; units, 127
Sociosensual: contact, 236; opportunities, 235
Soil, fertility, 43
Solidarity, 16
Sorcery, 32, 39, 59, 92, 130, 132; fear of, 132; social effect, 39; suspicion of, 92
Spade, introduction of, 228
Spiders, edible, 58-59
Staple: dietary, 54; taro, 105-106
Stinginess, 16
Stone implements, 17
Strategies, sampling, 249
String making, 50
Structured information, 249
Structure, sociopolitical (informal), 220
Subpopulations, divergence, 103
Sugar cane, 49-50, 62; ceremonial use of, 68
Supervision, child, 165
Sweet potato, 43, 48-49, 54, 62, 64, 69, 71, 73, 77; adoption of, 79; crop yields, 243; diffusion of, 92; impact of, 79; introduction of, 104, 244; movement, 106; northwestern route, 116; origin of, 79; replacement for taro, 79; route to the highlands, 79; yields, 54

T

Taboos, 15, 62; food, 59
Tactile: communication, 150, 204, 206, 208, 219; interaction, 151; interplay, 204, 207; response, 204
Tainoraba, 245
Tairora, 100
Takai, 22, 25, 33, 45, 58, 60, 82
Takari, 226
Tantrum, 177
Tapa: cloth, 50, 199; making of, 199
Taro, 43, 49-50, 62-63, 73, 244; grated, 69; growers, 106; movement, 105; replacement by sweet potato, 97; route into the Fore lands, 112; staple, 105-106
Territorial exclusiveness, lack of, 125
Teteyeguti, 31
Time and space constants, 249
Tobacco, 49-50
Toilet training, 177-178
Tomato, 50